Martin Dimnik

MIKHAIL, PRINCE OF CHERNIGOV AND GRAND PRINCE OF KIEV
1224-1246

In 1224 Mikhail Vsevolodovich, now the senior prince in the family of
Ol'govichi, became prince of Chernigov. During his reign he weakened
the influence of the Vsevolodivichi, princes of Rostov-Suzdal', over
Novgorod; he captured Galich from Daniil Romanovich, prince of
Galicia-Volyn'; and in 1235 he effectively terminated the supremacy of
the Rostislavichi, princes of Smolensk, over southern Rus'. Although
Daniil and the Vsevolodovichi formed an alliance against Mikhail, they
failed to defeat him and in 1236 Mikhail also became grand prince of
Kiev. It was the Tatars who, after invading the lands of the Rus' in 1237,
eventually drove him from Kiev. Mikhail continued to oppose the Tatars
and was the last prince to capitulate to their demands. In 1246 he finally
agreed to visit Saray to acknowledge the overlordship of Khan Baty.
Whereas the princes who had gone before him were given patents by the
khan to rule in their principalities, Mikhail was executed by the Tatars for
his faith. Later he was canonized by the Orthodox Church.

Historians are of the opinion that by the first half of the thirteenth
century the Ol'govichi had become ineffectual as a political force and that
the most powerful princes were the Romanovichi in Galicia-Volyn' and
the Vsevolodovichi in Rostov-Suzdal'. The accuracy of the accepted view
is now questioned. By 1235 when Mikhail defeated the Rostislavichi and
the Romanovichi and established his control over southern and southwest
Rus', the Ol'govichi were in fact the strongest family. After his martyrdom Mikhail became a model for the faithful in Rus' in their struggle
against their pagan oppressors. The epilogue examines the devotion to
Mikhail, how it developed in popular tradition and how it was
promulgated officially by the Orthodox Church and by the rulers of
Russia.

A contemporary icon of Saints Mikhail and Fedor,
"The Martyrs of Chernigov."

STUDIES AND TEXTS 52

MIKHAIL, PRINCE OF CHERNIGOV AND GRAND PRINCE OF KIEV 1224-1246

BY

MARTIN DIMNIK

PONTIFICAL INSTITUTE OF MEDIAEVAL STUDIES

TORONTO   1981

ACKNOWLEDGMENT

This book has been published with the help of a grant
from the Social Science Federation of Canada,
using funds provided by the Social Sciences and Humanities
Research Council of Canada

CANADIAN CATALOGUING IN PUBLICATION DATA

Dimnik, Martin, 1941-
  Mikhail, Prince of Chernigov and Grand Prince of Kiev, 1224-1246

(Studies and texts - Pontifical Institute of Mediaeval Studies ; 52 ISSN 0082-5328)

Bibliography: p.
Includes index.

ISBN 0-88844-052-9

1. Mikhail Vsevolodovich, Grand Duke of Kiev, d. 1245. 2. Christian saints - Russia - Biography. 3. Orthodox Eastern Church, Russian - Biography. I. Title. II. Series: Pontifical Institute of Mediaeval Studies. Studies and texts - Pontifical Institute of Mediaeval Studies ; 52.

BX597.M55D55   281.9´092´4   C80-094636-7

Pontifical Institute of Mediaeval Studies
59 Queen's Park Crescent East
Toronto, Ontario, Canada M5S 2C4

PRINTED BY UNIVERSA, WETTEREN, BELGIUM

Contents

Acknowledgments

This book had its origin in a doctoral thesis which was submitted in July 1976 to the Board of the Faculty of Mediaeval and Modern Languages of the University of Oxford. During the years of research and writing I received much needed assistance and encouragement. My greatest debt of gratitude is to my supervisor Prof. J. L. I. Fennell for the patience with which he assisted me through all the stages of my work. His advice was invaluable and his dogged endurance in reading and rereading the manuscript went far beyond the call of duty. My thanks go also to Prof. Dimitri Obolensky who helped during an important stage of the investigations. I benefited greatly from the counsel given to me by Rev. James K. McConica CSB who, at times, assumed the role of mentor. Rev. J. Reginald O'Donnell CSB gave me valuable advice for revising the thesis into book form. Jane Card kindly translated Latin texts and Irina Sergeevna Tidmarsh gave warm encouragement and valuable instruction in the Russian language. A generous post-doctoral grant from the Canada Council enabled me to visit Oxford in the summer of 1978 to complete my work on the book. As well as these, there are many other professors, librarians and friends who helped in various ways. I wish to express my heartfelt thanks to all of them.

Toronto   *Martin Dimnik* CSB
December, 1978

Abbreviations

Chteniya	*Chteniya v Obshchestve istorii i drevnostey rossiyskikh pri Moskov- skom universitete.*
NPL	*Novgorodskaya pervaya letopis' starshego i mladshego izvodov*, ed. A. N. Nasonov (Moscow-Leningrad, 1950).
Pskov	*Pskovskie letopisi*, ed. A. N. Nasonov, 2 vols. (A.N. SSSR, 1941, 1955).
PSRL	*Polnoe sobranie russkikh letopisey*, vols. 1-33 (Saint Petersburg, Leningrad, Moscow, 1841-1977).
RIB	*Russkaya istoricheskaya biblioteka*, vols. 1-39 (Saint Petersburg, 1872-1927).
s.a.	sub anno/under the year.
TL	*Troitskaya letopis', rekonstruktsiya teksta*, M. D. Priselkov (Moscow-Leningrad, 1950).
TODRL	*Trudy Otdela drevnerusskoy literatury* (A.N. SSSR, Institut russkoy literatury, Pushkinskogo Doma).
VOIDR	*Vremennik Obshchestva istorii i drevnostey rossiyskikh pri Moskov- skom universitete.*

Preface

This work is based on an analysis of the primary sources. The chronicles of medieval Rus' published in the series PSRL[1] have served as the chief materials for the reconstruction of the events of the first half of the thirteenth century. The problems facing an investigator using the chronicles are many and at times insurmountable. There is, for example, the problem of contemporaneity. No chronicle has survived which was written in the first half of the thirteenth century. Information for this period is preserved in various later chronicle compilations, the oldest being the Hypatian Chronicle, the Novgorod First Chronicle and the Laurentian Chronicle.

The chief source of information concerning southern Rus' for the first half of the thirteenth century is the Hypatian Chronicle.[2] It is named after its oldest manuscript from the beginning of the fifteenth century. The chronicle is also known as the "South Rus'sian chronicle *svod*" (*Yuzhno-russkiy letopisnyy svod*); the *svod* was probably compiled at the end of the thirteenth century. It can be divided into three parts, the last of which, from 1200 to 1292, is based mainly on information derived from the no longer extant "Galician-Volynian *svod*" compiled in Volyn' at the end of the thirteenth century.[3]

The Novgorod First Chronicle is primarily a record of local Novgorod information. Two if its manuscripts have been published – the "older redaction" (*starshiy izvod*) called the *Sinodal'nyy spisok* and the "younger

---

[1] *Polnoe sobranie russkikh letopisey*, izdannoe po Vysochayshemu poveleniyu Arkheograficheskoyu kommissieyu, 24 vols. (Saint Petersburg, 1841-1921). After 1921 the series continued to be published as: *Polnoe sobranie russkikh letopisey*, Izdavaemoe Postoyannoyu Istoriko-arkheograficheskoy kommissieyu Akademii nauk SSSR. Izd. 2, vols. 25-33 (Leningrad, 1925-1977). It is important to note that vol. 2, which was first published in 1843 contained the "Gustinskaya letopis'." The latter source was omitted when vol. 2 was reprinted in 1908. Akademiia nauk SSSR also republished some of the early volumes in new editions, namely, volumes 1, 4 and 5.

[2] "Ipat'evskaya letopis'," PSRL vol. 2, 2nd edition (Saint Petersburg, 1908).

[3] See L. V. Cherepnin, "Letopisets Daniila Galitskogo," *Istoricheskie zapiski*, vol. 12 (1941), pp. 228-53 and V. T. Pashuto, "Ocherk istorii letopisaniya yugo-zapadnoy Rusi," *Ocherki po istorii Galitsko-Volynskoy Rusi* (Moscow, 1950).

redaction" (*mladshiy izvod*) called the *Komissionnyy spisok*.[4] The *Sinodal'nyy spisok* was compiled in the fourteenth century at the court of the archbishop and can be considered to be the official Novgorod chronicle. It brings its consecutive yearly information up to 1330 after which date it records sporadic entries up to 1352. The *Komissionnyy spisok*, written in the fifteenth century, brings its information up to 1446. For the period of the first half of the thirteenth century it is much the same as the "older redaction."[5] When quoting from the Novgorod First Chronicle in this work two references are usually given: the first reference is to the *Sinodal'nyy spisok* and the second is to the *Komissionnyy spisok*.

The Laurentian Chronicle[6] is named after the monk Lavrenty who copied the manuscript in 1377 from an "old chronicler" (*vetkhiy letopisets*) which goes as far as 1305. This source is of special value to the investigation of the first half of the thirteenth century – mainly for events which occurred in northeast Rus' – as it incorporates the "*svod* of 1239" of Yaroslav Vsevolodovich as well as information from the chronicles kept at the court of Konstantin Vsevolodovich and his sons in Rostov (viz. the "*svod* of 1263").[7]

All remaining chronicles are compilations dating from the fifteenth to the seventeenth centuries which, for the most part, repeat the information given by the three chronicles mentioned above. On occasion they contain unique items of information concerning southern Rus'. It is difficult to establish what sources, now lost, were available to the compilers of the later chronicles. Two chronicles, the Sofiyskiy First and the Novgorod Fourth,[8] appear to have derived their information from the hypothetical "*svod* of 1448."[9] It contained information from southern Rus' different from that found in those chronicles (viz. the Moscow *svod* of 1479 and the Ermolinskiy, L'vov and Nikon Chronicles),[10] which used the common

    [4] *Novgorodskaya pervaya letopis' starshego i mladshego izvodov* (NPL), ed. A. N. Nasonov (Moscow-Leningrad, 1950).

    [5] See D. S. Likhachev, *Russkie letopisi i ikh kul'turno-istoricheskoe znachenie* (Moscow-Leningrad, 1947), pp. 440-4.

    [6] "Lavrent'evskaya letopis'," PSRL vol. 1, 2nd edition (Leningrad, 1926).

    [7] See Likhachev, *Russkie letopisi*, pp. 427-31 and Yu. A. Limonov, *Letopisanie Vladimiro-Suzdal'skoy Rusi* (Leningrad, 1967).

    [8] "Sofiyskaya pervaya letopis'," PSRL vol. 5, 2nd edition (Leningrad, 1925), and "Novgorodskaya chetvertaya letopis'," PSRL vol. 4 (Petrograd, 1915).

    [9] On the "*svod* of 1448" see Ya. S. Lur'e, "Obshcherusskiy svod-protograf Sofiyskoy I i Novogorodskoy IV letopisey," TODRL, vol. 28, pp. 114-39.

    [10] "Moskovskiy letopisnyy svod kontsa XV veka," PSRL vol. 25 (Moscow-Leningrad, 1949); "Ermolinskaya letopis'," PSRL vol. 23 (Saint Petersburg, 1910); "L'vovskaya letopis'," PSRL vol. 20 (Saint Petersburg, 1910) and "Patriarshaya ili Nikonovskaya letopis'," PSRL vol. 10 (Saint Petersburg, 1885).

source known as the "*svod* of Feodosy and Filipp."[11] In the few instances where such unique items of information are found in later compilations attention is drawn to them.

A major problem which arises when analysing the chronicle information recorded in principalities which were often rivals of Chernigov is one of tendentiousness. For example, how objectively did the chroniclers depict the activities of the princes of Chernigov who were opposed to their own prince? What additions and deletions did later compilers make when copying the information? How much information did later copyists and editors invent in their attempts to "clarify" what appeared to them to be unclear entries?

Another difficulty which an investigator of the chronicles faces is dating. All the chronicle sources which contain information for the years up to and including the fourteenth century use either the "March" (*martovskiy*) or the "Ultra-March" (*ul'tramartovskiy*) system of dating. The early calendar of Rus' was based on the Byzantine calendar which calculated its years from "the creation of the world," namely, 5508 years earlier than the birth of Christ. Thus, for example, a chronicle would enter the year 1224 as 6732 (i.e., 1224 + 5508). Unlike the Byzantine calendar which began its year in the autumn on 1 September, the medieval calendar of Rus' began its year in the spring on 1 March. This created a problem. There are six months between March and the beginning of the September year and there are also six months from the beginning of the September year to the following March. Therefore, the March year could begin either on the March six months before the September year and thus be "older" than the latter (i.e., Ultra-March year), or it could begin on the March six months after the September year and be "younger" than the September year (i.e., March year; see chart below).[12] The chronicles, up to

---

[11] A. N. Nasonov postulated a common source for the Ermolinskiy Chronicle and the Moscow *svod* of 1479 in what he calls the "Common Russian chronicle *svod* 1464-1472 of Metropolitans Feodosiy-Filipp"; see "Moskovskiy svod 1479 i ego yuzhnorusskiy istochnik," *Problemy istochnikovedeniya*, vol. 9 (1961), pp. 350-85 and "Moskovskiy svod 1479 i Ermolinskaya letopis'," *Voprosy sotsial'no-ekonomicheskoy istorii i istochnikovedeniya perioda feodalizma v Rossii. Sbornik statey k 70-letiyu A. A. Novosel'skogo* (Moscow, 1961), pp. 218-22. However, J. L. I. Fennell has suggested that the terminal dates of this hypothetical *svod* might be 1448 and 1472, and that as well as the Ermolinskiy Chronicle (and the almost identical L'vov Chronicle) and the Moscow *svod* of 1479, the Nikon Chronicle also derived from it; see "The Tale of the Murder of Michail of Tver'," *Studies in Slavic Linguistics and Poetics in Honor of Boris O. Unbegaun* (New York and London, 1968), p. 36 and "The Tver' Uprising of 1327: a Study of the Sources," *Jahrbücher für Geschichte Osteuropas*, Heft 2 (1967), pp. 168 ff.

[12] See E. I. Kamentseva, *Khronologiya* (Moscow, 1967), pp. 77-80.

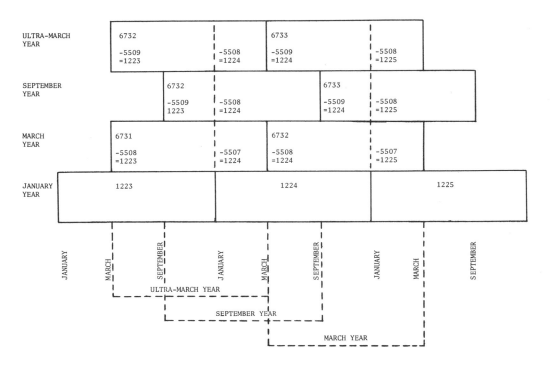

(Adapted from Berezhkov, *Khronologiya*, p. 12.)

and including the fourteenth century, used *both* March systems of dating. Unfortunately for the investigator, later compilers of chronicle *svods* complicated matters even further. These editors incorporated into their yearly accounts entries from various chronicles so that often one finds both March and Ultra-March information included under the same year.

Clearly, the difficulty which faces an investigator is to establish which system is being followed by a chronicle in each entry. In attempting to establish the correct dates for entries in the Novgorod First and the Laurentian Chronicles, N. G. Berezhkov's study was used as a guide.[13] However, no similar study has been made concerning the dates of the entries in the Hypatian Chronicle for the same period. The problem is accentuated in the case of the latter as the "Galician-Volynian *svod*" did not use the traditional manner of recording information, that is, it did not

---

[13] *Khronologiya russkogo letopisaniya* (Moscow, 1963).

date its entries. Although the compiler of the Hypatian manuscript attempted to date the information of the "Galician-Volvynian *svod*," he was not always successful; in some instances his dates are as many as four years off the mark.[14] As a result, much attention has been given in this work to establishing, where possible, the correct dates concerning events recorded in the Hypatian Chronicle.

Several other sources deserve individual mention. The Smolensk Chronicle, "Letopis' Avraamki," written by the monk Avraamka in 1495 (the oldest extant manuscript of which dates from the beginning of the sixteenth century), for the most part gives information concerning Smolensk and northern Rus' up to 1469.[15] Similar information is found in the "Sokrashchennaya Novgorodskaya letopis'" contained in the *Suprasl'skaya rukopis'*, a manuscript of the first half of the sixteenth century.[16] The Pskov chronicles, on the other hand – the hypothetical "*svod* of 1469" from which the *Tikhanovskiy spisok* written in the first half of the seventeenth century derived, and the *Stroevskiy spisok* written in the 1550s[17] – have mainly local Pskov information.[18] However, both the Smolensk and the Pskov chronicles contain information from southern Rus' derived from a common source which is not found in other chronicles.

The sixteenth-century Vladimir Chronicle[19] also contains certain unique items. According to L. L. Murav'eva, it derived its information from two independent sources – an "all-Rus'sian" source and a Novgorod source (also used by the Novgorod Fourth Chronicle). The "all-Rus'sian" source (viz. *Letopisets Velikiy Russkiy*) used by the Vladimir Chronicle was also used by the compiler of the Trinity Chronicle. This source provided both chronicles with unique information for the thirteenth and the fourteenth centuries. Since N. M. Karamzin who used the Trinity Chronicle extensively, as we shall see, did not preserve the entire text, only the Vladimir Chronicle has preserved all these items of information.[20]

---

[14] See Likhachev, *Russkie letopisi*, p. 433 and the Hypatian Chronicle (PSRL vol. 2, p. v).

[15] PSRL vol. 16 (Saint Petersburg, 1889); see Likhachev, *Russkie letopisi*, pp. 465-7.

[16] The manuscript was published by M. A. Obolensky in 1836.

[17] *Pskovskie letopisi*, ed. A. N. Nasonov, 2 vols. (A.N. SSSR, 1941, 1955).

[18] Concerning the Pskov chronicles, see A. N. Nasonov, "Iz istorii Pskovskogo letopisaniya," *Istoricheskie zapiski*, vol. 18 (1946), pp. 255-94 and Likhachev, *Russkie letopisi*, pp. 360-5.

[19] "Vladimirskiy letopisets," PSRL vol. 30 (Moscow, 1965).

[20] "Ob obshcherusskom istochnike Vladimirskogo letopistsa," *Letopisi i khroniki, sbornik statey 1973 g.* (Moscow, 1974), pp. 143-9.

The Trinity Chronicle has been used sparingly. This source, so named by Karamzin who used it in his *Istoriya gosudarstva Rossiiskago*,[21] was a chronicle "*svod* of 1408." Unfortunately it was destroyed in the Moscow fire of 1812. It has subsequently been published in a reconstructed form by M. D. Priselkov.[22] In reconstructing the third part of the chronicle, the years 1177 to 1305, he used the sixteenth-century Simeonovskiy Chronicle[23] and the Laurentian Chronicle. Priselkov used the latter in his reconstruction of the text as Karamzin himself was obliged to use it in place of the Trinity Chronicle which was apparently defective for various years of the first half of the thirteenth century (1224 to 1230,[24] 1235 to 1237, 1239 to 1249).[25]

One seventeenth-century source, the Gustinskiy Chronicle, is of special interest. Named after the manuscript belonging to the Gustinskiy Monastery in the district of Poltava southeast of Kiev, this chronicle was published as a supplement to the Hypatian Chronicle in 1843 in PSRL.[26] It is important because it incorporates in the first part of the chronicle a manuscript similar to the Hypatian manuscript.[27] Consequently, a comparison of this chronicle with the Hypatian Chronicle has been a help in determining the dates of events which transpired in southwest Rus'.

Chronicle information has also been obtained from other sources. The Polish historian J. Długosz wrote a twelve volume work entitled *Longini canonici Cracoviensis, Historiae Polonicae*[28] in which he incorporated excerpts from various chronicles of Rus'. Besides the Primary Chronicle he also used a "Lithuanian Chronicle" (i.e. from western Rus') and Kievan and Galician-Volynian chronicles. Certain information concerning southern and southwest Rus' during the first half of the thirteenth century is found only in his work.[29]

V. N. Tatishchev's *Istoriya Rossiyskaya* is another valuable fund of chronicle information. This work has been the centre of much controversy; it has been criticized, on the one hand, by Karamzin but

[21] See vols. 2-4, third edition (Saint Petersburg, 1950).
[22] *Troitskaya letopis', rekonstruktsiya teksta* (Moscow-Leningrad, 1950).
[23] "Simeonovskaya letopis'," PSRL vol. 18 (Saint Petersburg, 1913).
[24] TL, pp. 35, 40.
[25] TL, p. 42.
[26] "Gustinskaya letopis'," PSRL 2 (Saint Petersburg, 1843).
[27] M. N. Tikhomirov, "Istochnikovedenie istorii SSSR s drevneyshikh vremen do kontsa XVIII v.," *Kurs istochnikovedeniya istorii SSSR*, vol. 1 (Moscow, 1940).
[28] He discusses the first half of the thirteenth century in book 6 (Leipzig, 1711).
[29] Tikhomirov, "Istochnikovedenie," pp. 124-5; see also Yu. A. Limonov, "Pol'skiy khronist Yan Dlugosh o Rossii," *Feodal'naya Rossiya vo vsemirno-istoricheskom protsesse* (Moscow, 1972), pp. 262-8.

defended by S. M. Solov'ev and other historians.[30] A. A. Shakhmatov pointed out that all manuscripts of Tatishchev's *History* can be divided into two redactions differing greatly from one another. The first redaction was completed ca. 1739 while the second was compiled after 1748 (he died in 1750). The second redaction was a complete revision of the first. Although Tatishchev added information from new chronicles and foreign sources it is suspect. For example, he translated the chronicle entries into his contemporary language and thus frequently changed the sense of the original meaning; he also incorporated his own explanations into the text. These were intended to clarify vague passages and to provide continuity where it was apparently lacking.[31]

The changes which Tatishchev introduced in the second version of his *History* have drawn much criticism. He cannot be exonerated from this criticism for, as Shakhmatov points out, a comparison of the second redaction with the first shows that in the latter version Tatishchev was guilty of inventing information. However, he cannot be accused of inventing information for the first redaction and any inconsistencies found in it are there because Tatishchev found them in his sources. And, it must be remembered, he had access to sources many of which are no longer available.[32] This makes the first version of his *History* indispensable to the investigator.[33]

The seven volumes of Tatishchev's *Istoriya Rossiyskaya* published by the Academy of Sciences of the USSR (1962-8) include the first version of his *History*, published for the first time. This version which covers events up to 1237 is found in volume four; it has been used as the more reliable of the two versions and, where possible, quoted in preference to the second redaction. The latter is found in volume three. Volume five includes information from 1238 to 1462.

It has been noted that in his *Istoriya gosudarstva Rossiiskago* Karamzin used the Trinity Chronicle. Given the fact that he had access to this and, it appears, to other sources which have not survived, his *History* has been

[30] Concerning the controversy, see A. G. Kuz'min, "Ob istochnikovedcheskoy osnove 'Istorii Rossiyskoy' V. N. Tatishcheva," *Voprosy istorii*, part 9 (1963), pp. 214-8, also his *Ryazanskoe letopisanie* (Moscow, 1965), pp. 33-43 and M. N. Tikhomirov, "Vladimir Nikitich Tatishchev," *Istorik-Marksist*, book 6 (1940), pp. 43-56.

[31] S. S. Shakhmatov, "K vorposu o kriticheskom izdanii Istorii Rossiyskoy V. N. Tatishcheva," *Dela i Dni*, kniga pervaya (Saint Petersburg, 1920), p. 82.

[32] For example the *Raskol'nich'ya letopis', Letopis' Khrushcheva, Letopis' Eropkina, Letopis' Volynskogo* (or *Simonova*); see Kuz'min, "Ob istochnikovedcheskoy osnove 'Istorii Rossiyskoy' V. N. Tatishcheva," p. 218.

[33] Shakmatov, "K voprosu o kriticheskom izdanii," pp. 94-5.

consulted with special attention. On occasion it contains information which is not found in other sources.

Besides the chronicles, information is also contained in various *sinodiki* (i.e., lists of deceased ancestors of various families who were to be commemorated in prayers and in the liturgy). Although it was not possible to consult the *sinodiki*, Archbishop Filaret of Chernigov and R. V. Zotov used them extensively and in the instance of the *Lyubetskiy sinodik* reproduced the list of princes in it in its entirety.[34] They compared the lists of the princes of Chernigov found in the *sinodiki* with the names of the princes recorded in the chronicles. Thus, their work is helpful in determining the identities of various princes of the first half of the thirteenth century.

Hagiographic literature and religious accounts have also proven to be a source of useful information – viz. the "Life" of St. Merkury of Smolensk, the "Life" of St. Evfrosinia of Suzdal' and the account of the miraculous cure of Prince Mikhail Vsevolodovich as a youth.

In attempting to establish the identities of those princes which are not clear from the sources, especially when ascertaining succession in various families of princes, one fundamental criterion has been used. It has been assumed that seniority in a family followed the traditional pattern – it passed laterally from brother to younger brother and from the youngest brother to his eldest eligible nephew (i.e., the son of an *izgoy* – a prince debarred from competing for the title of senior prince – was not eligible). For convenience sake, the princes of a family are often referred to by using the plural of the name of their progenitor (e.g., Ol'govichi, the descendants of Oleg Svyatoslavich; Vsevolodovichi, those of Vsevolod Yur'evich, etc.). Throughout the work the following terms have been used: Rus' – to designate the Kievan state; Rous' (Роусь) – to designate its inhabitants; and Rus'sian (Русьскии) – has been used as the adjectival form.

Five genealogical tables which list all the important princes discussed in the monograph are included at the end of the work. Four maps have also been added to illustrate the geography of the major principalities. A chronological table juxtaposes the important events as they occurred in the various regions of Rus'. This is helpful since each chapter, for the most

---

[34] See R. V. Zotov, *O Chernigovskikh knyazyakh po Lyubetskomu sinodiku i o Cherni-govskom knyazhestve v Tatarskoe vremya* (Saint Petersburg, 1892), pp. 24-9 and Filaret, archbishop of Chernigov, *Istoriko-statisticheskoe opisanie Chernigovskoy eparkhii*, vol. 5 (Chernigov, 1861-74).

part, deals with only those events which occurred in the region under discussion. There is a glossary and a selected bibliography.

In footnoting, the first reference to a work is always given in its complete form. All subsequent references to it are given in abbreviated forms. The short form normally consists of the author's last name, a key word or words from the monograph plus volume and page references. Some abbreviations have been used; these are explained in the list of abbreviations at the beginning of the work.

Words or phrases which are vital to an argument have been given in the original form. Those words which recur often (e.g., *postrig* and *spisok*) or have become part of English usage (e.g. boyar), and Russian titles of articles and books, have been transliterated. The "British System" of latinization given in *The Slavonic and East European Review* has been used.[35] However, a few minor exceptions have been made to this system: e and ë have been transliterated as e (thus *ego* and not *yego*, *znanie* and not *znaniye*); ѣ has been transliterated as e and ѧ has been transliterated as ya; proper names ending in -iy have been transliterated as -y (thus Yury and not Yuriy); however, when proper names are used as qualifiers then -yy and -iy have been used (e.g., *Sinodal'nyy spisok* and *Lyubetskiy sinodik*). In the spelling of feminine names ending in -iya the form -ia is used (e.g. Evfrosinia).

When transposing proper names from the chronicles these have been transliterated, for the most part, from the form found in the index of the relevant chronicle (e.g., Igor', Yaroslavl', Volyn'; however, Galich for the town and Galicia for the principality). In the transliteration of Polish names the system found in *The Cambridge Medieval History of Poland* has been used; in the transliteration of Hungarian names – that found in *The Cambridge Medieval History*. For those foreign names which have commonly accepted forms in English, the latter have been used (e.g., John de Plano Carpini, Chingis Khan; but Baty for Batu and Tatar rather than Mongol, since Tatar is the name given in the chronicles).[36]

[35] W. K. Matthews, "The Latinisation of Cyrillic Characters," *The Slavonic and East European Review*, vol. 30, no. 75 (June 1952), pp. 542-3.

[36] G. Vernadsky points out that the Tatars became one of the leading tribes in Mongolia in the middle of the twelfth century after they defeated a neighbouring tribe called the Mongols. However, the future emperor Chingis Khan, who was born in the second half of the twelfth century, belonged to a Mongol clan. Therefore, after all the tribes of Mongolia were united under him, they became known as the Mongols. In Western Europe, the word Tatars (in the form Tartars), was applied as a generic name to all the Mongol invaders. But in Rus' the name was kept in the original form, that is, *Tatary*. For a detailed discussion see his *The Mongols and Russia* (New Haven: Yale University Press, 1953), pp. 11-12.

Introduction

HISTORIOGRAPHY

No monograph has yet appeared evaluating the historical importance of Mikhail Vsevolodovich, an Ol'govich[1] and grand prince of Kiev, at the time of the Tatar invasion of Rus' in 1237/8. Pre-revolutionary Russian academics' interest in the prince stemmed chiefly from their desire to ascertain his genealogy so as to establish the family trees of the various families of princes of the nineteenth century descended from him.[2] Soviet historians, however, have made only passing references to Mikhail while stressing the importance of his rivals. This lack of interest in his political significance is surprising, for, by the time of the Tatar invasion, Mikhail had succeeded in establishing the authority of the Ol'govichi over southern and southwest Rus' and making them the most powerful family of princes in all Rus'.

The failure of historians to evaluate the significance of the princes of Chernigov in the first half of the thirteenth century, especially after the Kalka battle in 1223,[3] is, in part, understandable. On the one hand, there is a glaring paucity of chronicle information recounting the activities of these princes.[4] On the other hand, the fact that the Ol'govichi were

---

[1] I.e., a descendant of Oleg Svyatoslavich (d. 1115), the grandson of Yaroslav "the Wise"; the Ol'govichi ruled in the principality of Chernigov. See Table 2:2.

[2] See, for example, P. Khavsky, *Istoricheskoe issledovanie o rodosloviyakh svyatago muchenika knyazya chernigovskago Mikhaila i rossiyskikh velikikh knyazey opochivayushchikh v Moskovskom Arkhangelsom sobore* (Moscow, 1862), and by the same author *Drevnost' Moskvy ili ukazatel' istochnikov eya topografii i istorii*, third edition (Moscow, 1868), pp. iii ff. (i.e., Introduction to the second edition); see also R. V. Zotov, *O Chernigovskikh knyazyakh po Lyubetskomu sinodiku i o Chernigovskom knyazhestve v Tatarskoe vremya* (Saint Petersburg, 1892). Some of the families of princes descended from Mikhail which still existed in the nineteenth century were "the Boryatinskie, the Gorshakovie, the Dolgorukie, the Eletskie, the Zvenigorodskie, the Kol'tsovy-Mosal'skie, the Obolenskie, the Odoevskie and the Shcherbatovie" (Filaret, archbishop of Chernigov, *Russkie svyatye*, third edition, vol; 3 [Saint Petersburg, 1882], p. 101).

[3] On the question of the dating of the Tatar invasion, see N. G. Berezhkov, *Khronologiya russkogo letopisaniya* (Moscow, 1963), pp. 317-8.

[4] Although chronicles must have been kept at the courts of the Ol'govichi, none has survived. On the contrary, it is the chronicles of their rivals, the princes who ruled in the southwest and the northeast of Rus', which have come down to us. Understandably, these sources make only passing and often deprecatory references to the princes of Chernigov.

eliminated as a political force shortly after the Tatar invasion and their
rivals, the Vsevolodovichi of Rostov-Suzdal',[5] emerged victorious, meant
that the latter, as the progenitors of the rulers of Muscovy, received the
attention of historians. Since the Ol'govichi were vanquished, historians,
consciously or unconsciously, relegated them to a place of minor
importance when writing about the history of Kievan Rus'.

Various general histories written before and during the nineteenth
century illustrate what little significance historians attributed to the
activities of the Ol'govichi in the affairs of southern Rus'. These works,
which frequently consist in a mere paraphrase of the sources, show the
primary goal of the princes as the winning of the "golden throne" of Kiev.
In this context they mention several princes of Chernigov merely as
successful contestants. None of these histories attempts to analyze the
nature of Ol'govichi policy as a whole – trace its continuity from one
senior prince to another as power passed from brother to brother in lateral
succession – or to consider the existence of a durable family structure.

One such history, which for the most part synthesized the available
chronicle information, was written by M. Pogodin.[6] However, his
observations concerning the activities of the Ol'govichi for the first half of
the thirteenth century were not correct. In the first volume of his work he
devoted a section to the history of the principality of Chernigov but only
up to the first Tatar invasion. He concluded that, "after 1217 and up to
1224, no information has been preserved in the chronicles concerning
Chernigov which, in the wake of its continuous wars, became too weak to
participate even to the smallest degree in the general events" of the
period.[7] As we shall see, in 1224, when Mikhail Vsevolodovich occupied
the throne of Chernigov, he became involved immediately in the affairs of
Kievan Rus' as one of its major powers. In view of this information it
would not seem to be the case that Chernigov became too weak to be an
important political force after 1217.

In the second volume of his work Pogodin discusses the period
between the two Tatar invasions, 1223 to 1237/8. First he observed that
the principality of Chernigov became fragmented and that eventually it

---

[5] Concerning the Vsevolodovichi, see Table 4.

[6] *Drevnyaya russkaya istoriya do mongol'skago iga*, 2 vols. (Moscow, 1872).
Examples of other general histories are: V. N. Tatishchev, *Istoriya Rossiyskaya*, 7 vols.
(Moscow-Leningrad, 1962-8); N. M. Karamzin, *Istoriya gosudarstva Rossiiskago*,
12 vols., 3rd edition (Saint Petersburg, 1830-31); S. M. Solov'ev, *Istoriya Rossii s
drevneyshikh vremen*, 29 vols. (Moscow, 1962-66).

[7] *Drevnyaya russkaya istoriya*, vol. 1, p. 384.

exhausted itself in its constant battles with Kiev.[8] Later he pointed out that, aside from the two Tatar invasions, the most important political activity during this period occurred in the principality of Galicia in the southwest and in Novgorod in the north. But he failed to observe that in Galicia where events centred around Daniil Romanovich's attempts to establish his rule over the principality, his chief rival in Rus' was Mikhail Vsevolodovich of Chernigov.[9] Pogodin also failed to note that during this period Mikhail was the major opponent of the Vsevolodovichi of Rostov-Suzdal' for control of Novgorod.[10] In view of the fact that Mikhail was able to challenge the claims of what were apparently the two most powerful families of princes in Rus', Pogodin's assertion that Chernigov had exhausted itself by 1217 and that it lay fragmented, does not stand.

In the second half of the nineteenth century and at the beginning of the twentieth century works appeared dedicated to the study of individual principalities for the period dating from the twelfth to the fifteenth centuries.[11] One such work, concerning the principality of Chernigov, was written by P. Golubovsky.[12] The author collected chronicle information referring to the activities of the Ol'govichi and presented it in a systematic fashion. In his analysis of their activities for the twelfth and the first half of the thirteenth centuries he arrived at a conclusion similar to that of Pogodin. Golubovsky believed that the principality of Chernigov had become politically impotent by the time of the Tatar invasion; internal strife led to the fragmentation of the principality and minor princes broke their ties of allegiance with the senior prince.[13]

In the nineteenth century various genealogists were motivated to study Mikhail Vsevolodovich not for his political significance but as the progenitor of various families of princes. Their efforts to ascertain the lineage of these families led the genealogists back to Mikhail and required

[8] Ibid. vol. 2, p. 1351.

[9] Ibid. pp. 1367-83.

[10] Ibid. pp. 1383-91.

[11] E.g., V. S. Borzakovsky, *Istoriya Tverskago knyazhestva* (Saint Petersburg, 1876); B. E. Danilevich, *Ocherk istorii Polotskoy zemli do kontsa xiv stoletiya* (Kiev, 1896); M. V. Dovnar-Zapol'sky, *Ocherk istorii krivichskoy i dregovichskoy zemel' do kontsa xii stoletiya* (Kiev, 1891); P. V. Golubovsky, *Istoriya Smolenskoy zemli do nachala xv st.* (Kiev, 1895); D. I. Ilovaysky, *Istoriya Ryazanskogo knyazhestva* (Moscow, 1858); D. Korsakov, *Merya i Rostovskoe knyazhestvo* (Kazan', 1872); V. G. Lyaskoronsky, *Istoriya Pereyaslavl'skoy zemli s drevneyshikh vremen do poloviny xiii stoletiya* (Kiev, 1897); N. Molchanovsky, *Ocherk izvestiy o Podol'skoy zemle do 1454 g.* (Kiev, 1885).

[12] *Istoriya Severskoy zemli do poloviny xiv stoletiya* (Kiev, 1881); cf. D. Bagaley, *Istoriya Severskoy zemli do poloviny xiv stoletiya* (Kiev, 1882).

[13] Golubovsky, *Istoriya*, pp. 189-92.

them to establish his identity as well, that is, his place among the descendants of Ryurik. One of the most valuable monographs to be published in connection with these studies was written by R. V. Zotov.[14] He set himself the task of establishing the identities of the princes of Chernigov from the time of the Tatar invasion to the occupation of southern Rus' by Ol'gerd of Lithuania (1362).[15] In order to achieve this end he had to ascertain the lineage of the princes of Chernigov from Yaroslav "the Wise" to the last senior prince in the pre-Tatar period, namely, Mikhail Vsevolodovich. Zotov's study is of special significance in that he not only relied on chronicle sources for his information, but compared them with a then little known source – the *Lyubetskiy sinodik*.[16] Unfortunately, since his purpose was to discover princely genealogies he did not analyze their activities and their policies.

This was done by the Ukrainian historian M. Hrushevsky.[17] He explains that from the time of Grand Prince Vsevolod Ol'govich (d. 1146), up to the destruction of Kiev in 1240, the prime motivation for the princes of Rus' was the desire to rule from the "golden throne" of Kiev. From the three generations succeeding Vsevolod Ol'govich, three senior princes of Chernigov became rulers of Kiev.[18] But, in his opinion, these were merely

[14] *O Chernigovskikh knyazyakh.*

[15] Ibid. p. 3.

[16] This manuscript belonged to the Monastery of St. Anthony in Lyubech (a town northwest of Chernigov on the Dnepr river). Zotov explains that along with this *sinodik* (a register of the deceased), there were five others which listed the names of the princes of Chernigov – the *Elitskiy*, the *Severskiy*, the *Kievskiy*, the *Il'inskiy*, and the *Gamaleevskiy sinodiki*. However, the *Lyubetskiy* is the most valuable. It is divided into four parts: (1) an introduction, (2) a list of eighteen commemorations, (3) a commemoration of all the princes of Chernigov (the source of Zotov's study), (4) a list of families to be commemorated. Zotov explains that when giving the names of the princes the *sinodik* not only provides their secular names, but, for the most part, also their Christian names. It distinguishes those who ruled in Chernigov by calling them "grand prince" (*velikiy knyaz'*). Together with the princes it often includes the names of their wives and even children. On occasion, as well as giving the patronymic, the manuscript also appends an historical note (ibid. p. 21). Of special value is the fact that the names are presented either in chronological order or in groupings, generation by generation, from the time of Ryurik. The register also preserves the order of succession of the senior princes of Chernigov (ibid. pp. 30-1). Zotov gives the text of the *sinodik* in his monograph, pp. 24-9.

[17] Although Hrushevsky touched upon the activities of the Ol'govichi in his work *Ocherk istorii Kievskoy zemli ot smerti Yaroslava do kontsa xiv stoletiya* (Kiev, 1891), his chief task in this work was to define "the fate of Kiev" and its lands (p. 428). Later he carried out a more comprehensive analysis of their activities from the eleventh to the thirteenth centuries in the second volume of his *Istoriia Ukrainy-Rusy*, 9 vols., second edition (L'vov, 1904-1931).

[18] Vsevolod's son Svyatoslav was grand prince from 1181 until his death in 1194; his son Vsevolod "the Red" ruled in Kiev on three separate occasions between 1206 and his

moral victories for the individuals concerned and had little significance on the overall fortunes and policies of the Ol'govichi. Svyatoslav Vsevolodovich and his son Vsevolod "the Red" (*Chermnyy*) were able to obtain control of Kiev solely because they were willing to compromise with their adversaries the Rostislavichi of Smolensk.[19] And Mikhail Vsevolodovich, he claims, occupied Kiev only momentarily; he peremptorily dismisses him as being of little significance.

As well as striving to win control over the "golden throne" the princes of Chernigov attempted to secure possession of Galich in southwest Rus'. The first Ol'govich to lay claim to this region was Svyatoslav Vsevolodovich and after him his son and Mikhail's father, Vsevolod. Finally, says Hrushevsky, after 1230 Mikhail and his son Rostislav made it their prime military objective to occupy Galich rather than Kiev. However, their ambitions were stifled by the Tatar invasion. He concludes his analysis by observing that during the course of one hundred and fifty years the Ol'govichi pursued a policy of expansion. Unlike most historians, he believes that they were a formidable political power throughout the twelfth century and the first half of the thirteenth century. However, he declines to comment on the activities of Mikhail Vsevolodovich – or on the significance of his attempts to pursue the traditional policy of his family.[20]

Soviet historians also have underrated the role of the Ol'govichi in the first half of the thirteenth century. They tend to concentrate their studies on the principalities of Galicia-Volyn' and Rostov-Suzdal' but to ignore the history of Chernigov.[21] One Soviet historian expresses a not uncommon view when he states that after 1208 the fortunes of the principality of Chernigov present no special interest.[22] The little importance which they attributed to the Ol'govichi is reflected in the fact that not one monograph has been devoted solely to the history of these princes.

---

death in 1215; the last Ol'govich to rule in Kiev was his son Mikhail. See Table 2:3, 7, 14, 27. (A fourth prince of Chernigov, Izyaslav Davidovich [d. 1161] became grand prince after Vsevolod Ol'govich; however, he was not an Ol'govich; see N. de Baumgarten, *Généalogies et mariages occidentaux des Rurikides Russes du xe au xiiie siècle* [*Orientalia Christiana*, vol. IX, no. 35, Rome, 1927], Table IV, no. 10, p. 18.)

[19] The Rostislavichi were the descendants of Rostislav Mstislavich (d. 1168), the grandson of Vladimir *Monomakh*; they ruled in the principality of Smolensk. See Table 3:4.

[20] *Istoriya*, vol. 2, pp. 321-4.

[21] See for example M. N. Tikhomirov and S. S. Dmitriev, *Istoriya SSSR*, vol. 1 (Moscow, 1948), pp. 55-6.

[22] B. A. Rybakov, "Chernigovskoe i Severskoe knyazhestva," *Istoriya SSSR*, ed. B. A. Rybakov, vol. 1 (Moscow, 1966), p. 597.

The most extensive treatment of the princes of Chernigov is found in *Ocherki istorii SSSR: Period feodalizma IX-XV vv.*, part one, (IX-XIII vv.), *Drevnyaya Rus', Feodal'naya razdroblennost'*.[23] Here again, V. T. Pashuto reiterates the traditional view that at the beginning of the thirteenth century the strongest unified regions in Rus' were Rostov-Suzdal' and Galicia-Volyn'.[24] However, he overlooks the statement which he made prior to this where he had noted that in their inter-princely relations during this period the Romanovichi of Volyn' became involved in a struggle for supremacy in southern and southwest Rus' with the princes of Rostov-Suzdal' and the princes of Chernigov.[25]

V. V. Mavrodin, who wrote the entry on the history of the principality of Chernigov in *Ocherki istorii SSSR*, concludes his account with the death of the senior prince Mstislav Svyatoslavich at the Kalka battle in 1223. He reiterates arguments similar to those presented by Pogodin concerning the fragmentation of the principality and its political insignificance in the first half of the thirteenth century.[26]

It appears that A. N. Nasonov was the first historian to challenge the traditional views concerning the significance of the Ol'govichi. He claims that the twelfth century and the beginning of the thirteenth century witnessed a struggle for the supremacy in Rus' between two of the strongest principalities – Chernigov and Rostov-Suzdal',[27] a rivalry which was terminated only with Mikhail's death in 1246.[28] In his opinion it was in Khan Baty's interest to support Mikhail's enemy Yaroslav Vsevolodo-vich of Rostov-Suzdal', as the former had adopted an uncompromising stand against the Tatars.[29]

[23] Gen. ed., B. D. Grekov (Moscow, 1953).

[24] "Vnutripoliticheskoe polozhenie Rusi v nachale XIII v.," pp. 770-1.

[25] *Ocherki po istorii Galitsko-volynskoy Rusi* (Moscow, 1950), pp. 207-8; later he also acknowledges the fact that Mikhail established his rule over all Galicia (p. 217).

[26] "Chernigovskoe knyazhestvo," p. 400. It must be noted that Mavrodin is not entirely consistent in his evaluation of the activities of the Ol'govichi. Two pages prior to this conclusion he expresses the view that in the struggle for control of Kiev, the Ol'go-vichi enjoyed significant success. He points out that beginning with the reign of Vsevolod Ol'govich and up to the time of Mikhail Vsevolodovich the princes of Chernigov were often chosen by the popular assembly or *veche* of Novgorod to rule in the town. All this, explains, Mavrodin, shows the political *strength* and significance of the principality of Chernigov (ibid. p. 398).

[27] "Vladimiro-Suzdal'skoe knyazhestvo," *Ocherki istorii SSSR*, p. 334.

[28] *Mongoly i Rus'* (Moscow-Leningrad, 1940), p. 27.

[29] Ibid. pp. 26-8. Besides naming Yaroslav Vsevolodovich the senior of all the princes of Rus', Baty went even further and ordered the execution of Mikhail in order to secure Yaroslav's "claims over all Rus'" ("общерусския притязания"). Therefore, Nasonov suggests, the reason for Mikhail's execution was not the usually accepted one – that he failed to comply with a Tatar pagan custom, but rather that his death stemmed from political motives.

The most recent article on the principality of Chernigov has been written by A. K. Zaytsev. He has adopted Nasonov's view that the strongest principalities in Kievan Rus' at the end of the twelfth century and the beginning of the thirteenth century were Chernigov and Rostov-Suzdal'. However, Zaytsev repeats the traditional view that the Ol'govichi achieved their greatest success in 1206 when they occupied the thrones of Kiev and Galich.[30]

Consequently, a survey of the works written on the Ol'govichi for the first half of the thirteenth century shows not only that there is a paucity of secondary material on the topic but that there are also conflicting views concerning the importance of these princes. The purpose of this monograph is to present a systematic investigation of the information, found chiefly in chronicle sources, describing inter-princely relations from 1224 to 1246. It will attempt to show that the significance of the political activity of Mikhail Vsevolodovich, prince of Chernigov and grand prince of Kiev, has been underestimated in the past.

MIKHAIL VSEVOLODOVICH BEFORE 1224

There is little information about Mikhail Vsevolodovich before he became senior prince of the Ol'govichi and prince of Chernigov in 1224. The exact date of his birth is not known since there is a discrepancy in the information concerning the time of his birth and the marriage of his parents. The eighteenth-century Russian historian V. N. Tatishchev, in the second recension of his *History*, states that Mikhail was born in 1179; his mother died on 6 August, soon after giving birth.[31] However, this contradicts information given in the first redaction of his *History* that Svyatoslav Vsevolodovich brought a bride for his son Vsevolod in the same year after 14 November "during the fast of St. Philip," that is, during advent.[32] Given these conflicting reports it may be assumed that Mikhail was born either in 1179 or soon after.[33] Although no reference is made to

---

[30] "Chernigovskoe knyazhestvo," *Drevnerusskie knyazhestva x-xiii vv.*, ed. L. G. Beskrovnyy (Moscow, 1975), p. 116.

[31] Vol. 3, p. 121; this information is not found in the first version of Tatishchev's *Istoriya*, cf. vol. 4, p. 294.

[32] Ibid., according to W. Dworzaczek the marriage occurred either on 11 October or 24 December 1178 but he does not give his reference (*Genealogia* [*Tablice*], [Warsaw, 1959], table 3).

[33] Dworzaczek claims that Mikhail was born ca. 1185 but he does not cite his source (ibid., table 29). Cf. G. A. Vlas'ev, *Potomstvo Ryurika: materialy dlya sostavleniya rodosloviy*, vol. 1 (Saint Petersburg, 1906), part 1, p. 26; he suggests that Mikhail was born

the prince's baptism, all the sources call him by his Christian name as Mikhail; if he had a secular name it is not known.[34] Mikhail belonged to the eleventh generation of princes descended from Ryurik and to the family of the Ol'govichi whose patrimony was the principality of Chernigov.

The chronicles make only elliptical references to Mikhail's father and fail to give his full name, that is, his name and patronymic. His paternity is spoken of in the following ways: Mikhail is referred to as Mikhail Vsevolodovich,[35] or Mikhail the son of Vsevolod grandson of Oleg,[36] or Mikhail the son of Vsevolod "the Red" (*Chermnyy*),[37] or Mikhail Vsevolo-

---

ca. 1194-96. Neither date, 1185 or 1194-96 is correct, to judge from the information that Mikhail underwent a miraculous cure in Pereyaslavl', in 1186 (see below p. 10); see Table 2:27.

[34] Traditionally each prince was given two first names: his secular name and his Christian name. The chroniclers customarily referred to him by his secular name. Various entries in the sources give evidence of this tradition. For example, under the year 1213, the Laurentian Chronicle informs us that a son was born to Yury Vsevolodovich and he was called Vsevolod, but "in holy baptism he was given the name Dmitry" (PSRL 1, col. 438). Subsequently the chronicles referred to him only as Vsevolod; see for example, s.a. 1219 (PSRL 1, col. 444), the Nikon Chronicle (PSRL 10, p. 85); s.a. 1221, the *svod* of 1479 (PSRL 25, p. 118); s.a. 1222, the Novgorod First Chronicle (NPL, pp. 60, 262), the Ermolinskiy Chronicle (PSRL 23, p. 69), the Sofiyskiy First Chronicle (PSRL 5, p. 202), the Novgorod Fourth Chronicle (PSRL 4, p. 200), the Vladimir Chronicle (PSRL 30, p. 85) and elsewhere.

Similarly, under the year 1210, the Laurentian Chronicle states that a son was born to Konstantin Vsevolodovich who was called Vsevolod, but "in holy baptism he was given the name John (*Ioan*)" (PSRL 1, col. 435). After this information the sources always refer to him by his secular name, Vsevolod. See for example s.a. 1212 (PSRL 1, col. 437); s.a. 1218, the "Rogozhskiy letopisets" (PSRL 15 [Petrograd, 1922], col. 26), the Ermolinskiy Chronicle (PSRL 23, p. 67), the *svod* of 1479 (PSRL 25, p. 115) and elsewhere.

Consequently, a prince whose secular name was Rostislav and Christian name was David (i.e., Rostislav-David) and whose father's name was Mstislav and Christian name was Boris (i.e., Mstislav-Boris) was called Rostislav Mstislavich. One chronicle would not speak of him as Rostislav Mstislavich and another as Rostislav Borisovich and still another as David Mstislavich or David Borisovich. However, should the chroniclers deviate from this traditional practice all of them would be consistent in using the same appellation, as was the case with Mikhail Vsevolodovich. Mikhail was always referred to by his Christian name, the name chosen after the Archangel Michael.

[35] Although the Laurentian Chronicle and the Hypatian Chronicle consider Vsevolod to be Mikhail's father and the son of Svyatoslav Vsevolodovich, they do not give his patronymic; they simply call Mikhail, Mikhail Vsevolodovich (e.g. PSRL 1, col. 448; PSRL 2, col. 741).

[36] *Komissionnyy spisok* (NPL, p. 268); see also Sofiyskiy First Chronicle (PSRL 5, p. 207) and the Novgorod Fourth Chronicle (PSRL 4, p. 203).

[37] The Novgorod First Chronicle (NPL, pp. 73, 284). *Chermnyy* is a sobriquet and means "dark red" or "the red."

dovich grandson of Svyatoslav Ol'govich,[38] or Mikhail son of Vsevolod "the Red" grandson of Svyatoslav and great-grandson of Oleg.[39] Despite the ambiguity in the chronicles concerning Mikhail's immediate progenitor, there can be little doubt that he was Vsevolod Svyatoslavich.[40] This is confirmed by information given by the register of princes in the *Lyubetskiy sinodik* which alone gives his full appellation, Vsevolod-Daniil Svyatoslavich.[41] Therefore, Mikhail's father was Vsevolod-Daniil Svyatoslavich "the Red", prince of Chernigov and grand prince of Kiev, who died in 1215.[42]

Mikhail's mother was a Polish princess[43] but there is some uncertainty concerning her name. According to the *Lyubetskiy sinodik* which has the most complete list of the princes of Chernigov and their spouses, it was probably Anastasia.[44] Mikhail had two sisters – Agafia and Vera. The first

---

[38] The *svod* of 1479 (PSRL 25, e.g., pp. 119, 136).

[39] The Nikon Chronicle (PSRL 10, pp. 92, 99, 102-3, 115).

[40] See also Zotov, *O Chernigovskikh knayazyakh*, pp. 67-8; no. 52, p. 279.

[41] Ibid. pp. 25, 240-1.

[42] Ibid. p. 273, no. 30; see Table 2:14.

[43] In the first redaction of his *History*, Tatishchev states that Svyatoslav Vsevodolovich brought the daughter of Casimir II of Poland (he does not give her name), as wife for his "middle son" Vsevolod (vol. 4, p. 294). However, in the second recension, he wrote that in 1179 Maria, the daughter of Casimir II, the Just, of Poland, and wife of Vsevolod Svyatoslavich, became ill and "entered a convent on 6 August and was buried in the church of St. Kirill which she herself had built." She died of complications arising from the birth of her son Mikhail (vol. 3, p. 121). The information given in both entries that the wife of Vsevolod Svyatoslavich was the daughter of Casimir II of Poland is correct. This is verified by subsequent chronicle entries. The Hypatian Chronicle states that when Mikhail was informed of the fall of Kiev in the winter of 1240/1, he and his son fled to Conrad, prince of Mazovia, in Poland (PSRL 2, cols. 783-4). After the Tatars passed through Poland Mikhail "left his uncle" and returned to Kiev (PSRL 2, col. 788). Conrad, the son of Casimir II (see Dworzaczek, *Genealogia [Tablice]*, table 3), must have been the brother of Mikhail's mother. Consequently, she was the daughter of Casimir II brought to Rus' to marry Vsevolod, Mikhail's father, in 1179.

[44] The confusion arises from the fact that Tatishchev calls her Maria in the second recension of his *History*. Since there is no mention in the sources that Mikhail's father remarried, thus eliminating the possibility that the two names refer to two different women, Tatishchev's information no doubt is erroneous. To be sure, he himself commented on the inconsistency of his information. He conceded that a discrepancy existed in the information concerning the death of "Maria" (who he claimed was Mikhail's mother), on 6 August, and the arrival of Vsevolod's spouse (i.e. Mikhail's mother) after 14 November of the same year. Significantly, he also notes that while some of the chronicles at his disposal recorded only news of "Maria's" death, others mentioned only the arrival of the bride, but no source incorporated both items of information into the same entry (vol. 3, p. 251, n. 526). Consequently, it may be concluded that Tatishchev, who alone combined both incidents into one account, erroneously identified "Maria" as Vsevolod's wife.

married Yury Vsevolodovich, grand prince of Vladimir in Rostov-
Suzdal', in 1211.[45] She was killed in the cathedral where she and her
immediate family and retinue sought refuge from the invading Tatars in
the winter of 1237/8.[46] The only reference to her sister Vera is that she
married Mikhail Vsevolodovich (or *Kir* Mikhail), prince of Pronsk in the
principality of Ryazan'.[47] Since none of the sources speak of Mikhail's
brothers, it is safe to assume that he was the only son of Vsevolod "the
Red".[48]

The single item of information which is preserved in relation to
Mikhail's childhood is concerning an incident that occurred in 1186; it has
strong undertones of pious folk tradition. In that year the prince was
cured of an infirmity through the prayerful intercession of Nikita the
stylite of Pereyaslavl', south of Kiev. After receiving a blessing from
Nikita and after donating gifts to the monastery in thanksgiving to God for
his cure, he returned home. Later, as a public sign of his gratitude,
Mikhail ordered that a cross be erected on the site of his cure. The
chronicler concluded his account by announcing that the cross was still
standing to that day.[49]

It becomes evident from information provided by another source that the two
entries were not related. The seventeenth-century Gustinskiy Chronicle, which is the only
other source to record the death of "Maria," but, under the year 1178, states that she was
"Maria the wife of Vsevolod, mother of Svyatoslav and daughter of Casimir, the king of
Poland, the monk, who entered the convent and was buried in the church of St. Kirill
which she herself had built" (PSRL 2, 1843 edition, p. 317). This no doubt is the correct
form of the original entry showing that the "Maria" who died was not Vsevolod
Svyatoslavich's wife but his *grandmother* (see Zotov, *O Chernigovskikh knyazyakh*,
pp. 263-3, no. 13). Therefore, it may assumed that the name of Mikhail's Polish mother, as
given by the *Lyubetskiy sinodik*, was Anastasia (see ibid. pp. 25, 240 and 273, no. 30;
Filaret, archbishop of Chernigov, *Istoriko-statisticheskoe opisanie Chernigovskoy eparkhii*,
vol. 5 [Chernigov, 1861-74], p. 38, no. 9).

[45] The Laurentian Chronicle (PSRL 1, col. 435).

[46] PSRL 1, col. 463.

[47] Only Tatishchev gives her name (*Istoriya*, vol. 3, p. 180); see Zotov, *O
Chernigovskikh knyazyakh*, p. 280.

[48] The register of princes in the *Lyubetskiy sinodik* supports this view; it lists Mikhail
as the only son (see Zotov, *O Chernigovskikh knyazyakh*, p. 25 and p. 241). Tatishchev,
mistakenly, lists two princes, Mstislav Vsevolodovich and Oleg Vsevolodovich,
presumably as Mikhail's brothers (*Istoriya*, vol. 4, s.a. 1224, p. 362 and vol. 3, s.a. 1227,
p. 221 respectively; see Zotov, *O Chernigovskikh knyazyakh*, pp. 279-80, nos. 51 and 53);
Filaret believed that Mikhail had a brother Andrey (*Opisanie*, vol. 5, p. 42, no. 29) as did
Solov'ev (*Istoriya*, book 1, chart no. 3b). If Mikhail had a younger brother the chronicles
surely would have referred to him since he, and not Mikhail's cousin Mstislav Glebovich,
would have succeeded him to the throne of Chernigov in 1236 (see below, p. 85).

[49] The seventeenth-century "Mazurinskiy letopisets" (PSRL 31 [Moscow, 1968], p. 65); a
narrative account of this event is also recorded in the "Kniga stepennaya tsarskogo
rodosloviya" (PSRL 21, chast' pervaya [Saint Petersburg, 1908], pp. 248-9); see below

In 1206, when Mikhail was in his middle twenties and his father was the grand prince of Kiev, the latter "sent his son to Pereyaslavl'" as prince. But soon after Ryurik Rostislavich, from whom Vsevolod had usurped the "golden throne," "drove Vsevolod 'the Red' from Kiev and his son from Pereyaslavl'."[50] Although Mikhail is not mentioned by name, the "son" referred to can be none other since he had no brothers. To judge from this information, Mikhail's sojourn in the town was his first involvement in inter-princely rivalry because he supplanted Yaroslav Vsevolodovich of Rostov-Suzdal' (his future rival for the town of Novgorod), whose family traditionally ruled in Pereyaslavl'. However, Mikhail's rule was short-lived. Soon after, probably before 1212,[51] he married the daughter of Roman Mstislavich, prince of Galicia and Volyn' in southwest Rus'.[52] The chronicles do not give her name but, to judge from the information given in the *Lyubetskiy sinodik*, she was called Elena.[53]

---

pp. 150-151. M. Pogodin claims that Mikhail ordered a "stone column" to be erected on 16 May 1186 (*Drevnyaya russkaya istoriya*, vol. 2 [Moscow, 1871], p. 640). Unfortunately, he does not give his source.

[50] The Laurentian Chronicle (PSRL 1, col. 428).

[51] According to Filaret's account of the Life of St. Evfrosinia (the religious name of Mikhail's daughter Feodula who became a nun in a convent in Suzdal'), she was Mikhail's eldest daughter (i.e., eldest child?, *Russkie svyatye*, p. 120) and was born in 1212 (ibid. p. 121, n. 221). Cf. Vlas'ev, *Potomstvo Ryurika*, vol. 2, vypusk 1, p. viii; he states that the second daughter of Roman Mstislavich married Mikhail Vsevolodovich either towards the end of 1211 or at the beginning of 1212; he does not give his source.

[52] The Hypatian Chronicle (PSRL 2, cols. 782-3); she is called the sister of Daniil Romanovich.

[53] Filaret points out that the *Kievskiy sinodik* calls Mikhail's wife Feofania (*Opisanie*, vol. 5, pp. 38-9, no. 12, n. 34; see also his *Russkie svyatye*, p. 121). According to Zotov the *Lyubetskiy sinodik* states that Oleg-Mikhail Svyatoslavich (d. 1115) was married to Feofania but it does not give the name of Mikhail's wife (*O Chernigovskikh knyazyakh*, p. 239, no. 4). Despite Zotov's contention that Mikhail's wife is not listed in the register, a closer look at it reveals that this was not the case. It is interesting to note that the majority of the princes named prior to Mikhail, especially the more prominent ones, are listed along with their wives; in one instance only, after the first prince named, Konstantin Mstislavich, there is appended the additional information that he built the Church of the Saviour (Transfiguration) in Chernigov. Significantly, the entry for Mikhail is the largest in the register. But, rather than recording his name and that of his wife, as was customarily the case, it states: "Grand Prince Mikhail of Chernigov, son of Vsevolod, grandson of Svyatoslav and his boyar Fedor, who refused to bow to the sun and would not walk around the bush (куст), killed by the Tatars for the Orthodox faith." The next entry reads: "Prince Mikhail and his princess Elena." On the one hand, it must be remembered that after their martyrdom Mikhail and Fedor were always venerated together, whether in the liturgy or in private devotion. The entry in the register, in keeping with this pious tradition, lists Mikhail and his boyar first, rather than Mikhail

The last reference to Mikhail before he became prince of Chernigov is made under the year 1223. At that time the princes of Rus' held a council in Kiev, prior to the battle with the Tatars on the Kalka river. From among the many princes who attended, the chronicles list the names of the three senior princes of southern Rus': Mstislav Romanovich, a Rostislavich from Smolensk and grand prince of Kiev; Mstislav Svyatoslavich of Kozel'sk (a town in the northern districts of the principality of Chernigov) and prince of Chernigov; Mstislav Mstislavich "the Bold" (*Udaloy*), another Rostislavich and prince of Galich. It also names three junior princes: Daniil Romanovich of Volyn', Mikhail Vsevolodovich an Ol'govich and Vsevolod Mstislavich son of the grand prince of Kiev.[54] The amalgamated armies of southern Rus' set out to confront the new invaders from the east. But the Tatars overwhelmed them at the Kalka river. Several of the princes were killed, including Mstislav Romanovich the senior prince of the Rostislavichi and Mstislav Svyatoslavich the senior among the Ol'govichi. Although Mikhail is not singled out as participating in the battle, he was probably present in his capacity as junior prince (i.e., the next in line to succeed to the throne of Chernigov), since he had also attended the council of war in Kiev.

This was Mikhail's first encounter with the Tatars but it was not to be his last. Ironically, his initial clash with the enemy who would ultimately destroy him was propitious to his immediate political career. He had set out on the campaign as heir apparent to the throne of Chernigov. However, Mstislav Svyatoslavich's death on the battlefield accelerated his succession to the throne. Mikhail returned from the rout not only as one of the fortunate survivors but also as the new senior prince of the Ol'go-vichi and prince of Chernigov.

His reign was to last until his death in 1246. Following the example of his father and other Ol'govichi before him, Mikhail was to challenge, successfully, three families of Monomashichi, the most powerful princes in the country, for control over Kiev and supremacy in Rus'. His activity in Novgorod would antagonize the Vsevolodovichi of Rostov-Suzdal'; his

---

and his wife. On the other hand, it is difficult to imagine that the name of the wife of such an illustrious saint would have been either forgotten locally, or omitted from the register of princes where the venerable memory of her husband enjoyed a prominent place. Although the *sinodik*, as a rule, does not repeat the names of princes, no doubt, in this case it made an exception: after listing Mikhail the martyr with his companion Fedor, it gave Mikhail the prince with his spouse Elena (ibid. pp. 24-5).

[54] The Hypatian Chronicle (PSRL 2, col. 741).

policy towards Kiev would bring him into conflict with the Rostislavichi of Smolensk; and his efforts to secure his hold over Galicia in the southwest would alienate the Romanovichi of Volyn'. Ultimately, the inter-princely rivalry was resolved through the intervention of a foreign power, the Tatars, who invaded Rus', for the second time, in the winter of 1237/8.

1

Mikhail's Policy in Novgorod

Mikhail Vsevolodovich became involved in the politics of Novgorod almost immediately after he acceded to the throne of Chernigov; this activity was to lead him into conflict with the Vsevolodovichi of Rostov-Suzdal'. By the beginning of the thirteenth century Novgorod had become not only the most important trading and commercial centre in Rus' but also in northeast Europe. Situated near Lake Il'men', it was the hub of extensive commercial enterprises; its trade was dispersed via several major trade routes, chief among them being the rivers Volkhov (to the north), Lovat' (to the south), Msta and Mologa (to the southeast). Located strategically on these major routes, near the boundaries of its lands, Novgorod had "vassal" towns which helped to regulate its flow of trade (e.g., Ladoga on the Volkhov river, Velikie Luki on the Lovat' river, and the towns of Torzhok [Novyy Torg] and Volok Lam'skiy on the southeast trade route).

Novgorod's wealth and significance as a trading centre enabled it to enjoy a unique position among the great towns of Rus' – it was governed by an "assembly" (*veche*) and it had no ruling family of princes. The population of the town was made up primarily of merchants, boyars (who were the major landowners), tradesmen and "common people." Members from the various classes constituted its government and met in the traditional *veche* which voted on issues of policy and resolved disputes. The chief appointed officer of Novgorod was its archbishop. His main functions were the following: he was the head of the Orthodox Church; he was also the supervisor of the ecclesiastical court and the overseer of commercial weights and measures. The archbishop, as perhaps the single largest landowner in the first half of the thirteenth century, was also a major legislator of foreign policy. The other appointed officers, the *posadnik* and the *tysyatskiy*, were the executive agents of the *veche*. Their chief functions were to oversee the internal administration and the foreign affairs of the town. The *posadnik* was the supreme judge; he appointed state officials; he supervised the activities of the prince; he accompanied the prince on campaigns as commander of the Novgorod army. The *tysyatskiy* was the *posadnik*'s primary assistant; he commanded the town militia and acted as judge at the commercial court.

The salient feature of Novgorod's autonomy was its right to invite (and to expel) a prince from any principality in Rus' to rule in Novgorod. His chief function was to provide an army both to quell internal unrest and to promote Novgorod's interests beyond its frontiers. The prince had limited jurisdiction over the courts and over internal administration; he was also forbidden to acquire Novgorod lands. Needless to say, princes were not always ready to accept all the terms demanded by the assembly. The stringency of the clauses imposed on a prince by the *posadnik* and the *veche*, therefore, reflected the strength of Novgorod. At times the selection of a prince fostered violent debates in the assembly since various factions were divided in their choice. However, there was general unanimity among the townsmen in their desire to curtail the authority of the prince; at the beginning of the thirteenth century, the *veche* was exceptionally powerful in this resolve. In the early 1220s, when the assembly agreed to invite the Vsevolodovichi of Rostov-Suzdal' to rule, the princes found it impossible to accept the terms imposed on them; at the same time, they did not wish to reject the invitation. It was this impasse which implicated Mikhail Vsevolodovich in the affairs of Novgorod soon after he became prince of Chernigov.

According to chronicle information, Mikhail was drawn into the politics of northwest Rus' in the following manner. In 1224, Prince Vsevolod Yur'evich and all his court fled at night from Novgorod and sought refuge in the town of Torzhok or Novyy Torg as it was also known. This was a border town of Novgorod located on its southeast trade route to the Volga river; it was the most important centre of commerce between Novgorod and the lands of Rostov-Suzdal'. Grand Prince Yury Vsevolodovich came to Torzhok to the aid of his son. He was accompanied by his younger brother Yaroslav, his nephew Vasil'ko Konstantinovich who brought troops from the town of Rostov, and his brother-in-law Mikhail Vsevolodovich who had come with his army from Chernigov. The inhabitants of Novgorod sent messengers to Yury asking him to send back his son Vsevolod and requesting him to depart from Torzhok. Yury, on his part, threatened to invade unless they surrendered certain of the boyars to him. Instead of complying with his demands the townspeople strengthened their fortifications and, the chronicler explains, resolved to die rather than hand over their "brothers." Yury sent messengers a second time but on this occasion proposed that they accept his "brother-in-law" (*shurin*),[1] Mikhail Vsevolodovich, as prince. They welcomed the compromise and sent men to receive Mikhail. Yury and the remaining princes withdrew from Torzhok but only after doing "much harm to the Novgorodians" and extorting "7,000 novuyu (новую)."[2] Later the chronicler explains that part of the "harm" which Yury inflicted on the merchants of Novgorod was to plunder their wares in Torzhok and also on the trade route in his own principality of Rostov-Suzdal'.[3]

The chronicle does not explain why Mikhail accompanied the grand prince to Torzhok. Since it is not known whether or not he had another purpose for visiting Yury Vsevolodovich other than to help him settle the dispute with Novgorod, it can be assumed only that Mikhail joined the Vsevolodovichi expressly to provide reinforcements against the obstinate townsmen. Although he alone was not a prince of Rostov-Suzdal', Mikhail was more than merely a political ally of the grand prince. The chronicler points out that he was Yury's "brother-in-law." Since this family tie is singled out it probably played a significant part in the political relationship between Mikhail and Yury.[4]

---

[1] Yury Vsevolodovich married Mikhail's sister in 1211; the Laurentian Chronicle (PSRL 1, col. 435), see Table 4:8. The *svod* of 1479 is the only chronicle source which gives the date 10 April for the wedding (PSRL 25, p. 108); cf. Tatishchev who gives the date as 29 April (*Istoriya*, vol. 4, p. 342).

[2] The Novgorod First Chronicle (NPL, pp. 63-4, 267-8). These events occurred in the year 1224/5. See Berezhkov, *Khronologiya*, pp. 268-9; see below n. 18. This is the only reference to "новая" in the chronicles. It was no doubt a unit of currency. A deed from the first half of the twelfth century stipulates that the archbishop of Novgorod received the sum of 100 "гривен новых коун;" see "Ustavnaya gramota novgorodskogo knyazya Svyatoslava Ol'govicha tserkvi sv. Sofiyi v Novgorode datoy 1136/37 g.," in Ya. N. Shchapov, *Drevnerusskie knyazheskie ustavy xi-xv vv.* (Moscow, 1976). Similarly, the entry under 1224 may be referring to 7,000 "гривен новых коун."

[3] NPL, pp. 64, 268, s.a. 1225.

[4] Chronicle information shows that in the early thirteenth century marriage relationships were often utilized as expedients for political action. In 1204, Roman Mstislavich of Galich imprisoned Rostislav Ryurikovich. Vsevolod Yur'evich grand prince of Vladimir came to Rostislav's rescue and demanded that Roman release his "son-in-law"; see the Laurentian Chronicle (PSRL 1, col. 421). In 1207, when Vsevolod Yur'evich summoned the princes of Ryazan' to march against the Ol'govichi, Mikhail Vsevolodovich of Pronsk (*Kir* Mikhail as he was known), begged to be excused because he did not wish to march against his "father-in-law," Vsevolod Svyatoslavich (PSRL 1, col. 431). Finally, before the battle on the Kalka river, Khan Kotyan of the Polovtsy came to Galich and asked Mstislav Mstislavich "the Bold" to help him against the Tatars (Kotyan was his "father-in-law"). Mstislav approached the princes of southern Rus' at Kotyan's request; see the Novgorod First Chronicle (NPL, pp. 62, 265).

The friendship between the two princes was a noteworthy reversal of the relationship which had existed between the Ol'govichi and Vsevolod Yur'evich "the Big Nest" (*Bol'shoe Gnezdo*)[5] as he was known. Two factors contributed most to lessening the hostility between the two families of princes. In 1211, as has been mentioned, Yury Vsevolodovich married Mikhail's sister thus drawing the two princes together through family ties.[6] The other factor was the political relationships which arose between the various princes of Rus' following the succession crisis of 1216 in Rostov-Suzdal'. At that time Konstantin Vsevolodovich, Yury's older brother, solicited the support of the prince of Novgorod, Mstislav Mstislavich "the Bold" (*Udaloy*), a Rostislavich from the principality of Smolensk, and of all the Rostislavichi, the traditional allies of the princes of Rostov-Suzdal'.[7] Yury, therefore, was obliged to seek support elsewhere; the princes of Chernigov were his most logical, if not the only possible choice.[8] Consequently, in 1224 Mikhail and Yury were drawn together both by marriage ties and by political necessity.

The grand prince's proposal to the Novgorodians that they accept Mikhail as their prince was not only an expression of the good will which existed between the two princes but, more important, it was an unprecedented tactic used by the grand prince of Vladimir. During the reign of Yury's father, Vsevolod, the princes of Rostov-Suzdal' had been the chief, but, not the sole contestants for control over Novgorod. His desire to establish suzerainty over northwest Rus' dictated that he keep

[5] During the thirty-six year rule as grand prince, Vsevolod supported the claims of the Rostislavichi to Kiev against those of the Ol'govichi. On at least two occasions (in 1195 and in 1207), he marshalled his forces to march against the Ol'govichi, but each time he failed to fulfil his threat; see the Laurentian Chronicle (PSRL 1, cols. 429-30) and the Hypatian Chronicle (PSRL 2, col. 689).

[6] See n. 1.

[7] The Novgorod First Chronicle (NPL, pp. 55-7, 254-7).

[8] It is unlikely, for example, that the princes of Ryazan' would have allied themselves with the Vsevolodovichi. Vsevolod Yur'evich had pillaged their lands in 1207, and then imprisoned the princes in Vladimir. They were released in 1212 by his son Yury; see the Laurentian Chronicle (PSRL 1, col. 437). On the other hand, Yury demonstrated his partiality to the Ol'govichi as early as 1216 when he was embroiled in a power struggle with his elder brother Konstantin. The rivalry became so bitter that it had to be resolved in warfare on the Lipitsa river north of Vladimir. However, prior to the encounter of the enemy forces, Yury, who anticipated a victory, distributed the land of Rus' among his allies in the following manner: he himself was to take the principalities of Vladimir and Rostov; Yaroslav, his brother, was to take Novgorod; his brother Svyatoslav was to be prince of Smolensk; the Vsevolodovichi were also to keep Galich; however, Yury proposed to give Kiev to the Ol'govichi; see the Sofiyskiy First Chronicle (PSRL 5, p. 196), and the Novgorod Fourth Chronicle (PSRL 4, p. 190); this information is not found in the earlier chronicles – the Hypatian, the Laurentian and the Novgorod First.

other families of princes out of the town. This policy had proven to be so successful against the Ol'govichi that they were not able to assume control over it, in effect, for over forty years.[9] Ironically, in 1224 Vsevolod's successor himself proposed to the inhabitants of Novgorod that they accept the prince of Chernigov to rule in their town. Thus, Yury acted contrary to his father's long-standing policy and, with his proposal, admitted that he was no longer capable of controlling Novgorod, as his father had done, solely with the resources of northeast Rus'.

Reasons for Yury's weakened authority over Novgorod are not difficult to find. In the winter of 1208/9, even before the death of Grand Prince Vsevolod Yur'evich, the Rostislavichi of Smolensk, whose principality was located immediately to the south of Novgorod, succeeded in making a successful bid for control over it. Their rule proved to be popular in Novgorod and they remained there almost without a break until 1221.[10] It appears that during this interim period of Rostislavichi presence the *posadnik* and the *veche* were able to strengthen their independence from the authority of the prince.[11] Furthermore, during this interval, the Vsevolodovichi were experiencing a time of internal strife as Konstantin and Yury, the two eldest sons of Vsevolod, struggled to gain control over the principality of Rostov-Suzdal'. In 1216, their rivaly culminated in a crushing defeat for Yury and his brother Yaroslav on the Lipitsa river northwest of Vladimir. Their armies were crushed by their elder brother Konstantin and his allies Mstislav Mstislavich, the Rostislavichi of Smolensk and the forces from Novgorod. Thus, when the Novgorodians requested Grand Prince Yury to send a prince in 1221, he was not able to renew that relationship which his father had enjoyed with them in 1210.[12] The fact that the Vsevolodovichi kept leaving Novgorod, in the early 1220s, shows not only that it was they who were not content with the

[9] Except for a six month soujourn made by Yaropolk Yaroslavich in 1197 (NPL, pp. 43, 236), the last Ol'govich to rule in Novgorod had been Vladimir Svyatoslavich, in 1181 (NPL, pp. 37, 227); see Table 2:12.

[10] Mstislav Mstislavich ruled in Novgorod on two occasions: from the winter of 1208/9 until the winter of 1214/15 (NPL, pp. 51, 53; 249, 252; the chronicle misplaces Mstislav's arrival at Novgorod under 1210; for the correct dating see Berezkhov, *Khronologiya*, pp. 255-6), and from 1216 until 1218 (NPL, pp. 57, 58; 257, 259). In 1218, he was replaced by Svyatoslav Mstislavich, the son of Grand Prince Mstislav Romanovich (NPL, pp. 58, 259). In 1219, Vesvolod Mstislavich replaced his older brother (NPL, pp. 59, 260). Finally, in 1221, Vesvolod Mstislavich was driven out by the Novgorodians (NPL, pp. 60, 262). The only interval during which a Rostislavich did not rule was from the spring of 1215 (NPL, pp. 53, 252) until February 1216 (NPL, pp. 55, 253) when Yaroslav Vsevolodovich was prince.

[11] See V. L. Yanin, *Novgorodskie posadniki* (Moscow, 1962), pp. 130-1.

[12] See Solov'ev, *Istoriya*, book 1, p. 621.

conditions imposed upon them by the *posadnik* and the *veche*, but, that they were also powerless to rectify the situation.[13]

In 1224, three years after the assembly had invited the Vsevolodovichi to return, they were still not able to agree to the terms of rule. Since neither side was willing to give in, the impasse nearly led to bloodshed. Yury threatened to attack Novgorod but the townsmen refused to be intimidated. They held to their position declaring that they were prepared to die for the Cathedral of St. Sofia and for *Posadnik* Ivan Dimitrievich[14] whom they had appointed to the office of *posadnik* in 1220.[15] Although both sides were prepared to resolve the dispute by a show of force, the grand prince was reluctant to attack before he exhausted all possible alternatives. Not wishing to relinquish his hold over northwest Rus' and,

---

[13] In 1221, Yury sent his seven year old son Vsevolod to rule in Novgorod "according to all the conditions set down by the Novgorodians" ("на всѣи воли новгородьстѣи"). However, it appears that the grand prince later changed his mind and recalled his son in the winter of 1222/3. The townsmen proposed that "if it does not suit you to rule Novgorod through your son, then give us your brother" ("оже ти не угодьно държати Новагорода сыномь, а въда ны брат"). He complied with their request and sent Yaroslav in 1223; see the Novgorod First Chronicle (NPL, pp. 60-1; 262-3); cf. the Laurentian Chronicle (PSRL 1, col. 445); concerning the correct dating see, Berezhkov, *Khronologiya*, pp. 251-2. However, Yaroslav departed in the same year even though the townsmen begged him not to go; the chronicler explains that he left "of his own accord." The people of Novgorod again asked the grand prince to send them his son and he sent Vsevolod (NPL, pp. 61, 263). Finally, Vsevolod who arrived in Novgorod, in 1224 (NPL, pp. 61, 264), fled secretly at night in the same year (NPL, pp. 63-4, 267-8).

[14] "хотѣша умрети за святую Софию о посадницѣ о Иванцѣ о Дмитровици"; see the Novgorod First Chronicle (NPL, pp. 64, 268). The *posadnik*'s policy, aside from the evident fact that he sought to curtail the authority of the prince, is not explained. To be sure, various theories have been proposed concerning the objectives of faction politics in Novgorod for the period covering the twelfth and the beginning of the thirteenth century. It has been argued that the townspeople were determined, at all costs, to protect their independence from the princes of Suzdal' (N. I. Kostomarov, "Severnorusskiya narodopravstva," *Sobranie sochineniya*, book 3, vols. 7 and 8 [Saint Petersburg, 1904], pp. 51-2). N. Rozhkov expressed the belief that the people of Novgorod were divided into two political parties: the "democratic" party, which was made up of merchants and the "common people" (*chernye lyudi*), opposed the "aristocratic" party comprising the boyars, the chief landowners ("Politicheskie partii v Velikom Novgorode XII-XVI vv.," *Istoricheskie i sotsiologicheskie ocherki, sbornik statey*, part 2 [Moscow, 1906], p. 38). Finally, there is the theory that internal unrest in Novgorod stemmed from the class conflict which is indigenous to a feudal society – the struggle of the "lesser people" (*men'shie lyudi*) for their rights (M. N. Tikhomirov, *Drevnyaya Rus'* [Moscow, 1975], p. 215).

[15] The Novgorod First Chronicle (NPL, pp. 60, 262). The chronicle also speaks of *Posadnik* Ivan under the years 1222, 1226, 1228 and 1229 in which year he was removed from office (NPL, pp. 60-68, 262-74). Apparently he held the office of *posadnik* continuously throughout these years.

at the same time, unable to reach an agreement with the *veche*, he was faced with the problem of finding a candidate who would support the interests of Rostov-Suzdal'. He offered Mikhail as prince, presumably, as a stop-gap measure.

Yury selected his brother-in-law to represent his interests chiefly because, aside from the Vsevolodovichi, he did not have many princes to choose from. He would have been reluctant to see the Rostislavichi back in Novgorod since they had been the most successful rivals to the princes of Rostov-Suzdal'. It has been noted that they ruled, almost continuously, from 1208/9 until 1221. There was probably a dormant faction in the town still favouring the return of the Rostislavichi. Furthermore, the memory of his defeat on the Lipitsa river, when the princes of Smolensk had joined forces with the Novgorodians, could not have been far from the back of Yury's mind. Mikhail, however, was his *shurin* and ally, and his principality was sufficiently far from Novgorod[16] to make him a much safer choice in 1224.[17] Thus, by not allowing a Vsevolodovich to capitulate to the terms of the *posadnik* and the *veche* Yury saved face and, at the same time, vented his displeasure against them by plundering their trade caravans and by extorting the sum of "7,000 novuyu (новую)."

Mikhail arrived in Novgorod in March of the following year. The chronicler states that after he took over command of the town "things were easier in the district of Novgorod." One of his main services to the *veche* was to lead a delegation of townsmen to Yury Vsevolodovich in Vladimir to "retrieve the goods" which the latter had sequestrated from the merchants of Novgorod. After returning with the confiscated merchandise Mikhail announced that he did not wish to remain in Novgorod and intended to return to his principality in southern Rus'. But, before he departed, he requested the citizens to allow foreign traders to come to him in Chernigov. Since their pleas to him to remain proved to be of no avail, they "saw him off with honour." Then, turning to the Vsevolodovichi once again, they sent messengers to the grand prince's younger brother, Yaroslav, who was prince in Pereyaslavl', a town located between Rostov and Suzdal'.[18]

---

[16] Novgorod was less readily accessible from Chernigov than from either Smolensk or Rostov-Suzdal'. If Mikhail wished to bring troops from Chernigov to the northwest he had to pass through the lands of Smolensk and in some instances also through the regions of Rostov-Suzdal'. See Map no. 1; see below, n. 40.

[17] Although the princes of Chernigov had ruled in Novgorod in the past there is no evidence to suggest that Mikhail agitated to become prince at this time.

[18] NPL., pp. 64, 268-9. The chronicle states that the people of Novgorod sent their envoys to collect Mikahil in 1224. He arrived in the town in the beginning of 1225. Since

To judge from chronicle information, the Novgorodians were content
with Mikhail's rule. Reasons for their satisfaction are readily evident: he
made no demands and appears to have cooperated with them. Since
"things were easier" after he arrived, he must have eased some of the
burdens imposed on the inhabitants by previous princes. The fact that he
successfully negotiated the return of those "goods" which Yury had
confiscated from the merchants of Novgorod also indicates that he was
able to restore some semblance of good will between the *veche* and the
Vsevolodovichi. In this way he helped to pave the way for their return to
Novgorod. Since Yaroslav accepted the invitation to be prince, Mikhail's
stay in the town served the purpose for which Yury had appointed
him – to restore a working order between the princes of Rostov-Suzdal'
and the assembly. According to two late sources, it was the inhabitants of
Novgorod who made concessions to the terms they had demanded in
1224, since Yaroslav returned the following year "according to all his
terms."[19]

Despite the harmony which existed between Mikhail and the *veche*,
and even though the townsmen asked him to remain in Novgorod, he
chose to return to his patrimony. The chronicle fails to give Mikhail's
motives for leaving the town but at least one reason is obvious. As the
new prince of Chernigov he was concerned about the state of affairs in his
own principality.[20] He evidently had Chernigov interests in mind when he
departed from northwest Rus'. Wishing to take advantage of the good
rapport which he had established with the merchants of Novgorod, he
made an agreement with them to ensure that, even after his departure,
foreign trade would continue to flow through Novgorod to his
principality. Since the Novgorodians sent for Yaroslav Vsevolodovich
immediately following his departure, Mikhail must have made a complete
administrative break with the town, not leaving any representatives (his
son, for example) to rule in his stead.

---

there appears to be no break in the sequence of events between the time that the citizens
accepted Mikhail and the time that he arrived in the town, the events probably transpired
at the turn of the March (*martovskiy*) year 1224 and the year 1225. Therefore, the
occupation of the town of Torzhok by Yury probably occurred around February of 1225,
and Mikhail went to Novgorod some time in March 1225.

[19] "на свеы своеы воли"; see the Tver' Chronicle (from the second half of the
sixteenth century), "Tverskaya letopis'" (PSRL 15 [Saint Petersburg, 1863], col. 345), and the
"Kholmogorskaya letopis'" (from the second half of the seventeenth century) (PSRL 33
[Leningrad, 1977], p. 65).

[20] Indeed, it is surprising that Mikhail chose to leave his patrimony and become prince
of Novgorod in 1225 so soon after becoming prince of Chernigov. Clearly there was no
unrest among the Ol'govichi and he did not experience any opposition to his succession.

During the following two years, 1226 and 1227, while Yaroslav was prince in Novgorod, nothing significant occurred in northwest Rus' to alter Mikhail's relations with the princes of Rostov-Suzdal'. But a crisis in Chernigov gave him an opportunity to consolidate his political alliance with Yury. The grand prince returned Mikhail's favour to him in Novgorod by coming to Chernigov in 1226 to help in an internal crisis.[21] As we shall see, Mikhail attempted to prevent one of the junior Ol'govichi, Oleg Svyatoslavich, whose patrimony was the town of Kursk in the eastern districts of the principality, from occupying the town of Novgorod Severskiy on the Desna river north of Chernigov, which was also his rightful patrimony. The dispute was resolved peacefully through the mediation of both Grand Prince Yury and the metropolitan who had come to Chernigov at that time.[22] In the following year, Mikhail and Yury strengthened their family ties further still when the latter sanctioned the marriage of his nephew, Vasil'ko Konstantinovich of Rostov, to Mikhail's daughter Maria.[23]

Over the period of the next five years, however, Mikhail's increased involvement in the affairs of Novgorod would alienate the princes of Rostov-Suzdal' from the Ol'govichi. In the autumn of 1228, while Yaroslav's sons Fedor and Aleksandr ruled in Novgorod, the chronicler explains that heavy rains fell continuously for almost four months from the Feast of the Assumption (15 August) until 6 December.[24] These caused much damage, especially by preventing the farmers from working in the fields and harvesting the grain. After Lake Il'men' had frozen over that winter, a south wind broke up the ice and, as it flowed down the Volkhov river, it washed away nine pillars from the bridge on 8 December.

[21] The Laurentian Chronicle (PSRL 1, col. 448).

[22] See below, pp. 56-57.

[23] The Laurentian Chronicle (PSRL 1, col. 450). The "Life" of St. Evfrosinia states that Mikhail had a second daughter named Feodula who was also engaged to be married in 1227 to a certain "prince of Suzdal'," Mina Ivanovich, concerning whom this appears to be the only reference. Presumably he was of Varangian descent and was a member of the bodyguard and retinue (*druzhina*) of the prince of Suzdal'. But Prince Mina died before his bride-to-be arrived in Suzdal'. She, however, did not return to Chernigov but entered the convent dedicated to "The Deposition of the Precious Robe of the Theotokos at Blachernae" (*Rizpolozhenskiy monastyr'*). Feodula adopted the religious name Evfrosinia and died as a nun in the same convent in 1250. See, V. T. Georgievsky, "Zhitie pr. Evfrosinii Suzdal'skoy, s miniatyurami, po spisku XVII v.," *Trudy Vladimiroskoy uchenoy arkhivnoy komissii*, book 1 (Vladimir, 1899), pp. 73-172; N. P. Barsukov, *Istochniki russkoy agiografii* (Saint Petersburg, 1882), cols. 179-81.

[24] From "Госпожькинъ день" until "Никулин дан" (NPL, pp. 66-7, 272).

The rains also precipitated a revolt: the "common people" (*prostaya chad'*) rose against Arseny who had replaced Archbishop Antony.[25] They convoked a *veche* in "Yaroslav's court" and marched to the "archbishop's court"[26] where they accused Arseny of being responsible for the warm weather and the rains. The rioters claimed that these had come because he had driven out Archbishop Antony[27] and that he had occupied his throne by bribing Yaroslav. Arseny barely escaped with his life and, on the following day, the people brought back Archbishop Antony. But this was not the end of the unrest. Assembling in a *veche*, the town rose up in arms against *Tysyatskiy* Vyacheslav who had supported Prince Yaroslav in the past. The mob plundered his court, the court of his brother and those of several other boyars. They also pillaged the house of one Dushilich, the "elder" (*starosta*) of Lipno, a village near Novgorod, and tried to hang him. He escaped and fled to Yaroslav in Pereyaslavl'. The townsmen accused Vyacheslav and the other boyars of "advising the prince to do evil," so they deprived him of his post and appointed to the office of *tysyatskiy* Boris Negochevich, a boyar opposed to the rule of the Vsevolodovichi in Novgorod.

After the townspeople removed Yaroslav's administrators from office, they invited him to rule according to a new agreement. They demanded: "abide by all our terms and by all the laws of Yaroslav."[28] Namely, he

[25] In 1223, while Yaroslav was prince of Novgorod, Archbishop Mitrofan died on 3 July and the monk Arseny was appointed to replace him. He was archbishop for two years until 1225 when Archbishop Antony – who was first appointed archbishop of Novgorod in 1211 (NPL, pp. 52, 250), and then sent to the town of Peremyshl' in the principality of Galicia in 1220 (NPL, pp. 60, 261) – returned to Novgorod as archbishop (NPL, 64, 269). Antony remained in office for three years until 1228 and then entered a monastery (NPL, 65, 270). He was replaced by Arseny who occupied the archbishop's throne until the autumn when he was driven out by the "common people" (cf. NPL, pp. 473-4).

[26] The town of Novgorod, situated on the Volkhov river a few miles north of Lake Il'men', was divided into two sides by the river – the "market side" on the right bank (east side) and "Sofiya's side." The former contained the market place or "Yaroslav's court"; "Sofiya's side" held the cathedral of St. Sofiya (after which it was named), and the archbishop's court which were surrounded by a defensive wall (*kremlim*). The town was subdivided into five "suburbs" (*kontsy*): two were located on the east side of the Volkhov river (the *Plotnitskiy konets* and the *Slavenskiy konets*) and three on the west (the *Nerevskiy konets*, the *Zagorodskiy konets* and the *Goncharskiy* or *Lyudin konets*).

[27] The first entry under the same year, 1228, states that Archbishop Antony went to the Monastery of the Holy Saviour of his own accord ("на Хутино къ святому Спасу по своеи воли"), (NPL, pp. 65, 270).

[28] "На всѣи воли нашеи и на вьсехъ грамотахъ Ярославлихъ." There is some uncertainty concerning the nature of these *gramoty*. Tikhomirov points out, convincingly, that they are not to be associated with either Yaroslav Vsevolodovich or Yaroslav Vladimirovich who ruled in Novgorod from 1182 until 1199. Instead, "Ярославли

must agree to cancel one of the taxes (забожницье)²⁹ and stop appointing judges throughout the lands of Novgorod. The townsmen concluded their offer with the customary formula which was tantamount to an ultimatum; they declared that if he did not wish to accept the terms then – "each to his own" ("ты собе, а мы собе").

Yaroslav was not intimidated by the *veche*'s ultimatum. Rather than give in to their demands he took the Novgorodians at their word; he ordered his sons Fedor and Aleksandr to leave the town. The chronicler states that they "fled" that winter, on the Tuesday of the week before Lent (i.e., 20 February 1229).³⁰ Then the townsmen resolved to invite a new prince since, they argued, it was not they who had broken their agreement with Yaroslav – they had neither expelled his sons nor had they acted unjustly when they punished their "brothers" (i.e., his corrupt supporters). In confirmation of their resolve to act in unison, they kissed the icon of the Mother of God and sent messengers to Chernigov for Mikhail Vsevolodovich. But the envoys had to pass through the principality of the Rostoslavichi and, when they came to the town of Smolensk, the prince, Mstislav Davidovich, would not allow them to continue south because he had been instructed by Yaroslav to detain them. Despite the blockade, Mikhail received the invitation while he and his son Rostislav were in the town of Bryn in the northern district of Chernigov, near the principality of Smolensk.³¹ He set out immediately for Novgorod and arrived in the town of Torzhok on Palm Sunday (i.e., 8 April).³²

грамоты" refer to the "Rus'sian law" ("Русская правда") promulgated by Yaroslav "the Wise" (*Drevnyaya Rus'*, pp. 221-2).

²⁹ Solov'ev interpreted this to mean "to stop new duties" (*Istoriya*, book 1, p. 622). Karamzin, however, assumed that it meant "to remove the Church tax" (*Istoriya*, vol. 3, p. 286). It would appear that Karamzin's interpretation is more correct. In 1217, there was a large fire in Novgorod. The chronicler reports that those merchants who fled to "stone chapels" ("камяныя божнице") perished along with their goods; "and in the chapel of the Varyagi (the name by which the peoples of the northern regions were known), all their innumerable goods were burned" ("а въ Варязьскои божници изгорѣ товаръ вьсь варязьскыи бещисла," NPL, pp. 57, 258). This suggests that certain stone chapels (божнице) in Novgorod also served as warehouses for merchandise which was either in transit or waiting to be sold. Yaroslav no doubt imposed a tax (забожницье) on such chapels. His legislation clearly raised the price of goods for the townspeople and increased their discontent.

³⁰ Concerning the correct dating, see Berezhkov, *Khronologiya*, p. 269.

³¹ This town was located in the northern regions of the principality of Chernigov on the Bryn river which flows into the Zhizdra river (N. Barsov, *Materialy dlya istoriko-geograficheskago slovarya Rossii* [Vil'na, 1865], p. 15; see Map no. 2).

³² The Novgorod First Chronicle (NPL, pp. 66-8, 272-4). Since Palm Sunday fell on 8 April 1229, Berezhkov points out that the messengers from Novgorod must have been detained in Smolensk in March 1229 (*Khronologiya*, p. 269).

To judge from the chronicler's detailed description of the unrest in Novgorod the masses revolted against a number of Yaroslav's supporters and accused them of corrupt practices. The "common people" drove Arseny from the bishop's residence because he had bribed the prince for his post.[33] Later, all the townspeople rose up in arms and plundered the court of Yaroslav's supporter, the *tysyatskiy* Vyacheslav, and deprived him of office. They justified their violence by accusing him and all the other boyars whose courts they pillaged of "advising the prince to do evil"; only one of the guilty men, the "elder" of Lipno, escaped to Yaroslav in Pereyaslavl'. The officials, presumably, had been advising the prince to adopt measures which were detrimental to the interests of the town. Since the *veche* required Yaroslav to cancel the "zabozhnits'e" (забожницье) and to stop sending judges throughout the land, the officials may have been implicated in these practices. Understandably, in order to keep their lucrative posts, they worked hand in glove with the prince. For example, the two main officials of Novgorod, *Posadnik* Ivan Dimitrievich and *Tysyatskiy* Vyacheslav, had given support to Yaroslav earlier in the year when he marched against the citizens of Pskov whom the Novgorodians called their "brothers."[34] To be sure, the reaction against Yaroslav's supporters in Novgorod may have been influenced by the actions of the citizens of Pskov against Yaroslav's faction in that town.

Early in 1228, Yaroslav fell out with the inhabitants of Pskov, an important frontier town of Novgorod located on the western border of its lands. It was not only the commercial centre for Novgorod's trade with the Baltic ports, but also the administrative focus for the fertile agricultural lands in its own districts. Pskov was the strongest of all Novgorod's "vassal" towns and in the course of time it won for itself a considerable degree of autonomy. Yaroslav alienated its citizens by attempting to assert

[33] Tikhomirov looks upon this revolt of the *prostaya chad'* as one of the most outstanding events in the history of the class struggle in Rus' during the period of feudal fragmentation (*Drevnyaya Rus'*, p. 216). He argues that this revolt was not only against Arseny but also against the *tysyatskiy* and the "*sofiyan*" – all those affiliated with the archbishop's palace (ibid. p. 217). He points out that the archbishop's palace was an institutional complex which owned much land and also many granaries. Given the heavy rains of the autumn of 1228 and the ensuing famine, the *prostaya chad'* attempted to obtain the grain stored in the archbishop's warehouses (ibid. p. 218). The chronicles do not explain whether or not the archbishop's grain was a reason for the revolt; indeed, given the rains, it is difficult to find a reason why the archbishop's warehouses would have had grain when all the others were empty. On the other hand, Tikhomirov appears to ignore the reasons for the unrest given by the chronicle, namely, the corruption of Yaroslav's officials.
[34] NPL, pp. 65-6, 271.

his control over it by coercion. Accompanied by the *posadnik* and the *tysyatskiy* from Novgorod, he marched on the town intending to bind in fetters its prominent citizens. But the townspeople barred their gates to him. Later he sent his messenger to Pskov claiming that his visit had been friendly and he asked them to join him on a campaign against Riga; he also demanded that they hand over to him those men who had spoken against him. But the citizens replied: "We bow to you prince and to our brothers the Novgorodians; but we will not go on a campaign and we will not hand over our brothers."[35] Then Yaroslav asked the inhabitants of Novgorod to march with him, but they answered that they would not go without their "brothers" from Pskov.[36] After he returned to his town of Pereyaslavl' the citizens of Pskov expelled those of their number to whom he had given a "pridatk" (придатъкъ), meaning, presumably, a bonus payment or a reward. They told the outcasts to go to Yaroslav in Pereyaslavl' since they were no longer their "brothers."[37] To judge from this accusation, the offenders were Yaroslav's henchmen in Pskov and, no doubt, were eager to promote the interests of the Vsevolodovichi in preference to those of their fellow citizens.

Thus, as we have seen, in the autumn of 1228 the citizens of Novgorod also took punitive measures against Yaroslav's supporters. But, unlike the citizens of Pskov, they did not exile the culprits and continued to call them "brothers."[38] This is significant for, to judge from the chronicler's consistent use of the term,[39] their corruption was a civil offence and not a

---

[35] NPL, pp. 66, 271.

[36] NPL, pp. 66, 272.

[37] "поидите по князи своемъ, намъ есте не братья" (NPL, pp. 66, 272).

[38] "братью свою есме казнили" (NPL, pp. 67, 274).

[39] The chronicler uses the term "brothers" in reference to the inhabitants of Novgorod and Pskov on the following occasions. In 1224, as we have seen, the Novgorodians would not hand over their "brothers" to Yury who wished to punish them (NPL, pp. 64, 268). Similarly, in 1228, the citizens of Pskov refused to give to Yaroslav those of their "brothers" who had spoken against him. In the same year, the Novgorodians said that they would not march on Riga with Yaroslav unless their "brothers" from Pskov accompanied them. Later, the citizens of Pskov told those of their number whom they had exiled that they were no longer their "brothers." Finally, in 1230, as we shall see, a splinter group in Novgorod supported Mikhail in preference to Yaroslav whom the *veche* had invited to return as prince; they, like Yaroslav's supporters in Pskov, were ostracized from Novgorod (NPL, p. 70; the *Komissionnyy spisok* does not have this information).

In all the above instances the term "brothers" is used in a specific sense, but it does not connote blood ties. First, the "brothers" of Novgorod and Pskov were equals on the social scale – they were the citizens of the towns, the freemen and the members of the *veche*. Second, "brothers" were allies sharing similar political objectives. We see, for example, that the Novgorodians and Pskovites did not hand over their "brothers" to the

political one. Consequently, their support of Yaroslav was not questioned nor was it considered to be a crime. To be sure, the *veche* was not opposed to having Yaroslav as prince; after the rioting was over it sent him an invitation to return. But, to judge from the conditions it imposed on him, the assembly was opposed to his coercive policy. Therefore, it presented him with an ultimatum – he would rule either according to all their terms or he would not rule at all.

Although requested to return, Yaroslav refused to be cowed into accepting terms which curtailed his authority; instead, he recalled his two sons from Novgorod. The prince was in a position to reject these terms because, in the long run, he had the advantage. Novgorod could not withstand foreign incursions for long without the military support of a powerful prince. At such a time the assembly would have to turn to the princes of Rostov-Suzdal' for help and, Yaroslav, who directed the affairs of the Vsevolodovichi, could dictate his own terms.

Yaroslav's rebuff evoked an important change in the policy of the *veche*. Just as the impasse in 1224 prompted Yury to send Mikhail to Novgorod, similarly the impasse in 1228, created by Yaroslav's stubbornness to make concessions, forces the Novgorodians to turn to Mikhail for help. To ensure that their decision would be backed by all the

---

princes for, even though the former had offended the princes, they had not acted against the interests of their fellow citizens. Similarly, in 1228, the Novgorodians refused to march with Yaroslav without their "brothers," the citizens of Pskov, because they feared that he would use the troops from Novgorod to attack their "brothers."

The political dimension of the term is illustrated better still in the last two examples quoted above. In 1228, Yaroslav's protégés were exiled from Pskov and told that they were no longer "brothers" of the Pskovites, because they had supported the interests of the prince in preference to those of the town. In 1230, Vodovik and his "brothers" were driven out of Novgorod because they opposed Yaroslav's rule even though the *veche* had voted to invite him back. The dissidents assumed, as it were, the characteristics of an opposition "party" to judge from the fact that the chronicler singles them out as "brothers," that is, as an identifiable group with a political objective different from that of the *veche*. In both instances, in Pskov and in Novgorod, the dissidents not only were deprived of their membership in the *veche* and their citizenship, but were also exiled.

It should be noted that in a few instances the chronicler's use of the term could be interpreted in a more general sense. For example, under 1228, he says that "God does not wish to see bloodshed between brothers," whereas "the damned one [i.e. the devil] takes delight in bloodshed between brothers" (NPL, pp. 67, 273). In his account, under 1230, he says that "God sees our lawlessness and hatred among brothers" and later he explains that "foreign towns and countries were full of our brothers and sisters" (NPL, pp. 69, 276-7). The meaning of the word in these cases could be interpreted in the biblical sense, that is, that all men are brothers in the sight of God. However, since the chronicler is speaking about the citizens of Novgorod in each instance, the word can also be interpreted, in the narrower sense, to mean a social equal and a political ally.

citizens, they took a pledge of solidarity. Anticipating such a move Yaroslav arranged to have their messengers detained in Smolensk.[40] But, despite the blockade, the envoys succeeded in relaying their message to Mikhail. Although he had declined to remain as prince in 1225, it appears that he readily accepted the invitation four years later. The reversal in his policy is not surprising. Whereas in 1225 Novgorod had welcomed him as the agent of the grand prince of Vladimir, in 1229, the *veche* invited Mikhail in his own name and, to be sure, in preference to the princes of Rostov-Suzdal'.

Mikhail arrived in Novgorod towards the end of April[41] in fulfillment of the wish of the whole *veche*. Then, somewhat unexpectedly, the chronicler describes his installation in considerable detail. He "kissed the cross"[42] and promised to abide by the terms set down by the Novgorodians and by all the "laws of Yaroslav" (i.e., the laws laid down by Yaroslav the Wise). "And what is more," he promised "not to coerce Novgorod."[43] Then he dispensed all the "peasants" (*smerdy*) who had fled to new lands from paying tax for five years;[44] those who had remained on their lands he ordered to pay tribute as had been prescribed by former princes.[45] Although the Novgorodians did not pillage the "courts" (*dvory*) of Yaroslav's supporters and, apparently, of the inhabitants of the

[40] The chronicle states that the prince of Smolensk detained the messengers "according to Yaroslav's instructions" (NPL, pp. 67, 274). Clearly, by 1228, the Rostislavichi of Smolensk were too weak to oppose Yaroslav. As we shall see, the influence of the Vsevolodovichi over the Rostislavichi would increase in the future. In 1236, they would be instrumental in evicting Vladimir Ryurikovich from Kiev (see below, pp. 75-76). Later, in 1239, Yaroslav would appoint the new prince of Smolensk; see the Laurentian Chronicle (PSRL 1, col. 469). Consequently, in 1228, the vulnerability of the political alliance between Novgorod and Mikhail was illustrated even before it was concluded. The fact that the principalities of Smolensk and Rostov-Suzdal' lay between the lands of Novgorod and Chernigov made any intercourse between the latter susceptible to intervention from the former.

[41] Mikhail arrived in Novgorod after "the week of St. Thomas" ("по ... Фоминѣ недѣли"). According to Berezhkov this week, the second after Easter, ended on 28 April 1229 (*Khronologiya*, p. 269).

[42] This was a symbolic gesture accompanying the taking of an oath. In some instances the townsmen required that the prince kiss the icon of the Mother of God, e.g., s.a. 1230, the Novgorod First Chronicle (NPL, pp. 70, 278); cf. s.a. 1228 (NPL, pp. 67, 274).

[43] "а боле того не изневолить Новагорода," the Sofiyskiy First Chronicle (PSRL 5, p. 208); see also the *svod* of 1479 (PSRL 25, p. 123) and the "Suzdal'skaya letopis' po Akademicheskomu spisku" (PSRL 1 [Leningrad, 1928], col. 511).

[44] The Novgorod Fourth Chronicle is the only source which gives the number of years as ten (PSRL 4, p. 208).

[45] Cf. the Novgorod Fourth Chronicle (PSRL 4, p. 208); the Sofiyskiy First Chronicle does not have this information); the Nikon Chronicle (PSRL 10, p. 97) and Tatishchev, *Istoriya*, vol. 3, p. 224.

"prince's residence"[46] they nevertheless extorted "much money" from
them and used it for building the "great bridge" above the site of the "old
bridge." At the same time *Posadnik* Ivan Dimitrievich, who had held his
office for nine years, was deprived of his post and replaced by the boyar
Vnezd Vodovik who supported Mikhail; in recompense they gave Ivan
the town of Torzhok. But, when he arrived there, the inhabitants refused
to receive him so he proceeded to seek sanctuary with Yaroslav in
Pereyaslavl'. The chronicler also points out that Mikhail advised the
citizens to choose a new archbishop, since Antony, who had replaced
Arseny in the previous autumn, was ailing. Of the three candidates
presented by the people, Spiridon, a monk and deacon from the Yur'ev
Monastery, was chosen by lot by Mikhail's son Rostislav.

Having supervised the reorganization of Novgorod's administration,
Mikhail returned to Chernigov, "to his brothers," accompanied by several
prominent citizens of Novgorod. He left his son to rule in the town
declaring that, God willing, he (Mikhail) would fulfill his agreement with
the *veche* but, should he fail, he would recall his son to Chernigov.[47]
Mikhail also dispatched two messengers to Yaroslav Vsevolodovich in
Pereyaslavl' demanding that he return Novgorod's frontier outpost of
Volok (i.e., Volok Lam'skiy),[48] and all the other territories which he had
appropriated from the town, and that he "kiss the cross." Yaroslav not
only sent a terse refusal but detained the messengers for the remainder of
the year. Finally, the chronicler states that in the winter, on 17 December,
the monk Spiridon went to Kiev to be consecrated archbishop by the
metropolitan.[49]

When Mikhail arrived in Novgorod in 1229, he was welcomed no
doubt as a "reformer." It must be remembered that he came after Yaroslav's faction had been removed from power for its corrupt practices and
also after the prince himself had refused to govern according to new
stipulations. Therefore, unlike Yaroslav who had returned to Novgorod in
1226, "according to all his terms,"[50] Mikhail accepted the conditions

[46] I.e., the "городищанох," presumably inhabitants of the "городище," the prince's
residence after the twelfth century, situated approximately two miles south of Novgorod
on the right bank (east side) of the Volkhov river.

[47] "А мнѣ, рече, даи богъ исправити правда новгородьская, тоже от вас пояти
сына своего" (NPL, pp. 68, 275); cf. Karamzin, *Istoriya*, vol. 3, pp. 293-4.

[48] For the importance of Volok Lam'skiy, see A. A. Zimin, "Novgorod i Volokolamsk
v xi-xv vekakh," *Novgorodskiy istoricheskiy sbornik*, vol. 10 (Novgorod, 1961), pp. 99-
101.

[49] NPL, pp. 68, 274-5.

[50] See above, p. 22.

imposed by the *posadnik* and the *veche* and, above all, promised not to coerce the Novgorodians as Yaroslav had done. When he passed the legislation to alleviate the tax burden of the serfs, the reforms, it appears, were those which Yaroslav had refused to implement and which had been a major source of the unrest. This is suggested by the fact that in 1228, when the *veche* asked Yaroslav to return, it had stipulated, as part of the agreement, that he cancel a special tax ("zabozhnits'e," забожницье), and that he no longer send judges through the land whose job it was, probably, to enforce payments from the serfs. Mikhail, however, complied with these demands. He declared a moratorium on the payment of tribute for all the peasants who had fled from their lands, presumably, because they could not pay the cumulating debts imposed by Yaroslav and his henchmen. Similarly, the *smerdy* who had remained on their lands were freed from the obligations laid on them by Yaroslav. Instead, Mikhail ordered them to pay the tribute which had been prescribed by princes in the past. Thus the tax and social reforms introduced by Mikhail were designed to ease the burden of the serfs previously imposed on them by the legislation of the princes of Rostov-Suzdal'.

All the other measures introduced by Mikhail and his supporters in 1229 were also directed against Yaroslav's administration. According to the chronicler, Mikhail attempted to re-establish the authority of the archbishop since Antony was incapacitated by ill health.[51] His infirmity, no doubt, served as a pretext for Mikhail to replace the invalid with someone who would support his reforms, since Antony had supported Yaroslav in the past.[52] By selecting an archbishop from among candidates who supported him, Mikhail assured cooperation between the Church and the newly appointed civil administrators. Yaroslav's protégé, *Posadnik* Ivan Dimitrievich, was deprived of office and replaced by Mikhail's supporter Vnezd Vodovik for the same reason. Finally, the townsmen sequestrated immense sums of money from Yaroslav's supporters to pay for the construction of the new bridge.[53]

---

[51] Karamzin points out that Antony had become mute, *Istoriya*, vol. 3, p. 285.

[52] In 1215, when Yaroslav came to Novgorod for the first time, he was welcomed by Antony; see the Novgorod First Chronicle (NPL, pp. 53, 252). In 1225, Yaroslav replaced Mikhail in Novgorod; immediately after this information the chronicler states that Antony returned to Novgorod from the town of Peremyshl' in southwest Rus' (NPL, pp. 64, 269).

[53] In relation to the fines which were allocated for the construction of the new bridge it is interesting to note the existence of the so-called "Statute of Yaroslav concerning bridges" (see Ya. N. Shchapov, *Drevnerusskie knyazheskie ustavy* [Moscow, 1976], pp. 149-152). It has been suggested that the prince in question was Yaroslav Vsevolodovich and that he passed the statute between 1230 and 1235. He attempted to free his own

The most daring step taken by Mikhail against Yaroslav was to challenge him personally; Mikhail demanded that he return the town of Volok [54] to Novgorod along with all the other districts which he had taken by force. Since the chronicler stressed the point that Mikhail promised not to coerce Novgorod, it is clear that this had been Yaroslav's practice. The latter had followed an aggressive policy in the town: he had imposed stricter tax laws ("zabozhnits'e/забожницье"); he had sent out judges to oversee the collection of the taxes from the serfs; and he had taken various territories by force, including Volok. Therefore, as well as repealing Yaroslav's restrictive statutes and evicting his protégés from office, the *veche* also asked Mikhail to repossess the territories which Yaroslav had occupied. Unfortunately for Mikhail, retrieving Volok in 1229 was not as simple a task as regaining the looted wares from Grand Prince Yury had proven to be in 1225. Yaroslav, unlike his brother, had not approved of Mikhail's appointment to Novgorod (presumably, on neither occasion to judge from subsequent information), and unequivocally refused to cooperate with one whom he considered to be his rival. Mikhail's legislation, his punitive measures and his demand for Volok were an open affront to Yaroslav; his tactics undermined Yaroslav's control over the *posadnik* and the *veche*. More important, his action weakened the efforts of the princes of Rostov-Suzdal' to establish their control over the trade passing from the Baltic Sea to the Caspian Sea. Consequently, Mikhail, by demanding the return of Volok, directly challenged the Vsevolodovichi for the first time since he had become prince of Chernigov.

After Mikhail made his demand to Yaroslav he returned to his "brothers" in Chernigov. This innocent interpolation made by the Novgorod chronicler is an important witness to the unity of the Ol'govichi. It is a rare reference to Mikhail and his "brothers." [55] The chronicler, as we

---

supporters from the burden of payment imposed on them by Mikhail's administrators and transfer it to all the inhabitants of the town (see L. V. Cherepnin, *Russkie feodal'nye arkhivy xiv-xv vv.*, part I [Moscow-Leningrad, 1948], p. 254).

[54] Yaroslav had occupied Volok on at least one previous occasion, in 1216 (NPL, pp. 56, 256), the Sofiyskiy First Chronicle (PSRL 5, p. 195), the Novgorod Fourth Chronicle (PSRL 4, p. 188). The Sofiyskiy First and the Novgorod Fourth Chronicles make a second reference to the fact that in 1216 Yaroslav had vented his antagonism against Novgorod by killing the inhabitants of Novgorod, Torzhok and Volok (PSRL 5, p. 199 and PSRL 4, p. 195); see Zimin, "Novgorod i Volokolamsk," p. 102. The fact that Yaroslav sought to cripple Novgorod by attacking Volok as well as Torzhok indicates that he believed them to be of special strategic importance to Novgorod.

[55] The only other instance when the term "brothers" is used in relation to Mikhail is found in the Hypatian Chronicle under 1235. At that time Mikhail and his ally Izyaslav Vladimirovich demanded from Daniil Romanovich of Volyn' that he release the "princes of Bolokhov" their "brothers" (PSRL 2, cols. 774-5).

have seen, uses the word to mean social equals and political allies without
any connotations to blood ties.[56] Therefore, when he speaks of Mikhail
returning to his "brothers" the chronicler means first, his equals who
were the other princes of Chernigov, and second, his allies with whom he
shared similar political objectives and with whom he lived in peace. It is
logical to assume that, if Mikhail was returning to his "brothers," he had
also come from them, that is, he had come from them not only as their
senior prince, but also as the representative of their policy. Consequently,
it may be concluded that he had the backing of the Ol'govichi for his
activities in Novgorod.[57]

The chronicler also points out that Mikhail returned to Chernigov in
1229 accompanied by prominent citizens of Novgorod. This is significant.
As we have seen, in 1224, when he was departing from the town he had
requested its inhabitants to continue sending foreign merchants to his
principality. Five years later when Mikhail set out from Novgorod, he
was accompanied by important townsmen. It is doubtful that they came
with him to Chernigov only to advise him on Novgorod policy. They
probably had the added duty of promoting trade relations with Mikhail
and his "brothers." Thus, to judge from this sparse chronicle information
and also from the lack of references to internal unrest in Chernigov,[58] it
may be assumed that the Ol'govichi were a united family during this
period.

Unlike the Ol'govichi, the princes of Rostov-Suzdal' were involved in a
violent quarrel over their policy in Novgorod. In 1229, the first time since
1216 when Konstantin and Yury, the two eldest sons of the late Grand
Prince Vsevolod, had been pitted against each other in a succession
struggle, the Vsevolodovichi were experiencing a crisis. According to the
chronicler, Yury's younger brother Yaroslav won the three Konstantinovichi (Vasil'ko, Vsevolod and Vladimir) over to his cause and with

---

[56] See above, p. 27, n. 39.

[57] The chronicles seldom name any other princes from Chernigov who accompanied
Mikhail on his campaigns and supported him in his policies. This is understandable since
most of the information concerning his activities, unfortunately for historians, has come
down to us through chronicles which were written in other principalities than Chernigov.
Consequently, the glaring lack of information concerning the Ol'govichi must not be
interpreted to mean that there were no other princes in the principality actively supporting
Mikhail. On the contrary, since the chroniclers were eager to record any disputes between
princes, their silence concerning the Ol'govichi implies that there were no rivalries
between them and that they worked in harmony during this period.

[58] As we have seen, the only crisis which the chronicles record was that between
Mikhail and Oleg Svyatoslavich of Kursk in 1226 (see below, pp. 56-57). The fact that it
was recorded suggests that had there been other conflicts they too would have been noted.

them plotted against Grand Prince Yury. He suspected his brother of treachery because he had "listened to lies" about him. Yury discovered the plot, and, summoning the conspirators to a "council" (*snem*) in Suzdal', succeeded in resolving their differences. Yaroslav and the Konstantinovichi promised "to acknowledge him as their father" and "kissed the cross" as a sign of their fidelity. They reached this agreement on 7 September.[59]

Although most chronicles give no reason for Yaroslav's conspiracy against his brother, one source associated the revolt with Mikhail's occupation of Novgorod. It states that Yaroslav plotted against the grand prince because he had been "informed by slanderers" that Yury had helped Mikhail to drive him out of Novgorod.[60] This explanation is no doubt correct. In Mikhail the Novgorodians had found a champion for their cause and a rival to Yaroslav. His willingness to rule according to their terms not only weakened Yaroslav's policy, but also jeopardized the latter's return to Novgorod. To make matters worse, Yaroslav was informed that his brother Yury had helped Mikhail assume control of the town. Yaroslav had grounds for suspecting Yury's complicity with Mikhail after the grand prince had appointed his brother-in-law to Novgorod in 1224. Although the sources do not mention whether or not Yaroslav disapproved of the appointment, to judge from his opposition to Mikhail's rule in 1228 and during this controversy, he probably thought that Yury had acted contrary to the interests of Rostov-Suzdal' in 1224 as well.

There is added evidence to suggest that the threat of Yury's interference in the affairs of Novgorod after 1225 would have prompted Yaroslav to conspire against his brother. As we have seen, between the years 1221 and 1224 the *veche* had always directed its requests for a prince to Grand Prince Yury.[61] However, after Mikhail departed from Novgorod in 1225, the townsmen did not ask Yury for a prince as was the custom; instead, their messengers went directly to his brother, Yaroslav, in Pereyaslavl'.[62] By by-passing the grand prince, the *veche* deviated from traditional protocol; its action reflected a change in its relationship with the Vsevolodovichi.

---

[59] The Laurentian Chronicle (PSRL 1, cols. 451-2).

[60] Tatishchev, *Istoriya*, vol. 3, p. 224. This information is not found in his first redaction; see vol. 4.

[61] The Novgorod First Chronicle (NPL, pp. 60-4, 262-8, s.a. 1222-4).

[62] NPL, pp. 64, 269; cf. the Laurentian Chronicle (PSRL 1, col. 448).

Mikhail may have been instrumental in bringing about the change even though the chronicles fail to mention it. Under the year 1225 they have little information concerning his mediation between the Novgorodians and the Vsevolodovichi; we are told merely that he travelled to Rostov-Suzdal' to retrieve the "goods" which Yury had taken from the merchants of Novgorod. The chronicles do not explain what agreements were reached by the princes, but, it was after Mikhail returned from Rostov-Suzdal' that the Novgorodians sent their emissaries directly to Yaroslav rather than to the grand prince. It was, perhaps, as a result of his meeting with Mikhail that Yury delegated the affairs of Novgorod exclusively to Yaroslav.

The sources show that, after 1225, Yury no longer played an active role in Novgorod but directed his attention, in the main, to southern Rus' and to the Volga river basin in the east. In southern Rus' he turned his efforts to fostering friendly relations with the princes of Chernigov and Kiev. As well as helping Mikhail in an internal crisis in 1226 Yury arranged marriage alliances; his nephews, the Konstantinovichi, married princesses from Chernigov, and his son married the daughter of the grand prince of Kiev.[63] He also continued to appoint princes to Pereyaslavl', the most important town south of Kiev, which traditionally belonged to the princes of Rostov-Suzdal'.[64] In the east, in the Volga river basin, he followed the expansionist policy begun by his father Vsevolod. The latter had organized several campaigns against the tribes in the eastern regions[65] in an effort to consolidate his control over trade coming up from the Caspian Sea. Following his father's example, Yury attempted to secure safe

[63] It has already been noted that Yury came to Mikhail's aid against Oleg Svyatoslavich of Kursk in 1226. He also arranged for the marriages of two of his nephews to Ol'govichi princesses. Vasil'ko Konstantinovich married Mikhail's daughter in 1227; see the Laurentian Chronicle (PSRL 1, col. 450). A year later Vsevolod Konstantinovich married the daughter of Oleg Svyatoslavich; see the Ermolinskiy Chronicle (PSRL 23, p. 72), s.a. 1227; the *svod* of 1479 (PSRL 25, p. 122), s.a. 1228 and the Nikon Chronicle (PSRL 10, p. 94), s.a. 1227. Yury also negotiated a marriage alliance with the grand prince of Kiev, Vladimir Ryurikovich in 1230, when his son Vesvolod married Vladimir's daugher; see the Laurentian Chronicle (PSRL 1, cols. 453-4).

[64] He sent his nephew Vsevolod Konstantinovich to rule in 1227; see the Laurentian Chronicle (PSRL 1, col. 450). A year later he appointed his brother Svyatoslav (PSRL 1, col. 451). Svyatoslav appears to have been the last prince to rule in Pereyaslavl' to judge from chronicle information. The Tatars razed it in 1239; they killed the bishop, set fire to the town and took many of the people prisoner (PSRL 1, col. 469). The chronicle makes no reference to a prince in 1239.

[65] For example, he marched against the "Great town" (Великий город) of the Volga Bulgars in 1183 (PSRL 1, col. 389, s.a. 1184; for the correct dating see, Berezhkov, *Khronologiya*, p. 82). He sent his troops against the Volga and the Kama Bulgars in 1205; see the Nikon Chronicle (PSRL 10, p. 50).

passage for all eastern trade. In 1221, he founded the citadel of Nizhniy
Novgorod,[66] a town strategically situated on the confluence of the Oka
and Volga rivers on the eastern frontiers of his principality. Its purpose
was to provide protection and sanctuary for trade caravans. In imitation of
its namesake in northwest Rus', Yury no doubt expected it to be the
eastern gateway for trade passing through Rostov-Suzdal' lands. Between
1226 and 1232 he organized several campaigns against the warring tribes
of the Mordva in the Volga basin regions.[67] Significantly, during the
period from 1225 to his death in 1238, Yury not once became personally
involved in any conflicts in northwest Rus'. His activities, therefore,
testify to the fact that he and his brother reached a working agreement
concerning the management of their external affairs. According to this
arrangement Yury oversaw their policy in southern Rus' and in the Volga
river region.

Yaroslav, to judge from chronicle information, was put in absolute
control over northwest Rus'. This is supported by the fact that after 1225
Yury not once sent one of his sons to be prince in Novgorod. Instead, after
Mikhail departed from the town, Yaroslav and his sons, Fedor and
Aleksandr, were the only princes of Rostov-Suzdal' to rule in it.[68] Just as
Yury was consolidating the control of the Vsevolodovichi over the
Mordva on the Volga river, similarly Yaroslav was busy fighting off both
the indigenous tribes of the northwest and the Germans who interfered
with the flow of trade.[69] He also attempted to extend Novgorod's com-
mercial influence over certain tribes by Christianizing them. To this end, it

[66] The Laurentian Chronicle (PSRL 1, col. 445).

[67] Against the Mordva tribes in 1226 (PSRL 1, cols. 448-9) and in 1228 (PSRL 1, cols.
450-1); the inhabitants of Nizhniy Novgorod, which he had founded, drove off the
Mordva in 1229 (PSRL 1, col. 451); and again against the Mordva in 1232 (PSRL 1, col. 459).

[68] During the period between the years 1226 and 1238, at times when Yaroslav
himself was not ruling in Novgorod, he appointed his sons Fedor and Aleksandr to
replace him, namely, in 1228 (NPL, pp. 66, 272), in 1231 (NPL, pp. 70, 278) and Aleksandr
in 1236 (NPL, pp. 74, 285). It appears that Grand Prince Yury had intended to give
Novgorod to Yaroslav as early as 1216. Before the battle of the Lipitsa river, Yury,
anticipating a victory, distributed the lands of Rus' among his allies; he gave Novgorod to
his brother Yaroslav; see the Sofiyskiy First Chronicle (PSRL 5, p. 196) and the Novgorod
Fourth Chronicle (PSRL 4, p. 190). Therefore, in 1225, Yury fulfilled the promise which he
had made to Yaroslav in 1216.

[69] Yaroslav defended Novgorod trade on several occasions between 1225 and 1238. In
1225, he pursued the Lithuanians who had attacked Torzhok (NPL, pp. 64, 269 and the
Laurentian Chronicle PSRL 1, cols. 447-8). He attacked the Em' tribes twice, once in 1227
(NPL, pp. 65, 270, cf. PSRL 1, col. 449, s.a. 1226; the campaign probably occurred in the
winter of 1226/7; thus the discrepancy in the dates given by the chronicles; see N. G.
Berezhkov, *Khronologiya*, p. 107) and again in 1228 (NPL, pp. 65, 270). In 1234, he
marched against both the Germans and the Lithuanians (NPL, pp. 72-3, 183-4).

appears, he adopted a program of evangelization. The Laurentian Chronicle states that in 1228 nearly all the people of Korela (Korila) were baptized by his missionaries.[70] Yaroslav's actions during this period suggest that he considered himself and his sons to be the only rightful claimants to the throne in Novgorod. Consequently, in 1229, when he was informed falsely that his brother had been instrumental in expediting Mikhail's return to the town, Yaroslav took strong exception to Yury's apparent breach of their agreement concerning northwest Rus'.[71]

The ease with which Yaroslav was influenced to suspect his brother, and, as well, his ability to win the support of the Konstantinovichi, exemplifies the volatile nature of internal politics in the principality of Rostov-Suzdal'. Yury had to remain on constant guard against a resurgence of those dormant hostile elements which had surfaced in the rivalry of 1216.[72] There can be little doubt that the boyars of Rostov, who advised the Konstantinovichi, still harboured ill feelings against the grand prince from the time of the succession crisis. Although they had supported Yury's victorious brother, they were despoiled of the fruits of their victory soon after by Konstantin's premature death.[73] Yaroslav's intrigue, there-

---

[70] PSRL 1, col. 449.

[71] It is not stated when Yaroslav began to stir up unrest against Yury. However, it is known that Mikhail arrived in Novgorod at the end of April 1229 and that Yaroslav agitated against his brother prior to 7 September since the princes pledged their alliance to Yury on that day. The span of just over four months between these two dates shows that Mikhail's activities in northwest Rus' and Yaroslav's plotting were more or less concurrent. This is further evidence to suggest that the crisis in Rostov-Suzdal' was connected with the events in Novgorod.

[72] See above, p. 18.

[73] Konstantin Vsevolodovich died on 2 February 1218; see the Laurentian Chronicle (PSRL 1, col. 442). The fact that there was a strong undercurrent of unrest in the principality of Rostov-Suzdal' during Yury's reign is reflected in the mystery surrounding his death. The enigmatic statement which records this event in the Novgorod First Chronicle suggests that all was not well between the towns of Rostov and Suzdal' even in 1238. It states that while Yury was making military preparations against the Tatars they arrived unexpectedly and forced him to flee. The Tatars caught up with him at the Sit' river (northwest of Rostov, see Map no. 3); "he ended his life there. God knows how he died; there is much talk about it. Rostov and Suzdal' then went their separate ways" (NPL, pp. 76, 288). The seventeenth-century Gustinskiy Chronicle appears to echo this oral tradition when it states that the Tatars massacred the princes of the "lands of Moscow" because "they refused to become reconciled with each other" ("не совгласившихся со собою") (PSRL 2, 1843 edition, p. 338, s.a. 1237).

A sixteenth-century redaction of the "Life" of Mikhail written by Pakhomy the Serb, called the *Chudovskoe zhitie*, is the source of unique information concerning Yury (see below, p. 153). This information is based on oral tradition and, as is the case with such material, there is uncertainty concerning its credibility. But for the few discordant notes concerning him given by the chronicles, the following information might be discounted as

fore, exposed the internal factionalism and the vulnerability of the apparently unified family of the Vsevolodovichi. Thanks to Yury's tactful intervention a tragic outcome was averted. Ultimately, the crisis appears to have confirmed Yury's position as grand prince and strengthened the political ties among the princes of Rostov-Suzdal' since, in the future, they were to act in concord against Mikhail.

Although Mikhail returned to Chernigov in 1229, he was back in Novgorod by the spring of the following year. He attended the initiation ceremony of his son Rostislav in the Cathedral of St. Sofia[74] on which occasion the new Archbishop Spiridon officiated over the ceremonial "cutting of hair" (postrig).[75] Mikhail then appointed his son as prince of Novgorod and returned to Chernigov.[76]

The chronicler implies that Mikhail made a special trip to Novgorod for his son's hair cutting ceremony. It is clear that he considered the event to be of great political importance. The ceremony itself, according to one source, was a carry-over from paganism and initiated the youth into civic life and to the status of a noble horseman. A young prince, at the age of four or five, underwent a hair cutting ceremony after which he was seated on a horse in the presence of the bishop, the boyars and the townsmen. His father, according to tradition, celebrated the event by holding

---

incredible. The *Chudovskoe zhitie* states that Grand Prince Yury was a completely unworthy man "who lived like a swine" ("Бѣ бо живуще ему свиньскы") "in sinful filth" ("въ мнозѣ кале грѣховнѣ"). He was proud, envious, miserly, unmerciful, he lusted after power, he indulged in drunkenness and debauchery – "in truth he lived like a beast" ("въистиниу скотско житие живы"). According to the *Zhitie*, Yury was a coward at heart and when he heard of the approaching Tatars he did not know what to do. Being in a quandary he sought advice from a hermit who could foresee the future. But the holy man refused to speak to him and only when the grand prince sent his daughter Feodora did he foretell the disaster which awaited the country. That night Yury had a vision and the next day he went to a different hermit, one who lived further from the town, but he also foretold the calamity which would befall his lands. And so it was that Yury and his sons, as well as all his relatives, were massacred by the Tatars and the whole land of Suzdal' pillaged (N. Serebryansky, *Drevnerusskiya knyazheskiya zhitiya [Obzor redaktsiy i teksty]*, [Moscow, 1915], Texts pp. 81-2).

[74] Tatishchev says that Rostislav Mikhaylovich was seven years old at the time of his *postrig* (*Istoriya*, vol. 4, p. 369). Three similar ceremonies are recorded in the chronicles prior to 1230, namely, the *postrig* of Yury Vsevolodovich s.a. 1192 (PSRL 1, col. 409), the *postrig* of Yaroslav Vsevolodovich s.a. 1194 (PSRL 1, col. 411) and the *postrig* of Vasil'ko and Vsevolod Konstantinovichi s.a. 1212 (PSRL 1, col. 437).

[75] Since Spiridon returned from Kiev on 19 May the ceremony must have occurred after that date; see the Novgorod First Chronicle (NPL, pp. 69, 276).

[76] NPL, pp. 69, 276. It was probably at this time that Mikhail promised to return to Novgorod by the Feast of the Exaltation of the Cross, 14 September, in order "to go to war" (NPL, pp. 70, 278). The chronicler does not state against whom this war was to be waged.

sumptuous feasts.[77] In the case of Rostislav the *postrig* gave him the legal status of prince. The ceremony also served the purpose, no doubt, to confirm cooperation between Mikhail and the new archbishop who had returned from Kiev not long before. From now on Rostislav would be prince of Novgorod through the power invested in him by Archbishop Spiridon and the *veche*; he would be the official liaison between the town and Mikhail. It would appear that the ceremony also inaugurated a new policy for Novgorod. Contrary to the long established practice of inviting the princes of Rostov-Suzdal', the townsmen asked the Ol'govichi to rule on a "permanent" basis since the latter were to provide a resident prince. The fact that the Novgorodians kissed the icon of the Mother of God in 1228, when they decided to invite Mikhail instead of Yaroslav, meant that they were bound by their pledge to support Mikhail's son Rostislav in 1230.

To judge from the brief entry given in the Novgorod First Chronicle concerning Mikhail's visit to Novgorod, there were no further developments in his relations with the princes of Rostov-Suzdal' in that year. However, this was not the case. Information given by the Laurentian Chronicle shows not only that the rivalry between Mikhail and Yaroslav escalated almost to the point of war, but that Mikhail's affairs in Novgorod suffered a permanent reversal. In 1230, Vladimir Ryurikovich, grand prince of Kiev, sent Metropolitan Kirill to Rostov-Suzdal' to Grand Prince Yury, to his brothers Yaroslav and Svyatoslav and to the Konstantinovichi. Mikhail, in his turn, dispatched Bishop Porfiry of Chernigov. The two prelates were also accompanied by *Igumen* Petr Akerovich[78] of the Holy Saviour Monastery at Berestovo near Kiev

---

[77] See Karamzin, *Istoriya*, vol. 3, pp. 154-5.

[78] The editors of the Laurentian Chronicle in PSRL 1 are of the opinion that Petr Akerovich was a boyar and that the *igumen* (Father Superior) of the Holy Saviour Monastery was a different person (p. 552). This was not the case. Immediately after the chronicler lists the names of the delegates who accompanied the metropolitan, he adds that the latter was accompanied by "these three," namely, Bishop Porfiry, *Igumen* Petr Akerovich and *Stol'nik* Georgy. If Petr Akerovich and the *igumen* had been two different persons the metropolitan would have been accompanied by four people. Furthermore, under the following year, 1231, the chronicle explicitly refers to "*Igumen* Petr of the Holy Saviour Monastery" ("игуменъ Петръ Спасьскыи") (PSRL 1, col. 456). This Petr could be no other than Petr Akerovich. Pashuto points out that it is not surprising that *Igumen* Petr Akerovich represents the interests of Mikhail Vsevolodovich. It appears that the Holy Saviour Monastery owned a "village" ("селце святого Спаса") near Chernigov; the Hypatian Chronicle (PSRL 2, col. 507, s.a. 1160), see *Ocherki*, pp. 57-60. According to S. Tomashiv'skiy, Petr Akerovich became the metropolitan of Kiev from 1241 until 1245. After being driven out of Kiev by the Tatars he attended the thirteenth General Council of the Church in Lyons convoked by Pope Innocent IV on 24 June. Tomashiv'skiy claims

and by Vladimir Ryurikovich's "courtier" (stol'nik) Gregory. The
metropolitan and his three associates endeavoured to reconcile Yaroslav
and Mikhail because, says the chronicler, he "had not been faithful to the
oath" which he had made to Yaroslav so that the latter wanted "to march
against Mikhail." Yaroslav was persuaded by the metropolitan, by Porfiry
and by Yury to conclude peace. After Yury and Yaroslav entertained the
metropolitan, Porfiry and the igumen of the Holy Saviour Monastery, the
prelates returned "each to his own prince."[79]

The chronicle does not describe the nature of the dispute which nearly
brought Mikhail and Yaroslav to open warfare. The high-powered
composition of the peace delegation from Kiev suggests that Yaroslav's
impending attack was to be a major campaign. Since the delegates
addressed themselves not only to Yaroslav, but also to his brothers, Yury
and Svyatoslav, and to the three Konstantinovichi, they also were
implicated in the hostilities. Such a campaign would have pitted the
principalities of Rostov-Suzdal' and Chernigov against each other for the
first time since the reign of Yury's father, Vsevolod. The seriousness of the
crisis reflected by the personages involved indicates that the issue at stake
was not merely Volok, which Mikhail had demanded that Yaroslav return
to Novgorod in the previous year. This is supported by the chronicler's
interpolation that Mikhail "had not been faithful to the oath" which he
had made to Yaroslav.[80] Since Yury was the grand prince, protocol would
require that Mikhail make an oath to him, especially one of a political
nature. But, as we have seen, Yury had placed Yaroslav in command of

that Petr Akerovich was a Roman Catholic archbishop who advocated union with Rome
("Predtecha Isidora. Petro Akerovich, neznaniy mitropolit rus'kiy [1241-1245]," Zapysky
chyna sv. Vasyliia Velykoho, vol. 2, vypusk 3-4, god 1926 [Zhovkva, 1927], pp. 221-313).
There is no indication given by the primary sources that Petr Akerovich was a Roman
Catholic archbishop of Kiev or that he went to Lyons.

    [79] The Laurentian Chronicle (PSRL 1, cols; 455-6). In the chronicle this information
constitutes the last entry under the year 1230. This suggests that the clerical mediators
travelled to Rostov-Suzdal' in the latter half of 1230.

    [80] "бѣ бо Михаилъ не правъ въ крстнмъ целованьи. при Ярославѣ.," the
Laurentian Chronicle (PSRL 1, col. 455). Unfortunately, the chronicler does not explain the
nature of the oath. However, the last occasion on which Mikhail was involved with the
Vsevolodovichi was, in 1224/5, when he was prince in Novgorod. At that time, as has
been noted, Yaroslav had probably objected to Mihail's appointment. Did Yaroslav agree
to support Yury's compromise provided that Mikhail promise not to rule in Novgorod in
his own name nor to appoint a resident prince in the town? The chronicles do not say.
However, the fact that Yaroslav intended to lead all the Vsevolodovichi against Mikhail
after the latter had officially installed Rostislav as prince in May of 1230 suggests that
Mikhail may have promised not to do that very thing.

all affairs in Novgorod. The fact that Mikhail made an oath to Yaroslav must mean that it was connected with his activities there. Consequently, in 1230, the dispute probably revolved around Mikhail's successful interference in Novgorod itself.

Yaroslav was determined to regain control of the town. He had been prepared even to march against his brother in the previous year, because he believed that Yury wished Mikhail to replace him there. To be sure, Yaroslav had growing cause for concern over Mikhail's prolonged control of Novgorod. The latter's return at the beginning of 1230 and his confirmation of Rostislav's rule in it, shows that its inhabitants were content with his administration, and it became evident that his stay might become protracted; indeed, in the spring of 1230 the Novgorodians elicited Mikhail's promise to return with his troops by 14 September. Yaroslav realized that such a move would diminish his hold over Novgorod since the town no longer would rely on him alone for military assistance. Thus, it was with growing consternation that Yaroslav observed how Mikhail, having replaced him as prince of Novgorod, was strengthening his position there. His only recourse lay in military action and in this he now received the backing of all the princes of Rostov-Suzdal'. This is attested to by the fact that on 7 September of the previous year the Vsevolodovichi had been reunited once again by the oath of fidelity which they all made to Grand Prince Yury. The fact that the envoys from Kiev directed their appeal not only to Yaroslav, but also to his brothers and to the Konstantinovichi, supports this view as well.[81] The Vsevolodovichi, however, were not Mikhail's only source of concern in 1230.

A look at the increasing opposition which Mikhail and his supporters had to face in Novgorod in 1230 will help to put the crisis between him and Yaroslav into better perspective. Towards the end of the year, while Rostislav was prince, bitter factional feuding erupted again amongst the

[81] A. E. Presnyakov points out that from 1215, when Yaroslav first appeared on the Novgorod political scene, he had a twofold aim, at least from the standpoint of the *veche*. He was the vigilant champion of princely rights against the spread of the Novgorod's autonomy on the one hand, and on the other he was a powerful agent in the struggle against the western enemies of Novgorod and in the subjugation of the Finnish tribes. However, the prince himself saw no dichotomy in his policy since he was representing the interests of the Vsevolodovichi and not those of the *posadnik* and the *veche* of Novgorod. Presnyakov observes that Yaroslav's activities in the northwest were not his personal initiative; he was supported by his brother, the grand prince, and by the other princes of Rostov-Suzdal' (*Obrazovanie Velikorusskogo gosudarstva* [Petrograd, 1918], pp. 39-40).

townsmen.[82] Stepan Tverdislavich, the son of the former *posadnik*, Tverdislav Mikhaylovich, who retired from office in 1220,[83] quarrelled with *Posadnik* Vodovik and summoned a *veche*. Spurred on by Stepan and his allies the Novgorodians plundered Vodovik's "court" (*dvor*). In retaliation Vodovik and his protégé, Semen Borisovich, who had replaced Stepan Tverdislavich's father as *posadnik*,[84] also convoked a *veche* and incited the whole town against those boyars who had conspired against them. Vodovik not only looted their homes, but had two of his opponents put to death. However, a certain Ioakim Blunkovich escaped and fled to Yaroslav in Pereyaslavl'.[85] These events occurred on 6 November.[86]

The feuding, however, was not yet over. Approximately one month later, on Sunday 8 December, *Posadnik* Vodovik and Rostislav Mikhaylovich went to the town of Torzhok. The following day the Novgorodians killed Vodovik's comrade and former *posadnik*, Semen Borisovich, and plundered Vodovik's and Semen's homes and "estates" (*sela*). They also looted the homes of the *posadnik*'s brother, Mikhail, of the *tysyatskiy* Boris Negochevich[87] and others. As soon as Vodovik heard of these reprisals he fled from Torzhok to Chernigov accompanied by his "brothers" – *Tysyatskiy* Boris and other boyars. After his flight the Novgorodians appointed Stepan Tverdislavich their new *posadnik* and ordered Rostislav Mikhaylovich to return to his father in Chernigov. They complained that his father had "kissed the cross" and promised to return to Novgorod with an army by 14 September, but the Feast of St. Nicholas (i.e., 6 December) had already passed and he had not yet arrived. Therefore, they sent an invitation to Yaroslav Vsevolodovich and he came

---

[82] The Tver' Chronicle alone introduces its account of the fighting by stating that "the *smerda* of Novgorod quarrelled" ("розопрешася смерди Новгородциь"), (PSRL 15, col. 355).

[83] The Novgorod First Chronicle (NPL, pp. 60, 261-2).

[84] In 1219, Semen Borisovich replaced Stepan Tverdislavich's father as the *posadnik* of Novgorod (NPL, pp. 59, 260).

[85] Six years later, in 1236, when Yaroslav occupied Kiev, Ioakim Blunkovich was one of the prominent citizens of Novgorod whom the chronicler singled out as accompanying the prince to his new appointment (NPL, pp. 74, 285).

[86] The *Komissionnyy spisok* of the Novgorod First Chronicle adds, "on the feast of our holy father, Paul the Confessor" (NPL, p. 276), i.e., 6 November.

[87] In this instance the chronicle simply refers to him as "*Tysyatskiy* Boris" and then in the next phrase again in the same manner. Although the editors of the Novgorod First Chronicle identify him only as *Tysyatskiy* Boris (NPL, p. 570), there is little reason to doubt that this was Boris Negochevich. The chronicle states that *Tysyatskiy* Boris fled to Chernigov with other Novgorodians in 1230. Under the year 1232 it states that Boris Negochevich departed from Chernigov (NPL, p. 71; the *Komissionnyy spisok* explicitly calls him Boris Negochevich *tysyatskiy*, NPL, p. 280).

"quickly" on 30 December. He convoked a *veche*, kissed the icon of the
Mother of God, and promised to abide "by all the laws of Yaroslav" and
by all the terms set down by the Novgorodians.[88] Two weeks later he
returned to Pereyaslavl', but he left his sons, Fedor and Aleksandr, to
govern in Novgorod.[89]

According to this information the faction backing Yaroslav, whose
power had been stifled temporarily by the revolt of the *prostaya chad'* and
by Mikhail's measures, reasserted its influence towards the end of the year
1230.[90] Even though the "brothers" of Novgorod had kissed the icon of
the Mother of God pledging to give unanimous support to Mikhail, Stepan
Tverdislavich succeeded in fomenting a strong undercurrent of opposition
to his rule. By 8 December this opposition gained sufficient momentum to
force *Posadnik* Vodovik to retreat from Novgorod with Mikhail's young
son. Stepan Tverdislavich and other supporters of Yaroslav then
reasserted their control over the town. Clearly the determining factor
which undermined the unanimity of the townsmen, and persuaded them
to withdraw their support from Mikhail, was the fact that he failed to keep
his promise to come to Novgorod with an army by 14 September.

The unrest in Novgorod and the crisis between Mikhail and Yaroslav in
1230 were not unrelated events. A juxtaposition of these developments
will give at least a partial explanation for Mikhail's failure to keep his
promise to Novgorod and, therefore, to remain there as prince. It appears
that Yaroslav conducted his offensive against Mikhail from two fronts,
namely, from Rostov-Suzdal' directly and indirectly from Novgorod. By
threatening to march against Mikhail, Yaroslav forced him to concentrate
his troops in Chernigov; at the same time, Yaroslav's supporters in Novgorod agitated against Mikhail on the grounds that he had failed to bring
the long-awaited troops. The final result was that Mikhail was successful
in negotiating peace with the Vsevolodovichi – perhaps by promising not
to take his troops to Novgorod – but he lost control of the town to Yaroslav and to his faction of boyars who were led by Stepan Tverdislavich.
After 1230 neither Mikhail nor his son Rostislav returned to Novgorod as
prince.

Yaroslav achieved his victory at considerable expense to his policy. In
1226, as we have seen, he had replaced Mikhail as prince of Novgorod

[88] Only the *Komissionnyy spisok* adds "and by all the terms set down by the people of
Novgorod" ("на всеи волѣ новгородчкои"), (NPL, p. 278; cf. p. 70).

[89] The Novgorod First Chronicle (NPL, pp. 69-70, 276-8).

[90] The fact that Ioakim Blunkovich, one of the *boyars* who sided with Stepan
Tverdislavich against Vodovik, flèd to Yaroslav in Pereyaslavl', indicated that Vodovik
was attacked by the supporters of Yaroslav.

"according to all his terms"; but, in 1230, the chronicle states that he agreed to abide "by the laws of Yaroslav and by all the terms set down by the Novgorodians." His capitulation to their demands was a direct consequence of Mikhail's diplomacy in Novgorod and of the latter's willingness to cooperate with the *veche* and to pass legislation to alleviate the stringent tax laws which, apparently, Yaroslav had imposed on the serfs. The reason why Yaroslav ultimately accepted the *veche*'s terms is obvious. In 1230, he did not wish to suffer another reversal to his rule similar to the one in 1228 when, after refusing to accept Novgorod's terms, he was replaced by Mikhail. Instead, Yaroslav welcomed his new invitation, and the chronicler states, he came "quickly." When he returned the struggle between Novgorod and the Vsevolodovichi, which had begun in 1221 when the latter had been invited to rule, was settled finally to the advantage of the townspeople. It is true that, by submitting to "all the terms set down by the Novgorodians," Yaroslav and the princes of Rostov-Suzdal' were able to establish their rule over northwest Rus', but, it appears, only at a loss to their former authority.[91]

[91] There has been considerable discussion among historians concerning the significance of Yaroslav's agreement with Novgorod in 1230. It has been suggested that, at that time, he finalized the arrangement according to which princes would rule (see L. V. Cherepnin, *Russkie feodal'nye arkivy xiv-xv vv.*, part I [Moscow-Leningrad, 1948], pp. 239-54 and A. B. Kuza, "Novgorodskaya zemlya," *Drevnerusskie knyazhestva x-xiii vv.*, ed. L. G. Beskrovnyy [Moscow, 1975], p. 161). This view appears to be supported by the deeds (*gramoty*) concluded between Novgorod and Yaroslav's son Yaroslav. In the *gramoty*, the Novgorodians stipulate that the prince, like his father Yaroslav Vsevolodovich, "kiss the cross" and rule according to the terms agreed upon by his father before him ("На семь ти, княже, хрьстъ цѣлов[а]ти, на цѣмъ то цѣловал[ъ хрьстъ] отець твои Ярославъ.," see "1264 g. – Dogovornaya gramota Novgoroda s tverskim velikim knyazem Yaroslavom Yaroslavichem," *Gramoty velikogo Novgoroda i Pskova*, ed. S. N. Valk [Moscow-Leningrad, 1949], p. 9; cf. pp. 10, 12).

The Soviet historian V. L. Yanin states that the form of the new agreement (новый формуляр), according to which princes would rule in Novgorod, was drawn up in 1230 when Yaroslav Vsevolodovich "kissed the cross" (*Posadniki*, p. 136; the Novgorod First Chronicle says that Yaroslav "kissed the icon of the Mother of God," NPL, pp. 70, 278). In light of Mikhail's activities in Novgorod, it appears that Yanin's observation should be modified. It is true, as he suggests, that in 1230 the so-called new agreement was new for the princes of Rostov-Suzdal'; by adopting it Yaroslav changed the traditional policy of the Vsevolodovichi in Novgorod. However, for the Novgorodians, it probably was not new because they had already concluded it with another prince, namely, Mikhail. In the previous year, the latter had "kissed the cross according to all the demands of the Novgorodians and according to all the laws of Yaroslav" (NPL, pp. 68, 274). As we have seen, after announcing the agreement, the chronicler listed the important "reforms" which he passed; clearly, the measures were legislated for the first time on that occasion. In 1230, wishing to return to Novgorod, Yaroslav finally agreed to rule according to all

Yaroslav's victory over the opposition in Novgorod itself appears to have been complete. *Posadnik* Stepan Tverdislavich, his protégé, was to hold his office without interruption for almost thirteen years.[92] Outside of Novgorod there was, however, a number of expatriated boyars who still posed a threat to his rule. In December 1230, *Posadnik* Vodovik, *Tysyatskiy* Boris and their "brothers" had fled to Chernigov.[93] This group of boyars, remaining faithful to their pledge of 1228, still hoped to obtain political backing from Mikhail. Therefore, they formed a potential nucleus for a resurgence of opposition to Yaroslav. In order to secure his hegemony, not only did he have to eliminate this faction but, more important, he had to persuade Mikhail to cease proffering his support.

In the light of the threat which Mikhail still presented to him, it is not surprising that Yaroslav attacked the principality of Chernigov in the following year. The Novgorod chronicler explains that Yaroslav, accompanied by his own troops and the Novgorodians, marched against Mikhail. He invaded the northern districts of the principality and set fire to the town of Serensk;[94] he also besieged the town of Mosal'sk (northwest of Serensk) but had to turn back after depleting his supplies and, significantly, without negotiating peace. The next and last entry under this year states that *Posadnik* Vnezd Vodovik died in Chernigov.[95] The Laurentian Chronicle, however, has different information. It states that Grand Prince Yury also went to Serensk but, for reasons not given, changed his mind before the forces entered the principality of Chernigov and returned to Vladimir;[96] meanwhile, Yaroslav and the Konstantino-

---

the demands of the *veche*. There can be little doubt that his agreement was identical to the one made by Mikhail in the previous year.

[92] Yaroslav's hold over Novgorod after 1230 is illustrated by the uninterrupted term of office of his supporter, *Posadnik* Stepan Tverdislavich. The latter held his post, according to the chronicle, "for thirteen years less three months," until his death on 16 August 1243 (NPL, pp. 79, 297-8).

[93] Just as the citizens of Pskov had evicted Yaroslav's supporters from the town in 1228 (see above, p. 27), two years later Vodovik and his "brothers" (i.e. Mikhail's supporters), were ostracized from Novgorod.

[94] Serensk was on the Serena river (Barsov, *Materialy*, p. 184); see Map no. 2.

[95] The Novgorod First Chronicle (NPL, pp. 71, 280).

[96] According to this source Grand Prince Yury set out for Serensk; he pitched camp "на Уполозѣх" and returned to Vladimir (PSRL 1, col. 459). Historians have not been able to determine the meaning of "Уполозѣх." The reference may be to the Poloz'e (Polozh'e? Poluzh'e?) district, that is, the region surrounding the Luzha river. The Luzha river is a tributary of the Protva river which flows into the Oka. It is approximately half-way between Moscow and Serensk. During the first half of the thirteenth century the northern boundary of the principality of Chernigov appears to have been located immediately to the south of it.

vichi advanced to Serensk, set fire to it and returned home after "much fighting."[97]

The sources give no explanation why Yaroslav attacked the principality of Chernigov. However, the fact that the last point of dispute between him and Mikhail had been Novgorod, and since the latter was harbouring boyars still hostile to Yaroslav, he probably invaded hoping to terminate Mikhail's prolonged involvement in the affairs of northwest Rus'. This view is supported by the information that he was accompanied also by Novgorodians. They obviously had a grievance against Mikhail, but the only townsmen who had suffered under his rule were Yaroslav's supporters. Just as they had taken punitive measures against Mikhail's faction in Novgorod in the winter of 1230, they no doubt wished to vent their displeasure against Mikhail himself by pillaging his lands.

Yaroslav's attack on Chernigov was also supported by the other Vsevolodovichi. Yury gave his approval by setting out on the campaign. Nevertheless, he remained faithful to what may be considered his policy of non-involvement in Novgorod affairs, which he adopted apparently in 1225 by not participating in the fighting. The Konstantinovichi who had shown their willingness to support Yaroslav already in 1229 against Yury, also accompanied him to Chernigov. The presence of so many princes from Rostov-Suzdal' implies that the controversy was not merely a personal vendetta between Yaroslav and Mikhail, but rather an issue of fundamental importance to the descendants of Vsevolod Yur'evich. Such a problem which brought both the Vsevolodovichi and the Novgorodians against Mikhail could only have been the question of the future of northwest Rus'. As long as Mikhail continued to support citizens opposed to Yaroslav's rule, the latter's control over Novgorod was in jeopardy. The

---

[97] PSRL 1 col. 459. Unlike the Novgorod First Chronicle, the Laurentian Chronicle has this information at the beginning of the year 1232. Berezhkov argues that the entry in the latter source is given under an Ultra-March year; therefore, the information belongs to the year 1231. All the remaining information under 1232, according to him, is given under a regular March year and falls under 1232 (*Khronologiya*, pp. 108-9). However, the entry in the Laurentian Chronicle is not in the Ultra-March year as Berezhkov suggests. Like the rest of the information under the year 1232, it is in the March year and belongs to 1232. The reason why this source records the raid under 1232 instead of 1231 becomes evident on closer scrutiny of the information. The Novgorod First Chronicle states that Yaroslav set out on the campaign in the autumn of 1231. The campaign lasted for a protracted period of time, but the chronicles do not state for how long. Therefore, it is highly probable that Yaroslav did not return to Rostov-Suzdal' until the beginning of 1232. In other words, the Laurentian Chronicle records the date of Yaroslav's *return* from the campaign rather than his *departure*. His attack on Mikhail therefore appears to have overlapped the two years, 1231 and 1232, in the winter common to both of them.

princes of Rostov-Suzdal' therefore raided the northern regions of Chernigov[98] in the hope of coercing Mikhail to withdraw his support of the Novgorod boyars whom he was harbouring at his court.

At the beginning of the following year, 1232, the Novgorodians departed from Chernigov. But, before they withdrew from the principality, *Tysyatskiy* Boris Negochevich and his compatriots succeeded in soliciting the support of Prince Svyatoslav of Trubchevsk (a town of minor importance located on the Desna river north of Chernigov through which the fugitives passed on their journey to the north).[99] When they arrived in Buytse, a southern outpost of Novgorod near the Pola river and a village belonging to the Yur'ev Monastery,[100] Prince Svyatoslav discovered that the Novgorodians had lied to him. He, therefore, returned home and they proceeded to Pskov.[101]

Again the chronicle gives no explanation as to why the boyars departed from Chernigov. But there can be little doubt that Yaroslav's attack must have served as a strong incentive to Mikhail to reconsider his involvement with the Novgorodians.[102] The death of *Posadnik* Vnezd Vodovik, the leader of the refugees,[103] could have given him the necessary excuse for severing his ties with them. Since his agreement with them had probably been made through the deceased *posadnik*, Mikhail could argue that Vodovik's death freed him from his obligation. The chronicle does not indicate that Mikhail pressured the Novgorodians into leaving his court,

[98] The region which Yaroslav chose to attack was that in which the town of Bryn was located. It will be remembered that Mikhail had been in Bryn when he was informed that the Novgorodians wished him to be their prince in the winter of 1228/9 (see above, p. 25). The fact that Yaroslav attacked this district, therefore, may have some connection with the events of the winter of 1228/9.

[99] This is the only reference in the sources to Svyatoslav of Trubchevsk; see Table 2:25. The last reference to a prince of Trubchevsk was made under the year 1196 when Vsevolod Svyatoslavich, prince of Trubchevsk, died; see the Hypatian Chronicle (PSRL 2, col. 696) and Zotov, *O Chernigovskikh knyazyakh*, p. 277, no. 44. Trubchevsk, or Trubetsk, is on the Desna river north of Novgorod Severskiy. See Map no. 2.

[100] Buytse was located in the vicinity of the source of the Pola river, which flows into Lake Il'men' from the south. See Map no. 1.

[101] The Novgorod First Chronicle (NPL, p. 280). This information is taken from the *Komissionnyy spisok*; it is fuller than the entry in the older *Sinodal'nyy spisok* (NPL, p. 71). The fact that the boyars fled, according to the chronicle, "in the middle of Lent," means that they departed from Chernigov some time in March, that is, soon after Yaroslav had withdrawn from the northern districts of the principality of Chernigov.

[102] As we shall see below, pressure from the Vsevolodovichi was only one reason which influenced Mikhail to adopt this course of action; his involvement in the politics of southern Rus' was the other and more important factor.

[103] Vodovik's death is placed after the information of Yaroslav's campaign (NPL, pp. 71, 280). Thus he probably died in the winter of 1231/2.

but there is every indication that he severed his support of them. This is suggested by their desperation; they had to trick Svyatoslav of Trubchevsk, a prince of apparently little political importance in the principality of Chernigov, to accompany them and, presumably, to help them in their cause against the Vsevolodovichi. Whatever the immediate reason for their departure from Chernigov, the exodus of Boris Negochevich and his compatriots signalled the end of Mikhail's commitment and Ol'govichi involvement, at least for a time, in the politics of Novgorod.

*
 * *

The following observations can be made concerning Mikhail's activity in Novgorod and his relations with the Vsevolodovichi between 1224 and 1232. In the early 1220s, the Novgorodians wanted to have the Vse-volodovichi as princes and, in turn, the latter wished to rule in Novgorod, but each group attempted to strengthen its position by imposing its demands on the other. Grand Prince Yury asked the *veche* to accept Mikhail as prince hoping that his brother-in-law would help the Vse-volodovichi win the desired concessions from Novgorod. In the short run, the stratagem enabled the princes of Rostov-Suzdal' to return to Novgorod in 1225; but in the long run, the tactic failed since the Novgorodians won the desired concessions from Yaroslav in 1230.

It appears that Yaroslav opposed Mikhail's appointment to Novgorod from the very beginning. Although the sources give no indication of this, it was no doubt through Yaroslav's insistence that Yury handed over to him the affairs of Novgorod in 1225. As a result of this arrangement, the grand prince was to oversee the affairs of the Vsevolodovichi in the east and southern Rus'. The division of power between the two senior princes of Rostov-Suzdal' shows the political objective of the Vsevolodo-vichi – they wished to establish control over the trade passing through their principality from Novgorod and the Baltic Sea to Nizhniy Novgorod and the Caspian Sea.

In opposition to the Vsevolodovichi, Mikhail also considered it vital to his interests to involve himself in the affairs of Novgorod for at least two reasons. First, he wished to tap the rich commercial resources of Nov-gorod. He made this intention clear in 1225 when he requested the merchants of the town to continue sending foreign trade to Chernigov. Second, he hoped to prevent the Vsevolodovichi from establishing their undisputed control over the east-west trade route and thus to weaken their power.

From 1225 to 1228 Yaroslav, as prince of Novgorod, followed an aggressive policy of consolidation. With the help of local officials he imposed severe demands on the serfs and attempted to coerce the townsmen into accepting his terms. His measures brought about civil unrest. In 1228, for the first time since the Vsevolodovichi returned in 1221, the people of Novgorod came to blows amongst themselves over Yaroslav's corrupt administrators and over his policy. Significantly, they did not revolt against Yaroslav, but asked him to return as prince provided he accept their demands. Yaroslav, confident that he could rule in Novgorod according to his terms, forced a confrontation by ordering his two sons to leave Novgorod. The impasse created by his decision was similar to the one in 1224.

Both he and the *veche* realized that only a prince had the legal power to abrogate the tax laws. Yaroslav was sure that no prince from Rostov-Suzdal' would countermand his statutes since he directed the policy of the Vsevolodovichi in Novgorod; he was confident also that the Rostislavichi of Smolensk, who had been princes in the town before the Vsevolodovichi had returned in 1221, were too weak to oppose him. However, Yaroslav, as well as the *veche* was aware that Mikhail was in a position to intervene. He was sufficiently powerful to challenge the Vsevolodovichi for control over Novgorod and to provide it with the military assistance which Yaroslav had withdrawn. Mikhail himself was not ignorant of his importance to the *veche* and of the threat which he posed to Yaroslav's control over the town. To be sure, he may have been expecting an invitation to return to Novgorod to judge from the fact that in 1228 the *veche*'s messengers found him conveniently available in the northern regions of his principality.

The Novgorod chronicler's elated account of Mikhail's administration reflects the welcome which he was given by the townspeople. In a passage which is unique in the chronicle accounts for this period – one couched in legal terminology and obviously derived from a "deed" (*gramota*) – the chronicler enumerates the new tax and social legislation passed by Mikhail. His measures bespeak the reasons for his willingness to go to Novgorod in 1229: Mikhail wished to weaken the control of the Vsevolodovichi in Novgorod by undermining Yaroslav's legislation and by removing the latter's supporters from office. Although there is little chronicle evidence, it appears that Mikhail and his "brothers" from Chernigov also derived commercial benefits as a result of his willingness to cooperate with the *veche*.

Yaroslav was infuriated with Mikhail's measures and readily believed false information concerning Yury's implication in Mikhail's return to

Novgorod. His ability to organize a revolt against Yury was an important revelation of the precarious unity of the princes of Rostov-Suzdal'. Fortunately for the Vsevolodovichi, Yury was able to restore family solidarity by convincing the rebels of his innocence. After Yaroslav was reconciled with his brother, he directed his unbridled hostility against Mikhail. To be sure, at the beginning of 1230 the latter gave Yaroslav even more cause for concern. Mikhail concluded an agreement with the *veche* not only to leave his son Rostislav as prince in Novgorod for an indefinite period of time, but also to return with his troops. It appears that with this arrangement Mikhail broke an oath which he had made to Yaroslav and the latter declared war. But, Mikhail misjudged Yaroslav's determination to regain control over Novgorod and the latter's aggressiveness forced him to back down. Taking advantage of his alliance with the grand prince of Kiev, Mikhail asked Vladimir Ryurikovich to help him conclude a truce with the Vsevolodovichi. The chronicles do not state what price Mikhail had to pay for peace in 1230 – perhaps he agreed not to take his troops to Novgorod. His failure to keep his promise to the Novgorodians enabled Yaroslav to return as prince.

When Yaroslav failed to give in to the *veche*'s demands in 1228, he discovered, to his great loss, that Mikhail could rule successfully in Novgorod. Consequently, two years later, he did not wish to chance another reversal to his policy. Rather than lose control over Novgorod again, he conceded to return with less authority, that is, he agreed to rule according to the demands imposed on him by the *veche*. He promised to adopt those measures which Mikhail had passed in the previous year. Therefore, in 1230, owing to Mikhail's successful rule in Novgorod, Yaroslav was forced to accept those conditions, presumably, which the *veche* initially had demanded from the Vsevolodovichi in the early 1220s. Although, ultimately, Mikhail was required to terminate his activity in Novgorod, his success in undermining the authority of the Vsevolodovichi was significant.

Yaroslav did not feel secure in his control over Novgorod even after Mikahil withdrew from the town in 1230 because the latter gave asylum to a faction of Novgorodians who opposed Yaroslav. Wishing to eliminate this opposition Yaroslav declared war on Mikhail a second time. Under his command the Vsevolodovichi pillaged the northern districts of Chernigov during the winter of 1231/2. But Mikhail refused to accept the challenge to go to war just as he had done in 1230. However, he evicted the Novgorodians from his lands and in this way broke his last tie with Novgorod.

Mikhail's unwillingness to go to war with Yaroslav either in 1230 or in the winter of 1231/2 must not be interpreted as weakness on his part. As we shall see, in 1228, before he returned to Novgorod, Mikhail and his ally, Vladimir Ryurikovich the grand prince of Kiev, attacked Daniil Romanovich, prince of Volyn'. It was because of their mutual interests in southwest Rus' that the grand prince helped Mikhail conclude a truce with the Vesvolodovichi in 1230. More important, the following year Mikhail broke his alliance with the grand prince and attacked Kiev. His action forced Vladimir Ryurikovich to seek help from his former enemy Daniil of Volyn'. Thus, between 1228 and 1232, Mikhail challenged not only the Vesvolodovichi in Novgorod, but also the most powerful princes in southern Rus'. Since, as we shall see, his primary objective was to establish the authority of the Ol'govichi over southern Rus', Mikhail did not wish to become involved in military conflicts with the Vesvolodovichi as well; such action would have made him vulnerable on two fronts. His ambitious policies in the late 1220s, both in Novgorod and in southern Rus', clearly placed him in a precarious position in his relations with the other major princes. Therefore, his success in weakening Yaroslav's hold over Novgorod, without having to engage the latter in open warfare, was not a sign of weakness on his part; on the contrary, it was proof of his diplomatic dexterity.

Consequently, in 1224, when the grand prince of Vladimir appointed Mikhail prince in Novgorod, the strategem proved to be a tactical error for the princes of Rostov-Suzdal'. Mikhail took advantage of the foothold he gained in the town to promote his own interests and to weaken the authority of the Vesvolodovichi. Similarly, the Novgorodians used Mikhail to help them assert their demands on the princes of Rostov-Suzdal'. It is doubtful that the townspeople, or the majority of them, wished to invite Mikhail to be prince on a permanent basis. On the one hand, Chernigov was too far from Novgorod to make such a relationship viable; on the other hand, Novgorod's geography as well as its commercial and political interests were linked more closely to the territory of Rostov-Suzdal' than to the distant principality of Chernigov.

2

Mikhail's Policy in Kiev

To judge solely from information given by the Novgorod First Chronicle, Mikhail Vsevolodovich terminated his involvement in the politics of northwest Rus' in 1232 chiefly owing to the opposition of Yaroslav Vsevolodovich and the Vsevolodovichi of Rostov-Suzdal'. This is only a partial explanation for his decision. Other sources suggest that he had another, more pressing reason for abandoning the northwest political arena. By the early thirties he had become implicated in a power struggle in southern Rus' which demanded his undivided attention. In 1231, even before Yaroslav and the Vsevolodovichi attacked Serensk and Mosal'sk,[1] Mikhail challenged Grand Prince Vladimir Ryurikovich, the senior prince of the family of Rostislavichi of Smolensk, for control of the "golden throne" and for the title of grand prince by attacking Kiev.

Kiev, the "mother of all towns in Rus'," was the seat of the grand prince, the eparchy of the metropolitan, the head of the Orthodox Church, and the commercial crossroad of the Kievan state. Kiev's political seniority – symbolically referred to as the "golden throne" – emanated, in part from its most eminent princes: Prince Vladimir the Christianizer of Rus' and his son Yaroslav "the Wise" the builder, the lawgiver and the patron of learning. As well as embodying the honourable memory of these architects of the Kievan state, the "golden throne" also carried with it the political authority which accrued to the prince of Kiev as the sovereign of the ecclesiastical centre of Rus' and the ruler of a wealthy principality.

Kiev became the object of inter-princely rivalry because, similar to Novgorod, it had no resident family of princes. After the death of Yaroslav "the Wise" in 1054, three of his sons, Izyaslav, Svyatoslav and Vsevolod, and their descendants after them, began to vie for control over the "golden throne." Although the townsmen of Kiev had a *veche* organization, unlike Novgorod they were not sufficiently strong to invite

---

[1] See above pp. 45-47.

the prince of their choice to govern them. Instead, families of princes competed with each other for possession of the town. The victorious family would appoint its senior prince to the grand princely throne for as long a period as it was able to maintain its supremacy over the rivals. Internecine conflicts for Kiev became exceptionally fierce at the beginning of the thirteenth century when the families of princes of the four major principalities of Rus' attempted to assert their influence over it, namely, the Romanovichi of Galicia-Volyn', the Vsevolodovichi (descendants of Vladimir *Monomakh*) of Rostov-Suzdal', the Rostislavichi (also Monomashichi) of Smolensk and the Ol'govichi of Chernigov. However, the chief contestants during the first half of the century were the Rostislavichi of Smolensk and the Ol'govichi of Chernigov.

The competition between these two families reached one of its most violent periods during the reigns of the fathers of Mikhail and Vladimir Ryurikovich – Vsevolod Svyatoslavich and Ryurik Rostislavich. When Grand Prince Svyastoslav Vsevolodovich, an Ol'govich, died on 25 July 1194, he was succeeded on the throne of Kiev by Ryurik Rostislavich.[2] During the first decade of rule his control over Kiev was challenged, not only by the Ol'govichi, but also by Roman Mstislavich prince of Volyn' and Galich who was the most powerful prince in southwest Rus'. However, after the latter was killed in Poland in 1205[3] Vsevolod Svyatoslavich became Ryurik's chief rival. He was able to wrest control of Kiev from Ryurik on three separate occasions between the years 1206 and 1212.[4] Finally, in 1212, the united forces of the Rostislavichi, led by Ryurik's nephew Mstislav Romanovich of Smolensk,[5] drove Vsevolod out of Kiev for the last time. With this victory the princes of Smolensk consolidated their control over Kiev; Mstislav Romanovich became grand prince and ruled from the "golden throne" until he was killed by the Tatars at the Kalka battle in 1223.

The Ol'govichi did not contest Msistlav Romanovich's control over Kiev during his ten-year reign. On the contrary, at times they deemed it advantageous to fight in alliance with the grand prince against common

---

[2] The Hypatian Chronicle (PSRL 2, cols. 680-1); see Table 3:6.

[3] The Laurentian Chronicle (PSRL 1, col. 425). This entry is misplaced in the chronicle under the year 1206. Berezhkov points out that the battle of Zawichost, at which the Poles finally stopped Roman's advance into their lands and at which he was killed, occurred on 19 June 1205 (*Khronologiya*, p. 88). See Table 5:9.

[4] There is some discrepancy concerning the exact dates of Vsevolod's rule in Kiev. See Zotov, *O Chernigovskikh knyazyakh*, p. 273.

[5] See Table 3:10. Concerning the correct date for the battle in 1212, see Berezhkov, *Khronologiya*, pp. 104, 257-8.

enemies.[6] The salient reason for their cooperation was the fact that during the suzerainty of Mstislav Romanovich, the princes of Smolensk reached the zenith of their political power.

During the period between 1212 and 1223 the Rostislavichi were able to extend their control over an area which extended far beyond the principality of Smolensk, their patrimony. The youngest Rostislavichi, descendants of Mstislav Rostislavich,[7] ruled in the town of Toropets north of Smolensk.[8] According to some sources the princes of Smolensk were the overlords of the principality of Polotsk.[9] The principality of Turov, situated along the upper reaches of the Pripyat' river, appears to have been under their suzerainty.[10] During Mstislav Romanovich's reign the

[6] The Hypatian Chronicle states that, in 1218, the Ol'govichi allied themselves to the Rostislavichi against the Hungarians in Galich (PSRL 2, col. 733); the chronicle misplaces this information under the year 1213, cf. the Novgorod First Chronicle (NPL, pp. 59, 260-1; for the correct dating, see Berezhkov, *Khronologiya*, pp. 259-260). According to the Laurentian Chronicle, in 1223, they and all the other princes of southern Rus' allied themselves to the Rostislavichi against the Tatars (PSRL 1, col. 446).

[7] See Table 3:8.

[8] The Laurentian Chronicle states, under the year 1209, that Mstislav Mstislavich went to Toropets "his own principality" (PSRL 1, col. 435). According to the Novgorod First Chronicle, David, Mstislav Mstislavich's younger brother and prince of Toropets, was killed in the winter of 1225/6 by the Lithuanians (NPL, pp. 64, 269).

[9] It is difficult to ascertain the precise extent of Rostislavichi control over Polotsk. Various sources suggest that this control was extensive. For example, the Novgorod First Chronicle states that, in 1222, "the Ярославици, the inhabitants of Smolensk, captured Polotsk on 17 January from the princes Boris and Gleb" (NPL, p. 263; this information is not found in the older *Sinodal'nyy spisok*). Golubovsky, in his monograph on Smolensk, claims that according to ancient tradition only the inhabitants of Polotsk called the descendants of Yaroslav "the Wise" Ярославици. In order to distinguish which Ярославици attacked Polotsk, the chronicler also added "the people of Smolensk" ("смольняне") (*Istoriya Smolenskoy zemli*, p. 198). J. Długosz states that in the same year in which David of Toropets was killed by the Lithuanians (i.e., in the winter of 1225/6), the latter also attacked Polotsk. Mstislav Davidovich prince of Smolensk marched to the defence of the inhabitants of the town with forces from Smolensk and came upon the Lithuanians by surprise. He killed most of them (*Longini canonici Cracoviensis, Historiae Polonicae*, book 6 [Leipzig, 1711], col. 619). This infirmation suggests that Polotsk, which had been captured by the Rostislavichi in 1222, was still under their control in 1226. Finally, the fact that in 1232, when the influence of the princes of Smolensk was already on the decline, Svyatoslav Mstislavich, the son of Mstislav Romanovich, was able to conscript the aid of Polotsk forces to help him obtain control of Smolensk (NPL, pp. 72, 281), indicates that the control of the Rostislavichi over Polotsk, at the height of their power, must have been secure.

[10] Tatishchev states that in 1214 Turov forces helped the Rostislavichi to drive out the Ol'govichi from Kiev (*Istoriya*, vol. 4, p. 345). In 1218 Rostislav Ryurikovich died in Turov, presumably as prince (ibid. p. 356). In 1218 troops from Turov again marched with the princes of Smolensk against the Hungarians in Galich (ibid. p. 359; Tatishchev misplaces this information under the year 1219).

Rostislavichi ruled over Novgorod, almost uninterruptedly, until 1221.[11] And, as well as obtaining control over the principality of Kiev, they won Galich from the Hungarians in 1218.[12] Thus, between the years 1218 and 1221, when they controlled the largest expanse of territory, the princes of Smolensk could boast of ruling lands which extended continuously from Novgorod in the northwest to Kiev and Galich in the south and south-west.

In the face of such overwhelming solidarity presented by the Rosti-slavichi, the Ol'govichi found it advisable to bide their time. However, in 1223, the arrival of the Tatars and the ensuing battle on the Kalka river disrupted the balance of power among the princes of southern Rus'. The invaders not only inflicted heavy losses upon the forces of various principalities but they also killed many of the princes. The deaths of the latter accelerated the cycle of the natural order of lateral succession both among the Ol'govichi of Chernigov and the Rostislavichi of Smolensk. Thus, after the death of Mstislav Svyatoslavich the senior Ol'govich and prince of Chernigov, Mikhail Vsevolodovich succeeded him to both posts since he was the next senior prince. Unfortunately, the chronicles do not say where Mikhail had been prince until then. Similarly, the grand prince of Kiev was succeeded by Vladimir Ryurikovich, the next Rostislavich in order of precedence. However, Mikhail and Vladimir inherited not only the titles of senior princes but with them responsibility for the long-standing rivalry which existed between their families for control over Kiev.

As the new policy maker for the Ol'govichi, Mikhail had two alter-natives open to him in formulating his relationship with the Rosti-slavichi:[13] he could continue to temporize with them as his predecessors

[11] See above p. 19, n. 10.
[12] The Novgorod First Chronicle (NPL, 59, 260-1).
[13] In 1224, Mikhail was pitted against the consolidated power of four branches of Rostislavichi. These were the descendants of the four sons of Rostislav Mstislavich of Smolensk – Roman, Ryurik, David and Mstislav. There is, however, disagreement among historians concerning the seniority of these princes. Baumgarten is of the opinion that David Rostislavich was older than Ryurik (*Généalogies*, Table IX, p. 39). However, the more general consensus of opinion appears to be that Ryurik was older than David ("Rodoslovnaya kniga," VOIDR, book 10 [Moscow, 1851], p. 52; Solov'ev, *Istoriya*, book 1, Table no. 4b, p. 739; Golubovsky, *Istoriya Smolenskoy zemli*, p. 203). The consistency with which the sources list Ryurik and his sons before David and his sons, when enumerating the princes of these families, supports the view that Ryurik was senior to David; see the Hypatian Chronicle (PSRL 2, cols. 469, 528, 680-1) and elsewhere; see also Table 3.

had done for the last decade, or he could revert to the policy of open warfare which his father, Vsevolod, had preferred. It appears that from the time that he assumed seniority and up to the beginning of the 1230s Mikhail chose to temporize. One reason for his decision, no doubt, was the fact that he became involved in the affairs of Novgorod.

The sources make no reference to any dealings between Mikhail and the grand prince of Kiev until after he returned from Novgorod.[14] In 1226 Mikhail had a dispute with Prince Oleg Svyatoslavich of Kursk.[15] At the time of the controversy the new metropolitan Kirill[16] was visiting Chernigov having been sent there by Vladimir Ryurikovich. He strove to reconcile Mikhail with Oleg and was assisted in his task by Yury Vsevolodovich, the grand prince of Vladimir, whom Mikhail requested to come to Chernigov in order to help him resolve the crisis. After they restored peace, Metropolitan Kirill accompanied Yury to Vladimir in Rostov-Suzdal'.[17]

The dispute between Mikhail and Oleg Svyatoslavich of Kursk was the first incident of internal unrest in the principality of Chernigov for fifty-two years.[18] Unfortunately, the chronicles do not state the nature of the

[14] During his first winter as prince of Chernigov in 1224/5, Mikhail was preoccupied with affairs in northwest Rus'. He did not return to Chernigov until later in 1225. See above pp. 16-22.

[15] Tatishchev claimed that Prince Oleg was Oleg Igorevich (*Istoriya*, vol. 3, p. 220). Zotov identified him as the son of Svyatoslav Igorevich (*O Chernigovskikh knyazyakh*, p. 282; see also Bagaley, *Istoriya Severskoy zemli*, p. 263). Baumgarten disagrees with Zotov and postulates that, although Oleg was Oleg Svyatoslavich, he was the son of a different Svyatoslav – Svyatoslav Ol'govich prince of Ryl'sk, a town located east of Chernigov on the Seym river (*Généalogies*, Table 4:59, p. 19). An analysis of the sources reveals that Oleg was the son of Svyatoslav Ol'govich prince of Ryl'sk; concerning the identity of Prince Oleg, see M. Dimnik, "Russian Princes and Their Identities in the First Half of the Thirteenth Century," *Mediaeval Studies*, vol. 40, pp. 158-165.

[16] Kirill, a Greek metropolitan, assumed office in Kiev on 6 January 1225; see the Laurentian Chronicle (PSRL 1, col. 447, s.a. 1224).

[17] PSRL 1, col. 448. This crisis probably occurred in the winter of 1226/7. The entry prior to this account is dated 22 May, while the last entry for the year begins with the phrase "that winter" (PSRL 1, col. 449). This dating is supported by the Tver' Chronicle which has this information as the first entry under the year 1227 and states that Yury went to Mikhail's aid in "the winter" (PSRL 15, col. 346), that is, the winter of 1226/7.

[18] The last time that the Ol'govichi had been pitted against each other was in 1174 when the grandfathers of Mikhail and Oleg, Svyatoslav Vsevolodovich and Oleg Svyatoslavich were at war. In that year Svyatoslav Vsevolodovich, prince of Chernigov, pillaged the principality of Oleg Svyatoslavich; see the Laurentian Chronicle (PSRL 1, col. 367). The chronicle has this information under the year 1175, but Berezhkov points out that the year in question is Ultra-March (*Khronologiya*, p. 74).

disagreement between the two Ol'govichi.[19] However, information relating to events which transpired in the principality between the years 1226 and 1228 shows that the dispute revolved around the question of the right of these princes to a district or principality (*volost'*).[20] This was not a question of Oleg's right to Chernigov, as has been suggested[21] but of his claim to the town of Novgorod Severskiy.[22]

Thanks to the intervention of Grand Prince Yury and Metropolitan Kirill who was visiting Chernigov at the time of the crisis, peace was restored. Unfortunately, the chronicle is silent concerning the nature of the metropolitan's visit and does not explain why he had been sent by the

---

[19] Tatishchev is the only source to described the controversy. He states that "Oleg Igorevich" returned from the Kalka battle and replaced Mstislav Svyatoslavich as senior prince among the Ol'govichi. He became prince of Chernigov and gave Mikhail an "appanage" (*udel*). But the latter believed himself to be unjustly deprived of his father's patrimony so he called upon Yury Vsevolodovich, his brother-in-law, to come to his aid (*Istoriya*, vol. 3, p. 220; this information is not found in the first redaction of his work; see vol. 4).

Tatishchev's explanation is questionable. Since he did not include this information in the first version of his *History* he probably interpolated it into his second recension as his own explanation of the controversy. Similarly, he added the patronymic Igorevich to Oleg's name only in the second redaction (vol. 3, p. 220). His identification is incorrect. Oleg Igorevich, the son of Igor of the epic work "Slovo o polku Igoreve," probably died soon after he was born, in 1175, since this is the only reference to him; see the Hypatian Chronicle (PSRL 2, col. 600).

Furthermore, there is some discrepancy in the chronology of events as presented by Tatishchev and by the chronicles. He claims that "Oleg Igorevich" occupied the throne of Chernigov when he returned from the Kalka battle. But the Novgorod First Chronicle records that in 1224 Mikhail came to Torzhok with the forces of Chernigov (NPL, pp. 64, 268). This would have been unlikely if "Oleg Igorevich" had been prince of Chernigov. The following year, before he departed from Novgorod, Mikhail told the people of Novgorod that he did not wish to rule in their town but desired to return to Chernigov and requested that they continue to send foreign merchants to him ("гост к мнѣ пускаите"), (ibid.). This again is not the language of a prince who was given only an "appanage" in the principality of Chernigov. Tatishchev also maintains that "Oleg Igorevich" challenged Mikhail's claim to the throne of Chernigov in 1224 whereas the chronicles record that the crisis did not arise until 1226. His chronology, therefore, does not correspond with that of the chronicles but, significantly, the latter are consistent with each other.

[20] In Metropolitan Kirill's entreaty to Yury Vsevolodovich presented in Tatishchev's account, the metropolitan gives the following reason for the cause of the dispute. He declares to Yury that they were prepared to wage war on each other because they had quarrelled over a district ("И вы ... будете друг на друга, которующеся о волость, ратовати"); see *Istoriya*, vol. 4, p. 365.

[21] Zotov was of the opinion that Oleg did in fact rule in Chernigov for a short time in 1226 (*O Chernigovskikh knyazyakh*, p. 100). Unfortunately he gives no chronicle reference to support his claim.

[22] See Dimnik, "Russian Princes," pp. 163-164.

grand prince of Kiev.[23] Since Vladimir Ryurikovich commissioned him to
go to Chernigov the grand prince was obviously desirous of preserving
peace in southern Rus'. The crisis, to judge from the sources, did not
jeopardize the relationship between Vladimir and Mikhail in any way.

Two years later, in 1228, an important event occurred which was to
influence significantly the alliance between the Ol'govichi and the
Rostislavichi. In that year Mstislav Mstislavich "the Bold" (*Udaloy*), a
Rostislavich, who had been prince in Galicia, was taken ill while travelling from his principality to Kiev. He adopted the monastic habit and died
soon after.[24] He was buried in the church of the Holy Cross in Kiev,
which he himself had built.[25]

Although the chronicles do not record any overt change in the relationship between the grand prince of Kiev and Mikhail at this time, the death
of Mstislav, one of the main architects of Rostislavichi supremacy in
southern Rus', weakened the political authority which they had enjoyed
over the other princely families since 1212. Without him the princes of
Smolensk were not able to assert their influence over southwest Rus'
where he had ruled.[26] Mstislav had also established important marriage
alliances. He had been the son-in-law of Khan Kotyan, the leader of a tribe
of Polovtsy living to the south of Rus' in the steppe along the Dnepr
river.[27] He had also been the father-in-law both to Daniil Romanovich of
Volyn'[28] and to Prince Andrew of Hungary.[29] When he died, therefore,

[23] Tatishchev claims that the grand prince sent the metropolitan to Yury Vsevolodovich after he had been informed that the latter had come to Chernigov to help Mikhail
against Oleg. The metropolitan addressed a long entreaty to Yury (and not to Mikhail),
beseeching him not to go to war. Tatishchev is the only source which presents the text of
Kirill's supplication to Yury. He is also the only source which places the blame for the
controversy on Mikhail. According to him, Kirill complained to Yury that Mikhail was
picking a quarrel with Oleg unfairly (*Istoriya*, vol. 4, p. 365).

[24] The Laurentian Chronicle (PSRL 1, col. 450). Concerning the correct dating of the
entry in the Laurentian Chronicle, see Berezhkov, *Khronologiya*, p. 108. The Hypatian
Chronicle misplaces this information under the year 1227 (PSRL 2, col. 752). It is noteworthy that several of the entries under the year 1228 in the Laurentian Chronicle give
the month in which the event they describe occurred. All of these months are presented in
chronological order (PSRL 1, cols. 450-1). Since the entry which records Mstislav
Mstislavich's death is placed between the last entry under the month of April and the first
entry under the month of September, it is reasonable to assume that he died between those
two months.

[25] Długosz, *Historiae Polonicae*, col. 623, s.a. 1218. He is the only source to provide
this information.

[26] The Hypatian Chronicle (PSRL 2, col. 750).

[27] The Novgorod First Chronicle (NPL, pp. 62, 265).

[28] The Hypatian Chronicle (PSRL 2, col. 732).

[29] PSRL 2, col. 748.

the Rostislavichi lost an important intermediary with the Polovtsy, with the Romanovichi and with the Hungarians. Furthermore, Mstislav's military prowess, epitomized in his sobriquet "the Bold," had been a byword in Rus' during the first quarter of the thirteenth century.[30] The esteem with which he was held not only among the Rostislavichi but also by the princes of Rus' was acknowledged even by his enemies on the battlefield near the Lipitsa river in 1216.[31]

In losing Mstislav the princes of Smolensk lost one of the bulwarks of their military supremacy. Consequently, their influence over the other families of princes, especially the Ol'govichi, suffered a setback. Mikhail must have begun to view the questions of Galicia and the supremacy of the Rostislavichi from a difference perspective after Mstislav's death upset the political equilibrium in southern Rus'. Indeed, he was obliged to re-evaluate the existing balance of power in all of Rus', especially his relationship to the grand prince of Kiev.

Although Mstislav's death was a great loss to the political fortunes of the Rostislavichi as a whole, it nonetheless enhanced the personal authority of Vladimir Ryurikovich. It is true, he had been the senior prince since 1224, yet there can be little doubt that his political decisions and actions concerning inter-princely relations were influenced by Mstislav.[32] Thus, soon after his death in 1228, Vladimir, wishing to assert

---

[30] Mstislav played a major role in the main clashes in Rus' in the first quarter of the thirteenth century. He helped his cousin Mstislav Romanovich to become grand prince of Kiev in 1212; see the Novgorod First Chronicle (NPL, pp. 53, 251-2). In 1216 he was instrumental in putting Konstantin Vsevolodovich on the grand princely throne of Vladimir in Rostov-Suzdal' (NPL, pp. 56, 257). Two years later he was one of the princes who drove the Hungarians out of Galich (NPL, pp. 59, 260-1). Finally, in 1223, he was one of the three senior princes to lead the campaign against the Tatars and, of the three, only he survived; see the Laurentian Chronicle (PSRL 1, col. 446), the Hypatian Chronicle (PSRL 2, col. 741), the Novgorod First Chronicle (NPL, pp. 62, 265).

[31] On that occasion a certain boyar tried to persuade the two Vsevolodovichi, Yury and Yaroslav, to make peace with their older brother Konstantin, whom Mstislav "the Bold" was helping. The boyar strove to deter the two princes from military action by enumerating Konstantin's military advantages. He concluded his argument by declaring: "and concerning Mstislav Mstislavich you yourselves know that in his family God has bestowed him with bravery which surpasses that of all the others"; see the Sofiyskiy First Chronicle (PSRL 5, p. 195), the Novgorod Fourth Chronicle (PSRL 4, p. 189), the Nikon Chronicle (PSRL 10, p. 71).

[32] See n. 52 below. According to the Hypatian Chronicle, the only time before 1228 on which Vladimir Ryurikovich participated in a campaign after he became grand prince was in 1225; at that time he assisted Mstislav against Daniil (PSRL 2, col. 746). In spite of his secondary role in the attack, Vladimir's action revealed already at that time his willingness to cooperate in a policy to curtail the power of the prince of Volyn'.

his new independence, inaugurated his own military policy by attacking Daniil Romanovich, Mstislav's son-in-law, in the principality of Volyn'.[33]

The Hypatian Chronicle describes the campaign in the following manner: Metropolitan Kirill came in the hope of restoring peace, but failed. After that Rostislav of Pinsk, a minor prince who was threatened by Daniil's expansionist policy because his lands bordered on the principality of Volyn', "did not cease to slander" (Daniil to Vladimir Ryurikovich?) since the former was holding his two sons captive. Therefore, Vladimir and Mikhail assembled their forces and prepared to attack Daniil because, says the chronicler, Daniil's father Roman had forced Vladimir's father to become a monk and because Vladimir had "a great fear in his heart." The grand prince also summoned Khan Kotyan and his Polovtsy to provide reinforcements.[34] When Vladimir assembled all the princes and the troops of Kursk, Pinsk, Novgorod Severskiy and Turov, they besieged the town of Kamenets on the eastern boundary of the principality of Volyn'. Daniil, feigning a desire to negotiate peace, escaped from the town and fled to Poland for help.[35] Meanwhile he dispatched a certain Paul to Khan Kotyan to persuade the latter not to attack. The khan deserted the Rostislavichi and the Ol'govichi and, after looting the lands of Galicia which were under the control of Prince Andrew of Hungary, withdrew to his own lands. The reason for Kotyan not wishing to return to the grand prince and Mikhail after his foray into

---

[33] He no doubt refrained from attacking Daniil while Mstislav was still alive since the latter was Daniil's father-in-law and appears to have become well disposed to his expansionist policy in southwest Rus'. To be sure, Mstislav had promised to help Daniil win Galich from the Hungarians; see the Hypatian Chronicle (PSRL 2, col. 752, s.a. 1227).

[34] Khan Kotyan was the leader of the Durut tribe of Polovtsy. This is the third and last occasion on which he is referred to by the source. The Hypatian Chronicle speaks of him under the years 1202 and 1226 (PSRL 2, cols. 717, 747 respectively) at which times he also participated in campaigns in southwest Rus'. This suggests that his tribe probably lived in the steppe along the Dnepr river (S. A. Pletneva, "Polovetskaya zemlya," *Drevnerusskie knyazhestva x-xiii vv.*, ed. L. G. Beskrovnyy [Moscow, 1975], p. 299). By the beginning of the thirteenth century the nomadic Polovtsy no longer posed a serious threat to the princes of southern Rus'. Finally, after the arrival of the Tatars in 1223, they were eliminated as a political force and the few surviving bands of Polovtsy were too weak to organize successful incursions into the principalities of Rus'. However, on occasion, the princes of various principalities used them as reinforcements for their internecine rivalries as was the case in 1226, 1228 and 1235; see the Hypatian Chronicle (PSRL 2, cols. 772-5).

[35] The seventeenth-century Gustinskiy Chronicle states that Daniil fled to King Leszek I the White for help (PSRL 2, 1843 edition, p. 336). However, Leszek was killed by Świętopełk prince of Pomerania on 24 November 1227 (see Pashuto, *Ocherki*, p. 208). The Gustinskiy Chronicle, therefore, is evidently wrong since, as has been noted, the attack on Kamenets occurred *after* Mstislav "the Bold's" death in 1228 (see above, p. 59).

Galicia was that the two princes were at peace with Andrew of Hungary.
Despite Daniil's flight, the princes failed to take Kamenets and returned
home. Then Daniil and his brother Vasil'ko retaliated by marching against
Kiev with the Poles. But before they reached the town they were
approached by a peace delegation sent out by Vladimir and Mikhail. A
truce was concluded and the Romanovichi returned to their lands.[36]

The chronicle begins its account of the unsuccessful campaign by
explaining that Metropolitan Kirill came with the hope of restoring peace
but failed. Although it does not elucidate whom the metropolitan
approached hoping to avert bloodshed, he must have come to the grand
prince. This is evident from the text: first it gives the metropolitan's plea
for peace, then it states that Rostislav of Pinsk did not stop "slandering"
Daniil and finally it declares that Vladimir assembled his forces.
Presumably both Kirill and Rostislav were addressing themselves to
Vladimir.[37]

If the reason given by the chronicler for the attack on the town of
Kamenets is to be taken at face value then the grand prince's motive was
merely revenge for the insult which his father had suffered at the hands of
Daniil's father in 1205.[38] However, it is difficult to imagine that Mikhail
agreed to march against Daniil, who was not only his brother-in-law but
against whom he had expressed no personal animosity previously, solely

---

[36] PSRL 2, cols. 753-4. Although the Hypatian Chronicle is very unreliable in placing its
entries under the correct year, it appears that in this instance it is correct. It has been noted
that Mstislav Mstislavich died between April and September of 1228 (see above, n. 24).
Not long before his death, to judge from information in the Hypatian Chronicle, Mstislav
gave Daniil his sanction to occupy Chertoryysk, northeast of Vladimir Volynskiy, the
possession of the princes of Pinsk. Daniil arrived at Chertoryysk on Easter Sunday and
occupied the town. (The last Easter before Mstislav's death was 26 March 1228; see
Berezhkov, *Khronologiya*, p. 108). After that Prince Rostislav of Pinsk, an ally of the
Rostislavichi, "spoke slanderously" against Daniil and as a result Vladimir Ryurikovich
and Mikhail marched against Daniil's town of Kamenets. Vladimir probably organized the
campaign soon after Mstislav died in 1228. (It may be presumed that the latter was dead
because the chronicle makes no mention of him during the campaign. Furthermore, the
grand prince would not have marched against Daniil had Mstislav still been alive, as
Daniil had had Mstislav's backing in his campaign against the princes of Pinsk.) Since
Mikhail accompanied Vladimir, the attack must have occurred prior to March 1229; at
that time Mikhail was already in Bryn in the northern districts of the principality of
Chernigov, and from there went to Novgorod (see above p. 25).

[37] This is supported by Karamzin, who (quoting perhaps from an unknown source)
states that the metropolitan approached the grand prince and sought in vain to end the
animosity. But Vladimir retorted that "such deeds are not forgotten" (*Istoriya*, vol. 2,
pp. 291-2).

[38] The Laurentian Chronicle (PSRL 1, col. 420). At that time Roman Mstislavich of
Galich compelled Grand Prince Ryurik Rostislavich to enter a monastery.

in order to satisfy Vladimir's honour. The true reason for the campaign no doubt stemmed from what the chronicler calls Vladimir's "great fear" ("boyazn' velika/боѧзнь велика").[39] The grand prince had good reason to be fearful of Daniil, for the latter had successfully consolidated his authority over the lands of Volyn' and this made him a serious political rival.[40] Vladimir hoped to curb his increasing power by attacking Kamenets and weakening his eastern stronghold.[41] Similarly, Mikhail attacked Kamenets because, as will be seen later, it was to his advantage to keep Daniil politically weak by containing his expansionist policy and thus preventing him from making a successful bid for control of Galicia.[42]

It is clear from the make up of their army that the grand prince and Mikhail considered the campaign to be of major importance. As has been noted, the Hypatian Chronicle states that Vladimir marched "with all the princes" including troops from the towns of Kursk and Novgorod Severskiy from the principality of Chernigov, and troops from Pinsk and Turov, the capital towns in their respective principalities. However, two other copies of the chronicle add – "and Mikhail with all the princes."[43] The fact that Mikhail assembled all the Ol'govichi is noteworthy. First, it underlines the importance which he attributed to restraining Daniil from asserting his influence over Galicia. Second, it shows the solidarity of the family of Ol'govichi as a political force. Mikhail's command over it as its senior prince was complete. This is intimated by the chronicler's reference to the troops from the towns of Kursk and Novgorod Severskiy; they were

[39] The Hypatian Chronicle (PSRL 2, col. 753).

[40] Daniil had taken Lutsk from Yaroslav Ingvarovich (PSRL 2, col. 751) and Chertoryysk from Rostislav of Pinsk (PSRL 2, col. 752).

[41] In 1196 Ryurik Rostislavich had attacked "Roman's principality around Kamenets" (PSRL 2, col. 698). In the years 1210 and 1211 Daniil and Vasil'ko, along with their mother, sought refuge in Kamenets when the chief towns of their principality, namely, Vladimir and Bel'z, were occupied by other princes (PSRL 2, cols. 728-9). Then in 1228 the allied forces of the Rostislavichi and the Ol'govichi attacked the same town. It must have been a citadel of some importance if, on the one hand, it was used as a place of sanctuary by the ruling family of Volyn' and, on the other hand, it was subjected to attacks from the grand princes of Kiev.

[42] Daniil sought to rule in the principality of Galicia which his father had held. According to the Hypatian Chronicle, Mstislav Mstislavich regretted the fact that he had bequeathed Galich to his son-in-law Prince Andrew of Hungary. He had been ready to march with Daniil against Prince Andrew in order to regain it and give it to Daniil (PSRL 2, col. 752). But Mstislav died before these plans materialized. Daniil's intentions concerning Galich no doubt made the Rostislavichi and the Ol'govichi apprehensive about their own ambitions in southwest Rus'. The threat of Daniil's occupation of Galich had become very real by 1228; by that time he had consolidated his control over the principality of Volyn'.

[43] The *Khlebnikovskiy spisok* and the *Pogodinskiy spisok* (see PSRL 2, col. 753, variant 16).

ruled by Oleg Svyatoslavich, thus confirming that he also was present with his family of princes.

Oleg's participation in the campaign was important to the Ol'govichi for he was the senior prince of the cadet branch of Ol'govichi and, as has been noted, had challenged Mikhail for control of Novgorod Severskiy in 1226. Oleg's presence in the company of all the Ol'govichi shows, therefore, that they all supported Mikhail's policy of cooperation with Grand Prince Vladimir and opposition to Daniil of Volyn'. Indeed, after 1228, to judge from later events and from the lack of references to any disputes, Mikhail continued to entertain the unquestioning support of the Ol'govichi. A year later, as we have seen above, the Novgorod chronicler also commented on the cohesiveness of the Ol'govichi. He stated that Mikhail returned to Chernigov to his "brothers," meaning the other princes of Chernigov with whom he lived in harmony. However, in 1228, despite the fact that "all the princes" accompanied both the grand prince and Mikhail, they returned from the campaign having been repulsed by the inhabitants of Kamenets.

The combined forces of the Rostislavichi and the Ol'govichi failed to weaken Daniil's hold over Volyn'; indeed, his successful defence of Kamenets enhanced both his control over his principality and his prestige in all Rus'. At the same time Vladimir's abortive attack did little to bolster his authority as the new policy-maker and commander-in-chief of the Rostislavichi. Since he had been accompanied by Mikhail the failure was also reflected on the Ol'govichi. However, soon after, Mikhail was given an opportunity to recoup much of the prestige which he lost at Kamenets.

In the winter of 1228/9 the Novgorodians summoned Mikhail to be their prince. He arrived there in April 1229 and then returned to Chernigov in the first half of the same year.[44] It is perhaps not without significance that he received this invitation after the death of Mstislav "the Bold." His death and the subsequent weakening of the influence of the Rostislavichi over the northwest probably encouraged Mikhail to accept the offer.[45] His decision was a milestone in his relationship to the other

---

[44] See above pp. 25 ff.

[45] The Rostislavichi had provided princes for Novgorod almost continuously from the winter of 1208/9 until 1221. During that period of time Mstislav had been prince for eight years, that is, from the winter of 1208/9 until 1215 and from 1216 until 1218; see the Novgorod First Chronicle (NPL, pp. 51, 53; 249, 252 and pp. 57, 58; 257, 259 respectively). No doubt he had supporters who favoured his rule in Novgorod since he had not only been a successful administrator (he left voluntarily to rule in Galich) but also because he had led the forces of Novgorod against Yury and Yaroslav in 1216 and thus helped the people of Novgorod further to undermine the influence of the princes of Rostov-Suzdal'

families of princes for it was tantamount to a declaration of independence from his allies – the princes of Smolensk and the princes of Rostov-Suzdal'. Mikhail demonstrated that he was prepared to take action which would conflict with their interests thus declaring that the Ol'govichi were no longer to be considered merely as second-class allies. The fact that Novgorod, the wealthiest town in northern Rus', turned to him for protection rather than to the Vsevolodovichi or the Rostislavichi, served to bolster Mikhail's political status to new heights.

He asserted his newly acclaimed independence almost immediately by challenging the princes of Rostov-Suzdal' on behalf of the *veche* in Novgorod. As we have seen, he implemented measures to countermand legislation which the Vsevolodovichi had passed and he demanded that Yaroslav Vsevolodovich return the outpost of Volok which he had taken by force. However, it appears that Mikhail may have overplayed his hand; his activities in Novgorod, for the first time, brought him to the verge of war with the Vsevolodovichi. Not wishing to engage in hostilities in northwest Rus' he attempted to reach a settlement. The grand prince of Kiev supported Mikhail in the peace negotiations, and a military confrontation with the Vsevolodovichi was averted, at least for a time.[46] The joint action of the princes of Kiev and Chernigov illustrates that, in spite of Mikhail's independent action in Novgorod, Vladimir Ryurikovich still wished to maintain his alliance with the former.

None of the sources state why Vladimir Ryurikovich implicated himself in the peace negotiations of 1230. As grand prince he sought no doubt to preserve the harmony which had existed between the Ol'govichi and the princes of Rostov-Suzdal' since 1207.[47] After the battle on the Lipitsa river, which resolved the power struggle in Rostov-Suzdal' in 1216, there had been no internecine wars between any of the three most powerful families of princes in Rus' – the Rostislavichi, the Ol'govichi and the Vsevolodovichi. Instead, these families confined their military energies to the peripheries of their principalities, chiefly, in attempts to

---

in Novgorod. After his death, Mstislav's supporters probably wished to find a substitute who could successfully challenge the Vsevolodovichi. The fact that they elected to choose such a prince from among the Ol'govichi rather than the Rostislavichi shows that they no longer considered the latter to be a serious threat to the princes of Rostov-Suzdal'.

[46] See above p. 39.

[47] In that year, Vsevolod Yur'evich marched against the Ol'govichi. En route to Chernigov, however, he diverted his march and attacked the princes of Ryazan' instead; see the Laurentian Chronicle (PSRL 1, cols. 429-31). The Novgorod First Chronicle has this account under the year 1209 (NPL, pp. 51, 247-8). For the correct dating, see Berezhkov, *Khronologiya*, p. 100.

consolidate their authority against external enemies. The Vsevolodovichi of Rostov-Suzdal', for example, directed their military efforts to the Novgorod and the Volga-Bulgar regions.[48] At the same time, the Ol'go-vichi, in alliance with the Rostislavichi, concentrated their energies against the Hungarians and the nomads in southwest and southern Rus'.[49] Thus, it may be concluded that in 1230, to judge from the policies and activities of the Ol'govichi and the Rostislavichi in the preceding two decades, Vladimir and Mikhail sent their messengers to the princes of Rostov-Suzdal' out of a common desire to preserve concord between the three families.

Furthermore, it is clear that a dispute between the Ol'govichi and the Vsevolodovichi would have placed the grand prince of Kiev in an embarrassing position. In such a war Vladimir would have been forced to choose between two allies. He could have elected either to maintain the unity of his own house, that is the house of Vladimir *Monomakh*, and ally himself to the Vsevolodovichi,[50] or, to support Mikhail. In view of the recent assistance which the latter had proffered to the grand prince against Daniil of Volyn', and in view of their common interests in southern Rus', Mikhail could have applied considerable pressure on Vladimir to help him against the princes of Rostov-Suzdal'. The success of the negotiations in 1230, therefore, saved the grand prince from the necessity of having to choose sides and at the same time from the risk of making new enemies. The latter must have been a very serious consideration for Vladimir given the steadily declining fortunes of the Rostislavichi.

Vladimir and Mikhail did not wish to become involved in a military conflict with the princes of Rostov-Suzdal' for another and more pressing

[48] In Novgorod they attempted to stem the flow of western incursions by Germans, Lithuanians and local indigenous tribes; see the Novgorod First Chronicle (NPL, s.a. 1222, pp. 60-1, 262-3; s.a. 1223, pp. 61, 263; s.a. 1225, pp. 64, 269; s.a. 1227, pp. 65, 270; s.a. 1228, pp. 65, 270). In the east and southeast of Rostov-Suzdal', they strove to subdue the Bulgars and the Mordva; see the Laurentian Chronicle (PSRL 1, s.a. 1220, col. 444; s.a. 1226, cols. 448-9; s.a. 1228, cols. 450-1).

[49] In southwest Rus' in 1219 they drove out the Hungarians from Galich in order to assert the influence of the grand prince of Kiev in that region; see the Hypatian Chronicle (PSRL 2, col. 733). In the south they sought to divert the incursions of the nomads from the steppe. To this end they amalgamated their forces in 1223 in an attempt to stem the tide of the Tatar invasion; see the Laurentian Chronicle (PSRL 1, col. 446), the Hypatian Chronicle (PSRL 2, col. 741), the Novgorod First Chronicle (NPL, pp. 62, 265).

[50] Earlier in the year 1230, on 14 April , Vladimir's daughter married Vsevolod, Yury's eldest son; see the Laurentian Chronicle (PSRL 1, cols. 453-4). This marriage alliance must have served as an added incentive to Vladimir to preserve peace between himself and Yury.

reason – the success of Daniil's expansionist policy in the southwest. This problem required such serious consideration that the majority of the princes of southern Rus' attended a congress (*snem*) in Kiev in the following year to determine a course of action. The Laurentian Chronicle, the only source which gives this information, states that on 6 April 1231 Kirill was consecrated bishop of Rostov in Kiev by the metropolitan and four other bishops. The ceremony was attended not only by the bishops and the senior clergy from Kiev and Chernigov, but also by the grand prince of Kiev and his son Rostislav. Various other princes were also present at the ceremony because, the chronicler explains, they were in Kiev attending a *snem*. He lists the following: "Mikhail, prince of Chernigov, his son (Rostislav), Rostislav Mstislavich, Mstislav, Yaroslav, Izyaslav, Rostislav Borisovich and many other princes" ("Михаилъ кнѧз Черниговьскыи. и снъ ѥго Ростиславъ Мстиславичь Мстиславъ. Ярославъ. Изѧславъ. и Ростиславъ Борисовичь. и ини мнози кнѧзи").[51] Unfortunately the princes listed are not all easily identifiable.

The five princes who are singled out, along with Vladimir Ryurikovich and his son Rostislav and Mikhail Vsevolodovich and his son Rostislav are the following: Rostislav Mstislavich, Mstislav, Yaroslav, Izyaslav and Rostislav Borisovich. They were either senior princes or ruled important principalities since the chronicle states that there were many other princes present beside the ones named. It may also be presumed that the chronicler followed protocol in listing these important princes as was done concerning the assembly held in Kiev in 1223.[52] Using these guideposts we can establish the identities of the five remaining princes

[51] PSRL 1, col. 457. The editors of the Laurentian Chronicle in PSRL 1, according to the classification given in the index to this volume, do not interpret this list of princes to read in the same manner. They identify the princes to be the following: Mikhail, prince of Chernigov, his son Rostislav, Mstislavich Mstislav, Yaroslav, Izyaslav and Rostislav Borisovich. Consequently they list only six princes where, it appears, there should be seven.

[52] According to chronicle information, the last such *snem* to be held in Kiev had been in preparation for the Tatar invasion in 1223; see the Hypatian Chronicle (PSRL 2, col. 741). In this instance the chronicle listed, in order of political seniority, the three senior princes of southern Rus', that is, the grand prince of Kiev Mstislav Romanovich, the prince of Chernigov Mstislav Svyatoslavich and the next Rostislavich of political importance, Mstislav Mstislavich "the Bold." (Evidently the chronicler followed the protocol of listing princes who enjoyed political seniority rather than merely hereditary seniority since Vladimir Ryurikovich, who participated in the battle, and who was the senior to Mstislav Mstislavich in the family of Rostislavichi, is not named as attending the *snem*.) In drawing up the list of participants for the congress of 1231 the chronicler, no doubt, followed a similar order, that is, he listed the Rostislavichi before their counterparts among the Ol'govichi since the former ruled in Kiev.

whom the chronicler lists; they were: Rostislav Mstislavich the prince of Smolensk and the second in seniority among the Rostislavichi after Vladimir Ryurikovich;[53] Mstislav Glebovich, an Ol'govich and the next in seniority after Mikhail Vsevolodovich;[54] Yaroslav Ingvarovich of Lutsk in the lands of Volyn', the senior prince of the Lutsk family of princes;[55] Izyaslav Vladimirovich, the senior prince among the Igorevichi, a cadet branch of the Ol'govichi;[56] and Rostislav Borisovich, prince of Polotsk and of minor political significance.[57]

The chronicle does not state what crisis prompted the grand prince to convoke such a major assembly. To judge from the fact that the last congress in Kiev, which was held in 1223, was called at the time of the Tatar invasion, a similar gathering in 1231 was presumably held also because of a common threat to the authority of the princes of southern Rus'. Since there appears to have been no external danger to the country in 1231 such as had existed in 1223,[58] it may be assumed that the crisis was internal.

The pressing reason which not only deterred the grand prince and Mikhail from becoming involved in a clash with the Vsevolodovichi in 1230, but also prompted Vladimir to assemble the *snem* in 1231, was the increasing strength of Daniil Romanovich in southwest Rus'. By 1231 the latter's attempts to consolidate the lands of Volyn' under his authority had been successful: Vladimir's ally Rostislav of Pinsk had already expressed his fears concerning Daniil's expansionist policy and his threat to the power of individual princes in Volyn' in 1228 after the death of Mstislav Mstislavich of Galicia;[59] Yaroslav Ingvarovich of Lutsk who attended the

---

[53] See Table 3:24.

[54] See Table 2:28.

[55] See Table 5:20.

[56] See Table 2:32.

[57] For a detailed discussion of the identities of these princes see Dimnik, "Russian Princes," pp. 165-80.

[58] There is no chronicle evidence to suggest that the princes were discussing the possibility of a renewed Tatar attack. If this had been the case Daniil would no doubt have been invited to attend as ruler of the largest principality in western Rus'. However, the first chronicle news concerning the return of the Tatars is not found until the year 1236 when they invaded the lands of the Bulgars on the Volga river; see the Laurentian Chronicle (PSRL 1, col. 460). Hrushevsky suggested that the purpose of the congress was to discuss Mikhail's controversy with Yaroslav Vsevolodovich in Novgorod; he also proposed that the conflict was resolved at this time (*Istoriia*, vol. 2, p. 245). To judge from the fact that Yaroslav attacked Mikhail's principality in the winter of 1231/2, their differences were not resolved at the *snem*.

[59] According to Karamzin, who appears to be quoting an unknown source, Rostislav turned to Vladimir for help in 1228 because he feared that after Mstislav Mstislavich's

snem, came no doubt to register his complaint against Daniil, since the latter had taken Lutsk from him;[60] furthermore, by 1231, Daniil had not only taken possession of Galich, but also successfully repulsed an attack by the Hungarians who attempted to regain possession of the town.[61] In the light of all these developments there is no doubt that the Rostislavichi and the Ol'govichi, as well as the other princes of southern Rus' who attended the congress, were chiefly concerned with the strategy to be adopted against the prince of Volyn'.

The *snem*, however, must have had an added and even more urgent purpose for the Rostislavichi themselves, whose former supremacy over southern Rus' had virtually disappeared. The princes of Smolensk, for various reasons, lost much of their political power and prestige after Vladimir became grand prince in 1224. Since they probably had provided the largest number of troops against the Tatars at the Kalka battle, the Rostislavichi also suffered the greatest losses. Four years later, when Mstislav Mstislavich "the Bold" died, they not only lost their influence over the territories of southwest Rus' but also much of the political prestige which had accrued to them thanks to the personal valour of Mstislav as a general. Then in 1230, after the death of Mstislav Davidovich the second senior prince after Vladimir Ryurikovich and prince of Smolensk,[62] there emerged the first visible signs of internal fragmentation among the Rostislavichi. Rostislav Mstislavich succeeded his father to the throne of Smolensk but, in doing so, he pre-empted seniority from his cousins, the sons of Mstislav Romanovich who were senior to him and the rightful heirs to the throne.[63]

---

death, Daniil would seek to assert his rule over the other princes of Volyn' (*Istoriya*, vol. 3, p. 291). Consequently, since Vladimir and the Ol'govichi attacked Daniil in 1228, it is obvious that his ambitions were already a primary concern to the former at that time.

[60] The Hypatian Chronicle (PSRL 2, col. 751).

[61] PSRL 2, col. 759. Although the entry is placed under the year 1229, it appears that Daniil's siege of Galich occurred in 1230. According to the account the opposing armies engaged in battle on ice, but in the evening the ice melted and the water rose on the Dnestr river. The fact that they fought on melting ice indicates that they engaged in battle in the spring of 1230.

[62] The Sofiyskiy First Chronicle (PSRL 5, p. 209); the Novgorod Fourth Chronicle (PSRL 4, p. 212); the *svod* of 1479 (PSRL 25, p. 125); the Nikon Chronicle (PSRL 10, p. 102); the Ermolinskiy Chronicle (PSRL 23, p. 73).

[63] Golubovsky observed that the rivalry which arose between the Rostislavichi in Smolensk split the family into two camps – the descendants of Mstislav Romanovich and the descendants of Mstislav Davidovich (*Istoriya Smolenskoy zemli*, p. 171). This crisis among the princes of Smolensk may have been one of the most urgent reasons why the grand prince convoked the *snem*. As the senior Rostislavich, Vladimir had to set his house in order before he could hope to reassert the authority of the Rostislavichi over southern Rus'.

Internal unrest among the princes of Smolensk was augmented by a natural disaster. In 1230, an early frost on the feast of the Exaltation of the Cross (i.e. 14 September)[64] caused havoc in all of Rus' "except in Kiev".[65] This was followed by a famine which lasted for two years and Smolensk suffered immense losses of population; some 32,000 inhabitants perished in the town and had to be buried in four mass graves.[66] Finally, the incursions of the Lithuanians on the lands of Smolensk played their part in sapping the resources of the Rostislavichi.[67] All these setbacks to the fortunes of the Rostislavichi were added reasons why Vladimir Ryurikovich convoked the *snem* in 1231 in the hope of renegotiating his alliances, especially with the Ol'govichi, and perhaps salvaging some of the former authority of the family.

This is the last recorded reference to an assembly of princes to be held in Rus' prior to the Tatar invasion of 1237/8. If it is to be taken at face value it reflects an impressive degree of unity among the families of princes in Kievan Rus' in 1231. Unfortunately, the chronicle not only fails to record the issues discussed but neglects to give what resolutions, if any, were reached by the congress. To judge from ensuing events, Vladimir was not successful in negotiating an agreement with the other princes concerning a policy to be adopted against Daniil. What is more, there is a strong indication that the *snem* did not even conclude in concord. According to the Hypatian Chronicle, in the same year, Vladimir sent word to Daniil, whom he and Mikhail had attacked three years previously, that the latter was marching against him in Kiev and requested Daniil to send him military assistance. Daniil came to the grand prince's rescue and restored peace between the Rostislavichi and the Ol'govichi.[68]

---

[64] The Novgorod First Chronicle (NPL, pp. 69, 277).

[65] NPL, pp. 71, 280.

[66] The Novgorod Fourth Chronicle (PSRL 4, p. 212); the *svod* of 1479 (PSRL 25, p. 125); the Nikon Chronicle (PSRL 10, p. 101); cf. the Sofiyskiy First Chronicle (PSRL 5, p. 209) and the Ermolinskiy Chronicle (PSRL 23, p. 73) where the number of dead is given as 33,000 and 30,000 respectively.

[67] The chronicles record four instances in the 1220s on which the Lithuanians attacked the principality of Smolensk either directly or in passing when raiding the lands of Novgorod. See the Novgorod First Chronicle (NPL, s.a. 1223, pp. 61, 263; s.a. 1224, pp. 61, 264; s.a. 1225, pp. 64, 269; s.a. 1229, pp. 68, 275).

[68] PSRL 2, col. 766. Mikhail and Vladimir probably fell out with each other at the *snem*. This can be deduced from the fact that prior to the congress the chronicles give no evidence of any animosity between them. The Hypatian Chronicle continues its account by stating that after Daniil had helped to settle the dispute between the two princes, and while he was still in Kiev, he was informed that Prince Andrew of Hungary had attacked

When Mikhail had agreed to become prince of Novgorod in 1229 he had acted independently of his allies and challenged the Vsevolodovichi; in 1231, however, he took even more ambitious measures and attempted to secure his control over southern Rus'. By attacking the Rostislavichi after the *snem* he repudiated his alliance with them and upset the existing balance of power. He also revived the struggle for supremacy in southern Rus' which had been dormant since the Rostislavichi had driven his father, Vsevolod, out of Kiev in 1212. After the congress, Mikhail resolved that the time of temporizing had come to an end and the Ol'govichi were again sufficiently powerful to challenge the princes of Smolensk. Subsequently, events would prove his decision to be well founded.

Mikhail's attack on Kiev exposed the vulnerability of the Rostislavichi. Vladimir could not defend the "golden throne" on his own nor could he rely on receiving the necessary reinforcements from Smolensk which was devastated by famine. The grand prince, in the last resort, was forced to solicit the aid of the prince of Volyn' whom he and Mikhail had attacked jointly only a few years previously. Mikhail's aggression, consequently, was instrumental in bringing about a major reversal of Rostislavichi policy by forcing the grand prince to turn to his former enemy for help. It also had significant consequences for Daniil as this was the first occasion on which he, as prince of Volyn', was brought into the arena of Kievan politics on an equal footing with the grand prince and with the prince of Chernigov. By asking Daniil to be his ally, Vladimir acknowledged him as one of the major rulers of southern Rus'. To be sure, it was thanks primarily to his intervention that Vladimir was able to retain possession of Kiev and to negotiate a truce with Mikhail, albeit a short one.[69]

---

his lands. Daniil marched against the Hungarians. They fought through the winter of 1231/2 until Holy Saturday 1232 (PSRL 2, col. 770). Mikhail must have attacked Kiev some time after the *snem* (the consecration of the bishop of Rostov was on 6 April), and before Andrew initiated hostilities against Daniil. Therefore, the attack must have occurred in the summer or autumn of 1231.

[69] Hrushevsky is correct in observing that the newly formed alliance between the grand prince and Daniil was not so much an alliance between equals as the protection of the grand prince by Daniil (*Istoriia*, vol. 2, p. 246). It appears that Vladimir relied so strongly on Daniil's protection, claims Hrushevsky, that his alliance with the latter even superseded his family ties. In 1234, when Aleksandr of Bel'z (a town south of Vladimir in Volyn') fled from Daniil to his father-in-law Vladimir, Daniil caught Aleksandr and imprisoned him. To judge from the account, Vladimir did not try to intercede in behalf of his son-in-law; see the Hypatian Chronicle (PSRL 2, cols. 771-2) and Hrushevsky, *Istoriia*, vol. 2, p. 247.

The truce concluded between Mikhail and Vladimir was still in effect the following year; there was no altercation between the two princes.[70] Then, in 1233, Daniil gave the grand prince an opportunity to strengthen their alliance in a joint campaign against the Hungarians; this venture precipitated a complete break between Vladimir and the Ol'govichi. According to the Hypatian Chronicle, the prince of Volyn' asked Vladimir for aid against Prince Andrew of Hungary. At the same time he secured the support of Izyaslav Vladimirovich, an Ol'govich and Mikhail's close ally,[71] and the Polovtsy. However, Daniil doubted Izyaslav's veracity and demanded that he take an oath of fidelity prior to the campaign. But his oath did not deter Izyaslav from betraying his two compatriots even before they encountered the Hungarians. He captured and pillaged the town of Tikhoml' in southwest Volyn'. Despite his perfidy, Daniil, Vladimir and the Polovtsy succeeded in repelling Andrew's attack.[72]

Daniil's invitation to both the Rostislavichi and the Ol'govichi to accompany him on the campaign appears strange at first sight given the growing animosity between the two families. However, his motives become apparent on closer scrutiny of the information. Since Daniil had helped the grand prince in 1231 he also wished to use the alliance to his advantage and, at the same time, to test Vladimir's readiness to come to his assistance. More significantly, Daniil's request forced the grand prince to re-evaluate his former relations not only with the Ol'govichi but also with the Hungarians who had been his allies in the past.[73] By asking him to march against Prince Andrew, Daniil pressured Vladimir into committing himself to his new alliance with him and renouncing his association with the former.

---

[70] It appears that the grand prince had domestic problems to cope with in that year. According to chronicle information, there was a conflict among the Rostislavichi in 1232. Svyatoslav Mstislavich, the next in seniority after Vladimir and the rightful heir to the throne of Smolensk, attacked the town with the help of forces from Polotsk and occupied it; see the Novgorod First Chronicle (NPL, pp. 72, 281; only the *Komissionnyy spisok* gives Svyatoslav's patronymic). This conflict is evidence of further deterioration in the crumbling structure of the family of the Rostislavichi.

[71] There is nothing unusual about the fact that Daniil asked Izyaslav Vladimirovich for assistance even though the latter was an Ol'govich and both an ally of the prince of Chernigov and on friendly terms with the Hungarians. During the first half of the thirteenth century it was common practice for princes and boyars to change their allegiance in order to suit their own interests.

[72] The Hypatian Chronicle (PSRL 2, col. 770).

[73] It has been seen that in 1228 when Vladimir and Mikhail attacked Kamenets, the Hungarians had been their allies (PSRL 2, col. 753).

Significantly, Daniil also asked Izyaslav Vladimirovich, Mikhail's close ally, to accompany him against the Hungarians, who were allies of the Ol'govichi. Although the sources give no indication as to whether or not Izyaslav had helped Mikhail attack Kiev in 1231, in the light of their subsequent relationship it is safe to assume that he concurred with Mikhail's action. Similarly, in 1233, when Izyaslav joined Daniil he would have been representing not only his own policy but also that of the prince of Chernigov. Therefore, to judge from Izyaslav's initial involvement in the campaign of 1233, the truce concluded between Vladimir and the Ol'govichi in 1231 was still in effect. Daniil may have asked Izyaslav to accompany him, not only because he wished to procure additional reinforcements, but also to test the tenor of the truce. The fact that Daniil made an Ol'govich take an oath shows that he obviously had little faith in Izyaslav's professed willingness to assist him. Izyaslav justified Daniil's suspicion of him, for it appears that he had no intention of marching against his allies the Hungarians; instead, he took the opportunity to pillage Daniil's principality. His attack on Tikhoml' had significant repercussions on the relations between the princes of southern and southwest Rus'. It not only broke the truce which existed between the Ol'govichi and the Rostislavichi but it also initiated rivalry between the princes of Chernigov and the princes of Volyn'.

Towards the end of 1234, and at the beginning of 1235, Mikhail and the grand prince were involved in several conflicts which completely altered the balance of power in southern Rus'. The Hypatian Chronicle states that while Vladimir was ruling in Kiev, he sent his son Rostislav to Galich where he concluded a peace treaty with Daniil. In spite of this agreement which boded ill for the Ol'govichi, Mikhail and his ally Izyaslav Vladimirovich continued their hostile action against him. As Mikhail once again prepared to lay siege to Kiev, Vladimir summoned Daniil to his assistance forcing Mikhail to withdraw to Chernigov.[74] Princes Vladimir and Daniil retaliated by attacking him at the beginning of 1235. The Hypatian Chronicle, however, has spurious information in its description of their siege of Chernigov.[75]

---

[74] PSRL 2, col. 772.

[75] The Hypatian Chronicle misplaced information describing the unsuccessful defence of Chernigov by Mstislav Glebovich (Mikhail's cousin and the next senior prince among the Ol'govichi), and its capitulation to the Tatars in 1239 into the account describing the attack made by Vladimir and Daniil on Mikhail in Chernigov in 1235. For a detailed analysis of this problem see, M. Dimnik, "The Siege of Chernigov in 1235," *Mediaeval Studies*, vol. 41, pp. 387-403.

The Novgorod First Chronicle has preserved the correct account of Mikhail's defence of Chernigov in 1235. It states that Vladimir and the troops from Kiev, along with Daniil and the forces from Galich, marched against Mikhail in Chernigov. While the princes were pillaging the district around Chernigov Izyaslav "fled" ("bezha/бѣжа") to the Polovtsy for reinforcements. Mikhail came out of the town and by means of a trick succeeded in killing many of the troops from Galich and in driving off the attackers. Daniil barely escaped with his life and Vladimir withdrew to Kiev.[76]

Although Mikhail defeated Daniil's forces and thereby also compelled Vladimir to withdraw from Chernigov, the princes did not reach any peace agreement. On the contrary, Izyaslav Vladimirovich who solicited the support of the Polovtsy returned with them and marched against the grand prince and Daniil in Kiev. The Hypatian Chronicle explains that Daniil's troops were war-worn since they had been ravaging the lands of Chernigov from 6 January to 14 May. He therefore wished to return home but Vladimir persuaded him to remain and fight the pagan Polovtsy. Their armies clashed near Torchesk, a town south of Kiev, and the Polovtsy were victorious. Vladimir and Daniil's *voevoda* Miroslav were captured owing to the treachery of many boyars from Galicia; but, explains the chronicler, Daniil escaped to Galich. However, when the boyars of Galich rose in rebellion he was forced to flee to Hungary.[77] Later in the winter he attempted, together with his brother Vasil'ko, to recapture Galich from Mikhail. They were not successful and had to withdraw to their capital of Vladimir in Volyn'.[78] The Novgorod First

---

[76] NPL, pp. 73-4, 284. Tatishchev who may be quoting an unknown source, alone gives more detailed information concerning the "trick" by means of which Mikhail drove off the attackers. He states that Mikhail, having mustered all the soldiers who were available, came out of Chernigov to Daniil and spoke to him "with much flattery." He promised Daniil many gifts if the latter would abandon the grand prince and persuade him to lift the siege. Daniil listened to Mikhail and attempted to convince Vladimir to end hostilities. Then at night Mikhail attacked Daniil and killed many of the Galicians so that Daniil himself barely escaped. After that the grand prince returned to Kiev (*Istoriya*, vol. 4, p. 372).

[77] According to a Hungarian source, Daniil was present at the coronation of Béla IV on "Sunday, the eve of the ides of October," that is, 14 October 1235 (*Historia critica regum Hungariae stirpis Arpadianae ex fide domesticorum et externorum scriptorum*, ed. S. Katona, vol. 5 [Posonii et Cassoviae, 1783], p. 754).

[78] PSRL 2, cols. 772-3. The chronicle has the information concerning Mikhail's attack on Kiev, Vladimir's and Daniil's siege of Chernigov and the sack of Kiev by the Polovtsy under the year 1234. It appears, however, that Mikhail attacked Kiev either in the fall or the winter of 1234, when Daniil came to Kiev in reply to the summons sent to him by

Chronicle gives additional information. When Izyaslav finally arrived with a large force of Polovtsy he was joined by Mikhail and his contingent from Chernigov. Together they marched on Kiev and captured it, and the Polovtsy took the grand prince and his wife prisoner. After this Mikhail occupied the throne of Galich and, says the chronicler, Izyaslav became the grand prince of Kiev. Later the Polovtsy released Vladimir and his wife for a ransom and the princes exacted ransom from the German merchants in Kiev.[79]

The events described above, which occurred between 1234 and 1236, present two problems of special interest. The first problem is one of identity. Most chronicles, in a way similar to the Novgorod First Chronicle, state that Izyaslav occupied Kiev but, unlike the latter source, they give him the patronymic Mstislavich; some of them add that he was the grandson of Roman Rostislavich of Smolensk.[80] Unfortunately, many of these sources, unlike the Hypatian Chronicle, claim that the prince who brought the Polovtsy to Kiev was also Izyaslav Mstislavich and not Izyaslav Vladimirovich. This inconsistency in chronicle information has created confusion among historians concerning the identity of the "Izyaslav" who participated in the inter-princely rivalries between the years 1234 and 1236. A close examination of the information given in all the available sources concerning "Izyaslav" reveals that there were *two* princes named Izyaslav active during this period.[81] The first, Izyaslav Vladimirovich, was an Igorevich who belonged to a cadet branch of the Ol'govichi and was Mikhail's close ally. He brought the Polovtsy to Mikhail's aid and attacked Kiev. The second, Izyaslav Mstislavich, the grandson of Roman Rostislavich, belonged to the family of Rostislavichi of Smolensk. It appears that he was the youngest prince of the senior branch of Rostislavichi[82] (i.e., the branch which would provide a suc-

---

Vladimir. It may be assumed that Daniil came to Kiev in December 1234 at the latest, since the Hypatian Chronicle states that he and Vladimir campaigned in Chernigov from Epiphany, 6 January 1235, until the Ascension, 14 May. After their failure to take Chernigov, they returned to Kiev in May. Izyaslav came with the Polovtsy after the princes had returned to Kiev. His attack therefore occurred some time after May in 1235.

[79] NPL, pp. 74, 284-285.

[80] See Table 3:22.

[81] For a detailed examination of this problem, see Dimnik, "Russian Princes," pp. 170-7.

[82] Izyaslav Mstislavich appears to have been the youngest of Mstislav Romanovich's sons; the eldest was Svyatoslav; see the Novgorod First Chronicle (NPL, pp. 59, 260). He occupied Smolensk by force in 1232 (NPL, pp. 72, 281). Izyaslav's other brother, Vsevolod, was placed on the throne of Smolensk by Yaroslav Vsevolodovich in 1239; see the Laurentian Chronicle (PSRL 1, col. 469).

cessor to Vladimir Ryurikovich as grand prince of Kiev);[83] he occupied the throne of Kiev (with Mikhail's approval), merely as a stopgap measure to maintain the authority of the Rostislavichi in Kiev while Vladimir was being held prisoner by the Polovtsy.

The second problem is one of chronology. There is, apparently, conflicting information concerning the princes who succeeded Izyaslav Mstislavich as grand prince in 1235 and 1236. For example, the Novgorod First Chronicle records that Izyaslav Mstislavich became grand prince of Kiev after Vladimir was captured but that the latter was released in the same year. Then under the following year, 1236, it states that Yaroslav Vsevolodovich of Pereyaslavl' occupied Kiev.[84] According to the Hypatian Chronicle, which apparently contradicts the above information, Yaroslav took Kiev from Vladimir and later Mikhail took it from Yaroslav.[85] Despite the confusing picture presented by the sources the following sequence of events is certain. Vladimir the grand prince was captured by the Polovtsy in 1235 and replaced on the throne of Kiev by his nephew Izyaslav Mstislavich; later in the same year he was released for a ransom. The controversy begins here – where did Vladimir return to?

Karamzin's explanation of the events – Vladimir after being released by the Polovtsy replaces Izyaslav in Kiev but is later obliged to hand it over to Yaroslav as a result of an agreement between Daniil Romanovich of Volyn' and Yury Vsevolodovich of Rostov-Suzdal'[86] – appears to have been based on some source which has not survived, and provides perhaps the key to the problem of the seemingly contradictory evidence of the known sources.[87]

To summarize, the following is the order of events which transpired after Mikhail withdrew to Chernigov in the winter of 1234. Vladimir Ryurikovich and Daniil of Volyń set out against Mikhail and campaigned in his lands from 6 January to 14 May 1235. They succeeded only in devastating the environs of Chernigov but were not able to capture the town because Mikhail tricked the attackers and forced them to withdraw to Kiev without reaching any peace agreement. Then Izyaslav Vladimiro-

---

[83] Vladimir Ryurikovich was the last surviving grandson of Rostislav Mstislavich. Consequently, according to the tradition of lateral succession, the grand princely throne would pass to the sons of Mstislav Romanovich; see Table 3:10.

[84] NPL, pp. 74, 284-5.

[85] PSRL 2, col. 777.

[86] *Istoriya*, vol. 3, pp. 312-3.

[87] For a detailed investigation of this problem see M. Dimnik, "The struggle for control over Kiev in 1235 and 1236," *Canadian Slavonic Papers*, vol. 21, no. 1 (1979), pp. 28-44.

vich, who had been soliciting reinforcements in the steppe during the
siege of Chernigov, returned with an army of Polovtsy after 14 May and,
joined by Mikhail and a contingent from Chernigov, marched on Kiev.
They defeated Daniil and Vladimir near Torchesk, captured the grand
prince and after razing Kiev exacted a ransom from the Germans. Kiev
was occupied temporarily by Vladimir's nephew Izyaslav Mstislavich, but
when Vladimir was released for a ransom later in the year, he returned as
grand prince of Kiev. Meanwhile, because Mikhail was consolidating his
authority over southwest Rus', Daniil and Grand Prince Yury of Rostov-
Suzdal' reached an agreement, persuaded Vladimir to vacate the "golden
throne" and designated Yaroslav of Pereyaslavl' to replace him as grand
prince. Yaroslav arrived with due ceremony early in 1236 but, not being
able to establish his control over the town, returned to Suzdal'; then
Mikhail came from Galich and became grand prince after him.

The sources do not give any explanation for the growing animosity
between the Ol'govichi and the Rostislavichi in the early 1230s which
eventually led to a full-scale conflict and to the victory of the Ol'govichi
over princes Vladimir and Daniil in the spring of 1235. However,
subsequent events show that Mikhail once again initiated the traditional
expansionist policy of his family. His objective, similar to that of his father
Vesvolod and his grandfather Svyatoslav Vsevolodovich, was to establish
the authority of the Ol'govichi over southern and southwest Rus' by
weakening the hold of the Rostislavichi over Kiev and by obtaining
control over Galicia.[88] He achieved his first notable victory in the spring of
1235 when the combined forces of the Ol'govichi and the Polovtsy not
only sacked Kiev but also drove out the Romanovichi from Galich.

Mikhail's victory over Kiev was a milestone in his career. It was the
first time that the Ol'govichi occupied the town since his father Vsevolod
had been grand prince in 1212. Over twenty years later, Mikhail's rivalry
with the Rostislavichi and the Romanovichi for control over Kiev is proof
that the commercial crossroad of Rus' was still a prime political objective
among the important families of princes. Not only did German trade from
the Baltic Sea continue to go down the Dnepr through Kiev to the Black
Sea, but the metropolis of Rus' was the gateway to the east for overland
trade caravans. The Franciscan monk John de Plano Carpini attested to
this fact some ten years after Mikhail's victory when he passed through
Kiev on his way to visit the Tatars and also on his return journey from

---

[88] Concerning the policies of Mikhail's father and grandfather, see above pp. 4-5.

Karakorum two years later, in 1247.[89] The account of his trip is indisputable testimony to the commercial importance of Kiev even after the Tatar invasion.

> To avoid any doubt arising in the minds of anyone as to our having been to the Tartars, we will write down the names of those with whom we came into contact there. ... The entire city of Kiev is a witness, for the inhabitants gave us an escort.... In addition there are as witnesses the merchants from Vratislavia [Bratislava], who accompanied us as far as Kiev and know that we were in the clutches of the Tartars, and also many other merchants, both from Poland and from Austria, who arrived in Kiev after we had gone to the Tartars. Further witnesses are the merchants from Constantinople who came to Russia via the Tartars. The names of these merchants are as follows: Michael the Genoese and Bartholomew, Manuel the Venetian, James Reverius of Acre, Nicolas Pisani, are the chief; the less important are: Mark, Henry, John, Vasius, another Henry Bonadies, Peter Paschami. There were many others, but I do not know their names.[90]

Carpini travelled with Czech merchants to Kiev and there he met others from Genoa, Venice and Acre in Palestine; after he departed from the town, merchants also came from Poland and Austria. Such intensive commercial activity in Kiev after, presumably, it had been razed by the Tatars, suggests that the traders were travelling along well established routes and that Kiev had been a flourishing emporium some ten years earlier.

In the 1230s, Kiev benefited not only materially but also intellectually and spiritually from its foreign contacts. According to a unique item of information given by the Polish historian J. Długosz, mendicant friars established themselves in Kiev for a time. He states that in 1233 Grand Prince Vladimir Ryurikovich, "fearing" the devout and exemplary life of the Dominican friars, expelled them from the Church of St. Mary in Kiev which had been signed over to them and in the neighbourhood of which they had their convent. The grand prince forbade Prior Martin of Sandomierz from Poland and his friars ever to return.[91] Unfortunately, the

---

[89] The Franciscan friar John de Plano Carpini, accompanied by Friar Benedict of Poland, was sent by Pope Innocent IV to Mongolia in the hope of converting the Tatars. He departed from Lyons in April 1245 and, travelling through Bohemia, Silesia, Cracow and Volyn', reached Kiev by February 1246. He departed from Karakorum in the middle of November 1246 and arrived in Lyons on 1 November 1247 (see G. Vernadsky, *The Mongols and Russia* [New Haven, Conn.: Yale University Press, 1953], pp. 62-4).

[90] C. Dawson ed., *The Mongol Mission* (New York, 1955), pp. 70-1.

[91] *Historiae Polonicae*, col. 649.

source does not state when the Order of Preachers arrived in Kiev[92] and who supported them in their mission by giving them a church and a convent. Significantly, the reason why Vladimir evicted them was not xenophobia or fear of western learning; to judge from the account, the prince, as an Orthodox Christian, "feared" their mendicant way of life and the success which they enjoyed in spreading the Roman Catholic faith. Although the presence of the Dominican friars and of the numerous trade caravans in Kiev in the 1230s are only two witnesses to its vitality, they are significant. The arrival of the first indicates that new intellectual and religious movements such as those of the mendicant preachers were not alien to Rus' but received support from the inhabitants of Kiev; and the activity of the merchants reflects the material wealth of the town. The presence of these foreigners, therefore, bespeaks a dynamic metropolis, one which maintained extensive contacts with Europe, with the Near East and, consequently, one which was still a prime political objective for the princes of Rus' in 1235.

According to the Novgorod chronicler, one group of merchants suffered as a result of Mikhail's attack on Kiev. After stating that Vladimir Ryurikovich was released by the Polovtsy for a ransom, the chronicler added that the princes also exacted ransom from the Germans. This information is interesting since the Novgorod chronicle is the only one to give it. To be sure, the Laurentian chronicle, which, for the most part, gives information concerning the princes of Rostov-Suzdal', states that in 1235 "it was quiet."[93] Its laconic entry indicates that the Vsevolodovichi were not affected directly by the crisis in southern Rus'. However, the fact that the Novgorod chronicler records the rivalry in much detail shows that the victory of the Ol'govichi had repercussions in Novgorod. Since he alone notes that the Germans were held for ransom, it was probably they who informed him of the fact. Unfortunately, he gives no information concerning the demands of the princes. Although they may have imposed similar fines on merchants from other countries, the chronicler does not say so.

It is ironic that Mikhail who in 1225 had asked the Novgorodians to continue sending foreign merchants to Chernigov, demanded a ransom from those very people ten years later. One obvious explanation for his action is that after Yaroslav Vsevolodovich came to Novgorod in 1230 he

[92] The Order of Preachers was founded in 1216; the friars, therefore, came to Rus' after that date.
[93] PSRL 1, col. 460.

demanded from the Germans that they no longer trade with the Ol'govichi in Chernigov even though they would continue to go to the Rostislavichi in Kiev. Therefore, by exacting a ransom from the Germans in 1235, Mikhail was not only disrupting the trade coming from Novgorod but also attacking Yaroslav. This observation is reinforced by the fact that, as we have seen, in the following year, 1236, Yaroslav occupied Kiev unexpectedly – the only occasion on which he did this. One of the reasons for his action may have been to reaffirm with Kiev the trade agreements of the Germans which Mikhail had disrupted the year before. Although the chronicler does not give details concerning the nature of Mikhail's punitive measures against the merchants, it may be assumed that he interfered with the trade arrangements which had existed under the Rostislavichi and imposed a new tariff, at least, on the Germans. Thus it would appear that Mikhail took advantage of the opportunity which presented itself to weaken the hold of the Vsevolodovichi over Novgorod once again.

Mikhail's victory over Kiev also bolstered his political status for he demonstrated the superiority of the Ol'govichi over the Rostislavichi. But, despite his success, it appears that he was not yet ready to rule in Kiev. Since the Rostislavichi no longer threatened his authority over southern Rus' he could, presumably, occupy the "golden throne" whenever he wished. The only family of princes who may have been sufficiently strong to challenge him were the Vsevolodovichi but Mikhail believed that they would not attack him. As we have seen, they were attempting to establish their control over the Volga river basin in the east and over the lands of Novgorod in the northwest. Furthermore, since they had not tried to assert their control over Kiev in the past, presumably, they would not attempt to do so in 1235. Consequently, Mikhail allowed the defeated Rostislavichi (i.e., Izyaslav Mstislavich) to remain in Kiev merely as figureheads. Meanwhile, he hoped to take advantage of Daniil's vulnerability, since the latter was on the run after his defeat near Torchesk, to extend his authority over Galicia as well.

Daniil had escaped from the battlefield but only after suffering severe losses. His forces from Galich had been crushed and his strongest ally, the grand prince of Kiev, was being held captive. Then he was driven out of Galich by disgruntled boyars, thus paving the way for Mikhail's arrival. The latter probably came before 14 October 1235 since Daniil was in Hungary at that time soliciting aid from the new king of Hungary, Béla IV.[94] But Daniil failed to win his support and returned to Volyn'; his

---

[94] See *Historia critica*, vol. 5, p. 754.

attempts to regain possession of Galich in the winter and spring of 1236 also proved to be fruitless.

Following Mikhail's unprecedented success in southern and southwest Rus', the year 1236 witnessed a major reversal in the political alliances between the princes. According to Karamzin, Daniil and Grand Prince Yury of Rostov-Suzdal' negotiated an agreement and resolved that it would best suit their interests to have Yury's brother, Yaroslav of Pereyaslavl', occupy Kiev. The immediate outcome of this decision was that the Rostislavichi were forced to leave Kiev; its long term objective, obviously, was to curtail the increasing power of the Ol'govichi. Although this was an unprecedented alliance, reasons for it are not difficult to find. The sack of Kiev in 1235 and Mikhail's occupation of Galich later in the same year established Ol'govichi supremacy over the whole of southern and southwest Rus' and drastically altered the balance of power among the princes.

Daniil, whose fortunes had been rising rapidly in the late 1220s and early 1230s, lost at one fell swoop the lands of Galicia and the support of his most powerful ally. And, failing to win the assistance of the King of Hungary, he was eager to make an alliance with anyone who could help him to curb the newly won supremacy of the Ol'govichi and to regain Galicia. For the first time during the course of his reign, he was forced to turn to the Vsevolodovichi of Rostov-Suzdal'[95] with whom the Romanovichi had, to date, been allied only in a marriage relationship.[96]

The Vsevolodovichi of northeast Rus' were also eager to diminish the authority of the Ol'govichi. Even though Yury had cultivated Mikhail's friendship in the early 1220s,[97] the growing animosity between the former and his brother Yaroslav over Novgorod also brought about a deterioration in Yury's relationship with Mikhail. By 1230, the Vsevolodo-

---

[95] The struggle of the Ol'govichi to regain control over Kiev began after the death of Svyatoslav Vsevolodovich in Kiev, in 1194; see the Laurentian Chronicle (PSRL 1, col. 412). At that time they became rivals of Daniil's father Roman Mstislavich and Vsevolod Yur'evich "the Big Nest," grand prince of Rostov-Suzdal'. Although both princes came into conflict with the Ol'govichi at one time or another between 1195 and 1205 (the year in which Roman was killed in Poland), at no time did the Ol'govichi become sufficiently strong to force Roman and Vsevolod to unite their forces against them. Therefore, Mikhail, after his victory, in 1235, was the first prince of Chernigov whose political success forced the princes of the southwest and the northeast to unite against the Ol'govichi.
[96] The "Tverskaya letopis'" (PSRL 15, col. 346); the "Kholmogorskaya letopis'" (PSRL 33, p. 65); the Gustinskiy Chronicle (PSRL 2, 1843 edition, p. 336). Cf. the Hypatian Chronicle (PSRL 2, col. 758).
[97] See above pp. 16-17, 23.

vichi, alarmed by Mikhail's success in Novgorod, were prepared to march against him, and in the winter of 1231/2 they invaded the principality of Chernigov. Even though the Vsevolodovichi and the Ol'govichi did not conclude peace in 1232, Mikhail withdrew his support from those Novgorodians who were opposed to the rule of the Vsevolodovichi and turned his attention to more immediate ambitions in southern Rus'. At that time he was not able to maintain an offensive on two fronts – in Novgorod against the princes of Rostov-Suzdal' and in Kiev against the princes of Smolensk.

However, in 1235, circumstances were different. Mikhail's unprecedented success against the Rostislavichi and the Romanovichi, his control over Kiev and his occupation of Galich, all boded ill for the Vsevolodovichi. The chronicles give no indication that Mikhail was interested in reasserting his claim to Novgorod but, as we have seen, in 1235 he exacted a ransom from the German merchants who had come to Kiev through Novgorod. The threat of his renewed intervention must have appeared menacingly real to the princes of Rostov-Suzdal'. Therefore, like Daniil, they hoped to curb Mikhail's expansionist policy in 1236. They agreed to send Yaroslav Vsevolodovich, who not only harboured personal animosity against Mikhail but who also had the most to lose through Mikhail's intervention in Novgorod, to challenge his supremacy in southern Rus' by occupying Kiev.

Yaroslav's mission reveals desperation on the part of the princes of Rostov-Suzdal' and the Romanovichi in face of the escalating power of the Ol'govichi. It was the first time that the Vsevolodovichi deemed it vital to their security in northeast Rus' to attempt to gain control of Kiev. To be sure, it was the first time since Andrey Yur'evich, *Monomakh*'s grandson, razed Kiev in 1168 that a prince of Rostov-Suzdal' attempted to occupy it. However, in 1236, Yaroslav's seizure of Kiev was less momentous. According to the Hypatian Chronicle, he was unable to establish his authority over it and "returned to Suzdal"; it was taken from him by Mikhail.[98] The latter, it appears, had little difficulty in occupying the town. However, even though Yaroslav lost Kiev, the Vsevolodovichi and especially the Romanovichi could derive at least one crumb of comfort from their stratagem: by drawing the prince of Chernigov and his retinue

---

[98] PSRL 2, col. 777. The Novgorod First Chronicle makes no reference to Yaroslav's departure from Kiev. The only other sources which mention that Mikhail came to Kiev in 1236 are the Nikon Chronicle (PSRL 10, s.a. 1238, pp. 113-4) and the Gustinskiy Chronicle (PSRL 2, 1843 edition, p. 338).

(*druzhina*) out of Galich, Yaroslav succeeded in weakening the position of the Ol'govichi in Galich.

Mikhail's first year of rule as grand prince in 1237 was uneventful. However, the regions of eastern and northeast Rus' were subjected to the first wave of the Tatar invasion. In the winter of that year they devastated the lands of Ryazan'[99] and then advanced to Vladimir destroying many towns in the principality.[100] On 4 March 1238, Grand Prince Yury was killed at the battle on the Sit' river northwest of Rostov.[101] The Tatars continued their invasion westwards until they came to within seventy miles of Novgorod and there stopped their advance.[102] As they returned south to the steppe via the lands of Chernigov, they besieged the town of Kozel'sk in the northern regions of the principality.[103] After this, the Laurentian Chronicle notes, all was quiet in Rus' for the remainder of the year.[104] In 1238, therefore, the principality of Chernigov remained unscathed by the Tatars except for Kozel'sk and its adjoining territories.

But the following year was disastrous for southern Rus' – it received the full onslaught of the Tatar invasion. Southern Pereyaslavl' was sacked on Thursday, in the middle of the week commemorating the veneration of the Holy Cross, that is, 3 March 1239.[105] Then prior to the fall of

[99] Ryazan' capitulated on 21 December 1237; see the Novgorod First Chronicle (NPL, pp. 75, 287).

[100] The Tatars reached Vladimir on 3 February 1238; see the Laurentian Chronicle (PSRL 1, col. 461). After taking Vladimir they proceeded to sack fourteen towns in the district of Rostov-Suzdal', all in the month of February (PSRL 1, col. 464).

[101] PSRL 1, col. 465. Concerning Yury's death see above (Ch. 1, n. 73). After Yury's death the new grand prince of Vladimir was his younger brother Yaroslav (PSRL 1, col. 467). According to the Nikon Chronicle Yaroslav came to Vladimir from Novgorod (PSRL 10, p. 113). However, a reading of one (faulty) version of the Nikon Chronicle states that he came from Kiev in 1238 (ibid.; cf. "Voskresenskaya letopis'," PSRL 7 [Saint Petersburg, 1856], p. 143). Nasonov apparently relied on this erroneous information. He stated that Yaroslav departed from Kiev in the year 1237/8 at the time when the Tatars attacked Rus' (*Mongoly i Rus'*, p. 23). As we have seen, Yaroslav departed from Kiev in 1236 (see above p. 81).

[102] The Novgorod First Chronicle (NPL, pp. 76, 288-9).

[103] The Hypatian Chronicle (PSRL 2, cols. 780-1). The chronicle, however, misplaces this information under the year 1237. The Tatars, it appears, pillaged not only Kozel'sk but also other towns of the principality of Chernigov which lay in the path of their retreat. This is attested to by archeological evidence which indicates, for example, that the town of Serensk (which Yaroslav had attacked in the winter of 1231/2) was devastated in 1238 (see T. N. Nikol'skaya, "Voennoe delo v gorodakh zemli Vyatichey [Po materialam drevnerusskogo Serenska]," *Kratkie Soobshcheniya*, no. 139 [Moscow, 1974], p. 35). Cf. Rashid al-Din, *The Successors of Genghis Khan*, trans. J. A. Boyle (New York and London, 1971), p. 60.

[104] The Laurentian Chronicle (PSRL 1, col. 467).

[105] The Pskov chronicles (*Pskov*, vol. 2, s.a. 1230, p. 79; cf. ibid. vol. 1, p. 11). See also "Letopis' Avraamki" (PSRL 16 [Saint Petersburg, 1889], col. 51) and "Sokrashchennaya

Chernigov in October of the same year, an incident occurred which reflects the extent of the discord still prevalent in inter-princely relations on the eve of the devastation of the principalities of Chernigov and Kiev.

A little over one year after the Tatars had razed the lands of Rostov-Suzdal' and Grand Prince Yury Vsevolodovich of Vladimir had beel killed near the Sit' river, his brother and successor Yaroslav [106] raided Kamenets, a town on the western borders of the principality of Kiev. [107] Information from the various sources concerning Yaroslav's attack can be reconstructed in the following manner. Mikhail and his wife were in Kamenets, visiting Izyaslav Vladimirovich, [108] some time between 3 March and the fall of Chernigov on 18 October 1239. [109] Grand Prince Yaroslav, informed of this visit, attacked Kamenets capturing Mikhail's wife and many of his boyars, but Mikhail escaped [110] and, it appears, returned to Kiev. When Daniil Romanovich received word of this incident he attempted to persuade Yaroslav to send Mikhail's wife, his sister, to him since, he advised Yaroslav, Mikhail was plotting against both of them. The grand

---

Novgorodskaya letopis', ot nachala zemli slavyanskoy do vzyatiya Moskvy Takhtamyshem v 1382 godu," *Suprasl'skaya rukopis'*, ed. M. A. Obolensky (Moscow, 1836), p. 31.

[106] There is some uncertainty concerning the identity of the Yaroslav who besieged Kamenets since neither the Laurentian Chronicle nor the Hypatian Chronicle gives his patronymic. It is generally believed by historians that he was one of two princes: Yaroslav Vsevolodovich, grand prince of Vladimir in Rostov-Suzdal' or Yaroslav Ingvarovich of Lutsk. However, there can be little doubt that this was Yaroslav Vsevolodovich, grand prince of Vladimir. For a detailed discussion of this problem see Dimnik, "Russian Princes," pp. 180-4.

[107] Kamenets was a town near the Khomora river between the principalities of Volyn' and Kiev. It was traditionally the patrimony of the Romanovichi; see M. Dimnik, "Kamenec," *Russia Mediaevalis*, vol. 4 (Munich, 1979), pp. 25-34.

[108] It appears that the town passed into the hands of the Ol'govichi, that is, to Izyaslav Vladimirovich an Igorevich, after Mikhail and Izyaslav defeated the combined forces of princes Vladimir and Daniil near Torchesk south of Kiev in 1235.

[109] Yaroslav's attack probably occurred at this time since all the sources which record the event, with the exception of the Hypatian Chronicle, place it under the same year, 1239. (The Hypatian Chronicle misplaces the information under the year 1238 following the account of Daniil's occupation of Kiev [PSRL 2, col. 782]. The latter event occurred in the winter of 1239/40; see pp. 87-88.) The Laurentian Chronicle places this information between the entry which records Baty's sack of southern Pereyaslavl' (3 March) and the account of the fall of Chernigov (18 October). The Vladimir Chronicle corroborates this information; it also placed the account of the fall of Chernigov immediately after the entry concerning Kamenets (PSRL 30, p. 90). Thus Yaroslav's attack took place between 3 March and 18 October 1239.

[110] The sixteenth-century Vladimir Chronicle alone has this item of information that "Prince Mikhail escaped" (PSRL 30, p. 90).

prince agreed to Daniil's request and sent Mikhail's wife to her two brothers, Daniil and Vasil'ko.[111]

This seemingly insignificant raid further illustrates the deep rooted hostility which existed between the princes of Rus' during the time of the Tatar invasion. It shows that Yaroslav, who had been opposed to Mikhail over Novgorod in the late 1220s, and who had attempted to take Kiev away from the influence of the Ol'govichi in 1236, was still campaigning against Mikhail in 1239 after his own principality had been ravished by the invaders. Furthermore, following the policy of cooperation established between his brother Yury and Daniil in 1236 against the Ol'govichi,[112] Yaroslav himself, as the new grand prince of Vladimir, elected to continue to work in cooperation with the Romanovichi against Mikhail. This alliance against the latter, renewed by the princes of Rostov-Suzdal' and Volyn' during the course of the Tatar invasion of southern Rus', did not augur well for the grand prince of Kiev. The hostility of his fellow princes would force Mikhail to go abroad in an unsuccessful search for aid against the invaders.

The second attack on southern Rus' came in the fall of that year after Yaroslav's sack of Kamenets. The Tatars stormed Chernigov,[113] pillaged the town, killed many of its inhabitants and looted the monasteries. According to this account, the princes of Chernigov fled to Hungary[114]

---

[111] See the Laurentian Chronicle (PSRL 1, col. 469) and the Hypatian Chronicle (PSRL 2, cols. 782-3).

[112] See above pp. 75-76.

[113] Information in the Hypatian Chronicle concerning the Tatar attack on Chernigov in 1239, which is misplaced under the year 1234, suggests that they came west along the northern bank of the Seym river. After Glukhov fell they attacked Khorobor, Sosnitsa, Snovsk and many other towns (PSRL 2, col. 772); see M. Dimnik, "The siege of Chernigov in 1235," p. 399. Since the chronicler gives the names of only three of the towns which were sacked, presumably, these were more important and may have had resident princes in them.

[114] The Laurentian Chronicle (PSRL 1, col. 469). This statement has been misinterpreted by various historians. Solov'ev believed that it was Mstislav Glebovich who defended Chernigov that fled to Hungary after being defeated (Istoriya, book 2, p. 143). Zotov was also of the opinion that the chronicle is referring to Mstislav Glebovich's flight to Hungary; however, he raises the question – who were the other princes who accompanied him in his flight? (O Chernigovskikh knyazyakh, p. 194). Although Mstislav Glebovich may have gone to Hungary, the Laurentian Chronicle is, no doubt, referring to the flight of Mikhail and his son Rostislav. From other sources it is known that Mikhail went to Hungary later in the winter of 1239/40 (see below p. 87); however, the Laurentian Chronicle fails to enter this information in the appropriate place. Consequently, in this entry the latter source must be referring to Mikhail's flight, which occurred after the sack of Chernigov. Furthermore, the Laurentian Chronicle states that the "princes" of Chernigov fled (i.e., more than one); presumably, it is referring also to

while Bishop Porfiry was captured and taken to Glukhov, a town approximately halfway between Chernigov and Kursk, where he was released. From Glukhov the Tatars returned to their camps.[115] Chernigov was sacked on Tuesday 18 October 1239.[116]

Immediately after the information that Bishop Porfiry was released, another source adds a significant item of information. It states that from there (i.e., Chernigov?) the Tatars came to Kiev in peace and negotiated a settlement with "Mstislav and Vladimir and Daniil."[117] This information suggests that the Tatars negotiated terms with the rulers of three of the most powerful principalities of southern Rus'. "Mstislav" was no doubt the Mstislav Glebovich who defended Chernigov unsuccessfully against the Tatars. As the second Ol'govich in precedence after Mikhail, he became prince of Chernigov when Mikhail had become grand prince in 1236. "Vladimir," the second prince listed, is none other than Vladimir Ryurikovich the senior Rostislavich. According to chronicle information he died in 1239,[118] apparently as prince of Smolensk.[119] And "Daniil" was

---

Mikhail's son Rostislav (see below pp. 105-107), information which is not found in its proper place in the source. Finally, aside from the reference made in the Laurentian Chronicle under the year 1239 that the "princes fled," there is no other information to suggest that Mstislav Glebovich may have gone to Hungary, whereas virtually all the chronicles record the flight of Mikhail and his son.

[115] The Laurentian Chronicle (PSRL 1, col. 469). The Hypatian Chronicle has a somewhat different version of the account. It states that Mstislav Glebovich confronted the invaders when they besieged Chernigov but was defeated. They killed many of his soldiers and, after capturing the town, set fire to it; the bishop of Chernigov was taken captive to Glukhov (PSRL 2, col. 782; it misplaces these events under the year 1237).
There is some confusion concerning the activities of Mstislav Glebovich during the siege of Chernigov. One manuscript of the Ermolinskiy Chronicle, the *Ermolinskiy*, states that Mstislav Glebovich "came out of Chernigov" (PSRL 23, p. 77). But both the *Uvarovskiy spisok* of the chronicle and the L'vov Chronicle state that he came "to Chernigov" (PSRL 23, p. 77, variant 11 and "L'vovskaya letopis'," PSRL 20 [Saint Petersburgh, 1910], p. 158). Hrushevsky believed that Mstislav was killed by the Tatars while he was defending Chernigov (*Istoriia*, vol. 2, p. 252), but various manuscripts of the Nikon Chronicle state that Mstislav "barely escaped" (PSRL 10, p. 114).
[116] This information is found in the Smolensk chronicle, "Letopis' Avraamkiy" (PSRL 16, col. 51), in the *Tikhanovskiy spisok* of the Pskov First Chronicle (*Pskov*, vol. 1, p. 12), in the *Stroevskiy spisok* of the Pskov Third Chronicle (ibid. vol. 2, p. 79) and in "Sokrashchennaya Novgorodskaya letopis'," p. 31.
[117] The Sofiyskiy First and the Novgorod Fourth Chronicles add this unique item of information evidently taken from some *svod* written in southern Rus' (PSRL 5, p. 219 and PSRL 4, p. 223). As it has been shown above, the Hypatian Chronicle had this information (in an adulterated form) under the year 1234 (see above, n. 75).
[118] The Pskov chronicles (*Pskov*, vol. 1, p. 12 and vol. 2, p. 79).
[119] "Rodoslovnaya kniga," VOIDR, book 10, p. 13.

the prince of Volyn'. Significantly the Tatars did not come to an agreement with the grand prince of Kiev, Mikhail.[120]

The elliptical reference to the peace agreement made by the source does
not reveal the nature of the settlement between the princes and the
invaders. However, the fact that they concluded peace with the Tatars
can only mean that they capitulated to their demands. Since both, the
principality of Smolensk[121] and the principality of Chernigov had been
devastated, the princes of those territories had little choice but to resign
themselves to unconditional surrender. But it is noteworthy that the lands
of Volyn' and Galicia had not yet been invaded; nevertheless, Daniil
Romanovich, according to the sources, also accepted the Tatar terms. He
was the only major prince of Rus' who reached an agreement with them
before his lands were invaded.

Mikhail, the grand prince of Kiev, was also approached by an envoy of
Khan Baty to accept terms of surrender. The Hypatian Chronicle states
that one "Mengu Khan" came to inspect Kiev and, standing on the
opposite bank of the Dnepr river in a village called "Sandy town"

[120] The Soviet historian S. K. Cherepanov states that this "unintelligible and im-
probable" information concerning the Tatar peace agreement with "Daniil, Vladimir ...
and Mstislav" must have been misplaced by the compiler of the "*svod* of 1448" from
which the Sofiyskiy First and the Novgorod Fourth Chronicles derived their information.
He suggests that the reference to a peace treaty must be to the agreement reached between
the princes in 1235 after Daniil and Vladimir attacked Mstislav in Chernigov as recorded
by the Hypatian Chronicle (PSRL 2, col. 772); see "K voprosu o yuzhnom istochnike
Sofiyskoy I i Novgorodskoy IV letopisey," TODRL, vol. 30 (1976), pp. 281-2. As has been
noted; Mstislav Glebovich was not involved in the defence of Chernigov in 1235 nor did
the princes conclude peace at that time (see above p. 72). The account which Cherepanov
quotes from the Hypatian Chronicle under the year 1234 is an adulterated text of the
information describing the sack of Chernigov by the Tatars in 1239 as given by the two
chronicles stemming from the "*svod* of 1448." Thus, rather than undermining the
credibility of the latter, the entry of the Hypatian Chronicle – which also speaks of the
same peace agreement – corroborates the information stemming from the hypothetical
svod, since the Hypatian Chronicle, which has a more complete text of the account,
apparently received its information from another source written in southern Rus':

[121] There is no chronicle information concerning the fate of the principality of
Smolensk at the hands of the Tatars during the years 1238 to 1241. However, according to
popular tradition, Smolensk was besieged by the Tatars but was defended successfully by
a certain Merkury of Smolensk. (Concerning this legend see M. Skripil', *Russkie povesti
xv-xvi vekov* [Moscow-Leningrad, 1958], pp. 106-7, 276-8, 441-5; L. T. Beletsky,
"Literaturnaya istoriya povesti o Merkurii Smolenskom," *Sbornik otdeleniya russkago
yazyka i slovesnosti Rossiiskoy Akademii nauk*, vol. 99, no. 8 [Petrograd, 1922], pp. 55-7.)
Although the town itself may not have been subjected to a direct attack, there is little
doubt that some of the lands of the principality were pillaged. This must have occurred in
1238 when the Tatars withdrew from Novgorod and retreated to the steppe via Kozel'sk
in the northern districts of the principality of Chernigov. At that time the Tatars had to
pass through the lands of Smolensk.

("gradok Pesochnyy/градък Пѣсочний"), marvelled at the sight of it. He sent messengers to Mikhail and to the citizens of Kiev intending to cajole them into surrendering.[122] But the grand prince and the townsmen refused to listen.[123] Then, in face of the impending attack, Mikhail fled to Hungary, just as his son had done before him.[124] The "golden throne" was later occupied by Rostislav Mstislavich of Smolensk but he was driven out by Daniil of Volyn' who appointed his military "commander" (*voevoda*), Dmitry, to defend it.[125]

It may be concluded from this information that, after the fall of Chernigov on 18 October 1239, the sequence of events in southern Rus' was as follows: the Tatars withdrew east to the town of Glukov and from there (or directly from Chernigov) dispatched a contingent to Kiev led by "Mengu Khan" to negotiate peace with Grand Prince Mikhail.[126] According to one group of chronicles Mikhail not only refused to reach a settlement but killed the Tatar envoys. However, other sources state that three of the princes from southern Rus' did come to an agreement with the invaders; after this Mikhail fled to Hungary, probably in the winter of 1239/40. After he vacated Kiev, Rostislav Mstislavich of Smolensk[127]

[122] There is evidence in the chronicles to suggest that Khan Baty attempted to negotiate peace with Mikhail on two separate occasions. But this information is found only in later sources. Of these, only the Gustinskiy Chronicle gives the information as a chronicle entry, whereas other sources incorporate it into their Church narrative accounts of Mikhail's (and his boyar Fedor's) death. Thus, the former states that when Baty sent his military commander (*voevoda*) to inspect Kiev, he *again* sent envoys to Mikhail (PSRL 2, 1843 edition, p. 339); cf. the *svod* of 1479 (PSRL 25, p. 136) and the Nikon Chronicle (PSRL 10, p. 130).

[123] PSRL 2, col. 782; the Hypatian Chronicle misplaces this information under the year 1237.

[124] The Ermolinskiy Chronicle, the L'vov Chronicle, the *svod* of 1479 and the Nikon Chronicle state that when Mengu Khan's envoys arrived in Kiev, Mikhail put them to death; after that he fled (PSRL 23, p. 77; PSRL 20, p. 158; PSRL 25, p. 131; PSRL 10, p. 116). The fact that this information is found in the chronicles which stem from the hypothetical all-Rus'sian "*svod* of Feodosy and Filipp" and is not found in the Sofiyskiy First and the Novgorod Fourth Chronicles which stem from the hypothetical "*svod* of 1448" clearly indicates that the former *svod* had a source from southern Rus' not used by the "*svod* of 1448."

[125] PSRL 2, col. 782. Since Chernigov was sacked on 18 October 1239 all these events must have occurred soon after.

[126] The Tatars probably sent their envoys to the Rostislavichi and to Daniil at the same time. Nasonov believed that the messengers were sent to Mikhail in 1237/8 (*Mongoly i Rus'*, p. 23).

[127] Concerning Rostislav Mstislavich see above pp. 66-67. Hrushevsky thought that he was a prince in the district of Kiev before he occupied Kiev (*Istoriia*, vol. 2, p. 250). Pashuto claims that Rostislav came to Kiev in 1238 and replaced Vladimir Ryurikovich after the latter died (*Ocherki*, p. 220).

occupied it for a time until he was driven out by Daniil; the latter appointed his own commander to defend it against the expected siege.

A parallel may be drawn between the attitudes of the grand princes towards the Tatars during the invasion of southern Rus' in 1223 and in 1239. Just as Mstislav Romanovich challenged the invaders in 1223, so Mikhail chose to oppose them fifteen years later. Mstislav and the princes of Rus' killed the Tatar envoys sent to negotiate peace;[128] Mikhail similarly had the messengers put to death. There is no evidence to show that Mikhail deliberately imitated Mstislav's treatment of the envoys in 1223. But, it must be remembered that he attended the council of war in Kiev at that time as a junior prince, and he no doubt recalled Mstislav's negotiations with the Tatars. Although Mikhail, like his predecessor, executed the messengers, he did not entertain the support of the princes of Rus' as Mstislav had done. Whereas the latter, in his campaign at the Kalka river, had had the backing of not only his own family the Rostisla- vichi, but also the Ol'govichi, the princes of Volyn' and others, Mikhail found himself denied support not only from the Romanovichi, Rostisla- vichi and Vsevolodovichi, but also from his own patrimony of Chernigov since it lay devastated.

Grand Prince Mikhail stood isolated in his resolve to oppose the Tatars and if, in the hope of confronting them, he sought to convoke a *snem* similar to the one assembled in Kiev in 1223, the chronicles make no mention of it. If he did, he received little cooperation from the other princes. In 1239 the senior princes of Rus' were, it appears, too confirmed in their antagonism towards him in fear of his supremacy. Instead, Mstislav Glebovich his cousin, Vladimir of Smolensk and Daniil of Volyn', rulers of three of the most powerful principalities in Rus', acted contrary to Mikhail's policy of opposition to the Tatars; they made peace with the enemy. Their action destroyed any hope which the grand prince may have entertained of mustering a united opposition in southern Rus'. Since there was no help forthcoming from the other princes, and faced with the inevitable Tatar reprisal, he fled to Hungary. He hoped to solicit aid from King Béla IV with whom, as we shall see, he had been on friendly terms during the 1230s.

Mikhail's departure from Kiev in the winter of 1239/40 sparked off a brief rivalry between his enemies, namely, the Rostislavichi and the Romanovichi, who had been allies until then. In the wake of his flight,

---

[128] The Novgorod First Chronicle (NPL, pp. 62, 265).

Rostislav Mstislavich occupied Kiev in an act of desperation, by means of which he hoped to revitalize the declining power of his family. But Daniil encountered little difficulty in removing him from the throne. By this action he severed his political affiliation with the Rostislavichi and thereby deprived them of their strongest ally in southern Rus'. He dashed any hopes which they may still have retained of remaining a primary political force.

When Daniil drove Rostislav out of Kiev, the rivalry for control over the grand princely throne between the Ol'govichi and the princes of Smolensk was terminated. This defeat was the culmination of a long process of decline for the Rostislavichi. Their political fortunes had waned drastically in less than two decades owing to natural as well as political causes. The Ol'govichi, however, by 1236 had achieved a position of power comparable to the one which the princes of Smolensk had held under Mstislav Romanovich until 1223. Thus, by 1240 the prince of Smolensk was too weak to compete with the prince of Chernigov. Another reason for the termination of their rivalry was the fact that after the Tatar invasion the princes of Rus' were confronted with a threat to their very existence. Competition for control over the "golden throne" was relegated to the background – at least for Mikhail, as he attempted to safeguard his lands from future Tatar attacks.

Unlike the Ol'govichi, neither the Rostislavichi nor the Romanovichi appear to have been deterred by the threat of a renewed attack, and both families attempted to win control over Kiev.[129] Daniil of Volyn' ultimately won. The sources do not state why he wished to take possession of Kiev whose destruction was clearly impending. Since he did not occupy it personally, he obviously had no intention of becoming grand prince at

---

[129] The fact that both the Rostislavichi and the Romanovichi attempted to win control over Kiev, after Mikhail had fled, suggests that the two families enjoyed some guarantee of immunity from the invaders. Such a promise could have been given to them in 1239 when the senior princes made peace with the enemy. It is noteworthy that although Kiev, which had supported Mikhail's decision to oppose the Tatars, was to be razed completely, its commander, Daniil's man, was not put to death; see the Hypatian Chronicle (PSRL 2, col. 785). According to the chronicler, the commander Dmitry was not killed because of his bravery; it is more likely that he was spared by Baty because of the agreement which Daniil and the Tatars had concluded in 1239; see below, pp. 109-112. (The inhabitants of Kiev, however, had been instrumental in the execution of Tatar envoys before the sack of Kiev in 1240 and, therefore, were massacred by the invaders.) Consequently, as a result of some agreement reached by the Romanovichi and the Rostislavichi with the enemy, both Rostislav Mstislavich and Daniil may have believed themselves to be secure in taking possession of Kiev since they expected preferential treatment from the Tatars. The Ol'govichi, however, could not anticipate leniency from the enemy, since Mikhail was the only senior prince in Rus' who still opposed them.

this time. However, despite the time of crisis, Kiev was still the "mother of all towns in Rus'" and the fact that he was able to occupy it for the first time, and in doing so drive out the princes of Smolensk, enhanced his reputation. It made him, and not the Rostislavichi, the chief rivals to Mikhail. In the light of later developments it may be conjectured that Daniil sought to gain control of Kiev, at least in part, so that he could use it as a bargaining point against the Ol'govichi for his claim to Galich.[130]

Mikhail's trip to the king of Hungary did not prove to be successful. As he did not receive the military support which he needed from Béla iv, he was forced not only to flee to Poland but also to conclude peace with Daniil, especially in view of the fact that the latter had occupied Kiev in his absence. Daniil agreed to hand back the town but Mikhail found it imprudent to return on the eve of the Tatar attack. Therefore, as we shall see, he remained in the principality of Volyn', a guest of his enemy, an exile from both Kiev and Chernigov, waiting helplessly for the Tatars to renew their onslaught. The anticipated attack on Kiev finally came in the winter of 1240; the Tatars pillaged St. Sofia and all the churches and monasteries. They killed the inhabitants of the town from the youngest to the oldest. "This evil," states the chronicler, "was perpetrated on the feast of St. Nicholas," 6 December 1240.[131]

As the Tatars proceeded to plunder their way through the principalities of Volyn' and Galicia, Mikhail and his retinue were forced to seek sanctuary in Poland and in Germany. It was not until after the Tatars withdrew from Hungary and retreated to their heaudqarters in the steppes that he was free to come to Rus' some time in the year 1241. According to the Hypatian Chronicle, when he returned, he "lived on the island below Kiev"[132] but, it appears, no longer enjoying his former capacity as grand prince; before Khan Baty had departed for Vladimir in Volyn' at the beginning of 1241, he apparently appointed his own commander to rule in Kiev.[133] It is not known how long Mikhail remained on the island but certainly not longer than 1243. In that year Grand Prince Yaroslav

---

[130] See below p. 108.

[131] The Laurentian Chronicle (PSRL 1, col. 470). Most chronicles which give a date for the fall of Kiev give 6 December, St. Nicholas' Day. However, several manuscripts contain information mainly from northern Rus', and which apparently had the same source for their information from southern Rus', give a different date. According to "Letopis' Avraamkiy" the Tatars came to Kiev on 5 September and besieged it for ten weeks and four days before they finally succeeded in taking it on Monday 19 November (PSRL 16, col. 51; cf. "Sokrashchennaya Novgorodskaya letopis'," p. 32). The Pskov chronicles give only the date 19 November (*Pskov*, vol. 1, p. 12 and vol. 2, p. 80).

[132] The Hypatian Chronicle (PSRL 2, col. 789).

[133] The Nikon Chronicle (PSRL 10, p. 117).

Vsevolodovich of Rostov-Suzdal' returned to Rus' from his visit to Khan Baty after the latter had appointed him senior prince among all the princes of Rus'.[134] This decree severed Mikhail's last tie with Kiev since he was not in a position to challenge the edict of the Tatar khan.

*
* *

Whereas Mikhail's intention in Novgorod had been to undermine the authority of the princes of Rostov-Suzdal', his policy in southern Rus' was more ambitious – he successfully challenged the Rostislavichi for control over Kiev. Once he became grand prince no rival in Rus' was able to depose him.

Mikhail did not challenge the Rostislavichi immediately after he became prince of Chernigov. As we have seen, in 1224 his first action in the sphere of inter-princely relations had been to intervene in the affairs of Novgorod; he continued his involvement there until 1232. In southern Rus', however, he chose to bide his time until the late 1220s. During this period the Rostislavichi were still a formidable power owing chiefly to the military expertise and strength of Mstislav Mstislavich "the Bold." The latter was not only their ablest general but, as prince of Galich, he had the resources of southwest Rus' at his disposal. Finally, Mstislav's death in 1228 gave both the Ol'govichi as well as the Rostislavichi the occasion to initiate hostilities against his son-in-law Daniil Romanovich of Volyn', when the latter attempted to assert his control over Galicia. Mikhail and Vladimir Ryurikovich formed an alliance against Daniil and attacked him in Kamenets attempting unsuccessfully to curb his increasing power.

After the *snem* convoked by Grand Prince Vladimir in 1231, Mikhail betrayed his ally and attacked Kiev. He considered the time ripe to challenge the Rostislavichi for control over southern Rus' for the following reasons. Daniil, who was preoccupied establishing his authority over southwest Rus', alienated the princes whose territories he confiscated. His policy also brought him into conflict with powerful boyars in Galicia and with the Hungarians who hoped to take possession of the territory. Therefore, he would not be in a position to challenge the Ol'govichi. Thanks to Mikhail's interference in Novgorod, the unity of the Vsevolodovichi had been shaken in 1229 and, two years later, they were

---

[134] The Laurentian Chronicle (PSRL 1, col. 470). Although the chronicles do not state explicitly that Yaroslav Vsevolodovich established his control over Kiev soon after he returned from Saray, this may be assumed. When Daniil passed through the town two years later on his way to visit the khan, the chronicler states that it was governed by Dmitry Eikovich, Yaroslav's commander; see the Hypatian Chronicle (PSRL 2, col. 806).

still attempting to settle their differences with the *veche* in Novgorod; at
the same time, Grand Prince Yury was busy asserting his control over the
Volga river basin in the east. Consequently, they also were not likely to
become involved in the affairs of southern Rus'. By 1231, the fortunes of
the Rostislavichi had declined steadily owing to the deaths of important
princes, to internal dissension in Smolensk, to wars and to natural
calamities. As a result of these setbacks, Grand Prince Vladimir relied
heavily on the cooperation of the Ol'govichi. By attacking Kiev in 1231,
Mikhail effectively isolated the Rostislavichi and upset the balance of
power which had existed in Rus' since 1214.

Mikhail's action forced Vladimir to seek aid from his former enemy,
Daniil of Volyn'. The two allies, it appears, received tacit support from the
Vsevolodovichi since the latter felt threatened by Mikhail's interference in
the affairs of Novgorod. Consequently, by 1231, Mikhail had challenged
three of the most powerful families of princes in Rus' (the Vsevolodovichi, the Rostislavichi and the Romanovichi), and had made a bid for
control over southern Rus' relying solely on the resources of the Ol'govichi. After 1226, the latter presented a cohesive family structure as they
adhered faithfully to the traditional system of lateral succession.

The princes of Chernigov were a united family and presented a
consolidated military force. Although there had been a crisis in 1226
between Mikhail and Oleg Svyatoslavich of Kursk, to judge from
chronicle information, the Ol'govichi – both the senior and the cadet
branches of the family – supported Mikhail's expansionism. For example,
in 1228 all the princes of Chernigov, including Oleg Svyatoslavich and his
towns of Kursk and Novgorod Severskiy, helped Mikhail attack Daniil in
Kamenets. Later, in the winter of that year, messengers from Novgorod
found Mikhail in Bryn, a town in the northern districts of the principality
of Chernigov; these territories probably belonged to the princes of
Novgorod Severskiy. The fact that Mikhail was able to travel freely
through the lands belonging to other Ol'govichi is further proof that they
lived in harmony. As we have seen, the Novgorod chronicler also testifies
to the unity of the Ol'govichi. He states, under 1229, that Mikhail returned
to his "brothers" in Chernigov, meaning, to his allies with whom he lived
in concord. Furthermore, two years later, Mikhail, his son Rostislav, his
cousin Mstislav Glebovich and other princes from Chernigov attended the
snem in Kiev where they discussed the strategy to be adopted against
Daniil. Their presence at the congress bespeaks their unity of purpose.
Consequently, there can be little doubt that Mikhail had the backing of all
the princes of Chernigov when he attacked Kiev in 1231 in his bid to
establish the supremacy of the Ol'govichi over southern Rus'.

Mikhail, along with his ally Izyaslav Vladimirovich, continued his aggression against the Rostislavichi even after Grand Prince Vladimir formed an alliance with Daniil. When he attacked Kiev again, in 1234, Vladimir and Daniil retaliated by marching on Chernigov. Mikhail repelled their attack, pursued them to Torchesk, a town south of Kiev, and defeated them. His victory was decisive; Vladimir was captured, Kiev was sacked and the trade which had been coming from Novgorod to Kiev was disrupted. Although Mikhail allowed a junior prince of the Rostislavichi to rule in Kiev the appointment was nominal. The princes of Smolensk, in effect, became pawns in the hands of other princes.

Even though Kiev was the "mother of all towns in Rus'," Mikhail did not occupy it immediately after defeating the grand prince but, instead, he attempted to secure his hold over Galicia. After he occupied Galich his cousin Mstislav Glebovich became prince in Chernigov. However, it appears that Mikhail misjudged the desperation of his rivals and the measures which they were ready to adopt in order to curb his increasing power. Contrary to his expectation, the Vsevolodovichi, who were interested primarily in establishing their control over northern Rus', intervened in the affairs of Kiev for the first time. Similarly, Daniil considered his position sufficiently precarious that he turned to the Vsevolodovichi for help; this was the first occasion on which he was forced to seek assistance from the distant princes of Rostov-Suzdal'. Daniil and Grand Prince Yury concluded an alliance and in 1236 they forced the powerless Rostislavichi to vacate Kiev. The two allies appointed Yury's younger brother Yaroslav to the "golden throne."

Despite the apparent strength which the alliance gave them, Yury and Daniil were not able to establish their control over Kiev. Presumably the inhabitants of the town did not give Yaroslav their support. This is not surprising. Just as Mikhail had to travel through the principalities of Smolensk and Rostov-Suzdal' when he ruled in Novgorod in the late 1220s, similarly Yaroslav and his troops from Pereyaslavl' in northwest Rus' had to pass through the lands of Chernigov to reach Kiev. Since Mikhail would not give Yaroslav free passage through his lands, the inhabitants of Kiev realized that an arrangement with Yaroslav was not viable. Therefore, he departed soon after he arrived in 1236 and was replaced by Mikhail. There is no information concerning Mikhail's reign in Kiev; presumably, it was peaceful. The inhabitants of the town made no attempt to depose him and, aside from Yaroslav's attack on Mikhail when the latter was in Kamenets in 1239 the princes of Rus' were not strong enough to challenge him.

After Chernigov was sacked by the Tatars in the autumn of 1239, Mikhail went to Hungary to solicit support but failed. His ally King Béla IV refused to give him military assistance. The king's unwillingness to help is understandable in view of the fact that Mikhail had been deserted by the major princes of Rus' – Daniil of Volyn', Vladimir Ryurikovich, who ruled in Smolensk after 1236, and Mstislav Glebovich of Chernigov – who capitulated to the Tatars. Therefore, Mikhail fled to Poland and returned to Rus' only when the Tatars had departed after sacking Kiev. He was not to rule from the "golden throne" again. The Tatars, it appears, appointed a commander to govern Kiev so that when Mikhail returned he lived on an island below the town. Finally, in 1243, after Khan Baty gave Yaroslav Vsevolodovich a patent to rule in Kiev, Mikhail was forced to return to Chernigov.

Mikhail lost the title of grand prince because of the Tatar invasion and not because a more powerful adversary in Rus' defeated him, as had been the customary form of transfer of power between grand princes until then. The Tatars, wishing to subjugate completely their newly conquered territories in Rus', took decisive action against Mikhail. Having nullified his military effectiveness by razing his lands and alienating him from the other princes, they also wished to appoint a puppet prince to the throne of Kiev. Yaroslav Vsevolodovich proved himself to be such a one by being the first prince to visit Baty and promise his allegiance. Mikhail, however, remained constant in his opposition and by 1243 was the only senior prince in all Rus' who still had not come to terms with the Tatars.

To be sure, by 1243 Mikhail had not given up hope of regaining control over Galich. His success in southwest Rus', after 1235, as we shall see, was considerable. Also, in 1239, after the lands of Chernigov were devastated, many of the boyars fled to Galicia where they were given estates by the supporters of the Ol'govichi. Thus, Mikhail had the backing of a strong faction of boyars in Galicia which, in effect, served as a fifth column. After Kiev was sacked, and even before the Tatars returned from Hungary in the early 1240s, Mikhail sent his son Rostislav to Galicia to reassert the authority of the Ol'govichi. In the light of his activities in southwest Rus', it is not surprising that, in 1243, Mikhail refused to acknowledge the overlordship of the Tatars, even after they had deprived him of his title of grand prince.

3

Mikhail's Policy in Galich

After the Ol'govichi had established their superiority over the Rostislavichi in 1235, Mikhail Vsevolodovich attempted to extend his authority over Galich in southwest Rus' as well. Consequently, he revived a policy initiated by his grandfather Svyatoslav Vsevolodovich and, after 1205, continued, with limited success, by his father Vsevolod "the Red" (*Chermnyy*). In that year, after the boyars of Galich selected Prince Daniil Romanovich to succeed his father, Vsevolod allied himself to the Rostislavichi of Smolensk and unsuccessfully attempted to expel Daniil from Galich.[1] Undaunted by their initial failure Vsevolod and the Rostislavichi tried to win possession of Galicia a second time in the following year. But on this occasion the boyars of Galich, acting independently of the princes of Volyn' (i.e., the Romanovichi) and their ally the king of Hungary, invited the Igorevichi (a junior family of princes among the Ol'govichi), to become their rulers. The princes accepted the offer in 1206. At the same time Mikhail's father, Vsevolod, wishing to capitalize on the unexpected good fortune of his family, betrayed his ally, Grand Prince Ryurik Rostislavich, and attacked Kiev.[2] Thus, by securing both towns, Galich and Kiev, the Ol'govichi succeeded in achieving temporary hegemony over southwest and southern Rus'.

But Vsevolod's hold over Kiev proved to be too tenuous to make it a lasting victory. He lost control over it on three occasions and was driven

---

[1] The Laurentian Chronicle (PSRL 1, cols. 425-6); the chronicle places this event under the year 1206. Concerning the dating, see Berezhkov, *Khronologiya*, p. 88.

[2] The Laurentian Chronicle (PSRL 1, cols. 426-7). Concerning the dating, see Berezhkov, *Khronologiya*, p. 99. It it noteworthy that the mother of the Igorevichi was the daughter of Yaroslav *Osmomysl'*, prince of Galich; see Zotov, *O Chernigovskikh knyazyakh*, no. 24, p. 270. Neither the Ol'govichi nor the Romanovichi had an undisputed right to rule in Galich. It was traditionally the patrimony of the descendants of Vladimir Yaroslavich, the eldest son of Yaroslav "the Wise." However, his family became extinct just before the turn of the thirteenth century with the death of Vladimir Yaroslavich, the uncle of the Igorevichi, who died in 1199. See Baumgarten, *Généalogies*, Table III, p. 15.

out for the last time in 1212.[3] Concomitantly, the Igorevichi also enjoyed only a limited success in Galicia. The boyars revolted in 1212 and, after deposing the princes, killed a number of them.[4] Consequently, Mikhail's father, Vsevolod, lost control over both Kiev and Galich before he died in 1215.

Twenty years later, in 1235, Mikhail reasserted the hegemony of the Ol'govichi over southern and southwest Rus'. In the spring of that year he won the most important military victory of his life. With the aid of Izyaslav Vladimirovich, the senior Igorevich, and the Polovtsy, he defeated not only the grand prince of Kiev, Vladimir Ryurikovich, but also the latter's most powerful ally Daniil Romanovich, who at that time was prince of both Volyn' and Galicia. By taking Vladimir prisoner and by sacking Kiev, Mikhail struck the fatal blow to the supremacy of the Rostislavichi in southern Rus'. At the same time, by vanquishing Daniil he expedited his own occupation of southwest Rus'. Daniil's defeat weakened his hold over Galich and forced him to flee to Hungary in search of aid; his departure enabled Mikhail to occupy the town for the first time.[5]

After the Igorevichi were overthrown in 1212 no Ol'govich succeeded in occupying Galich. Even Mikhail, who had attacked the Romanovichi prior to 1235, made no attempt to assert his control over the region before that date.[6] But his victory near Torchesk gave him an unprecedented advantage over his rivals and he judged the time ripe to challenge both the princes of Volyn' and the king of Hungary. There were several factors which prompted Mikhail to take such determined action.

Hungary's hold over southwest Rus' had been weakened by two deaths. In the winter of 1233/4 Prince Andrew died in Galich while

---

[3] According to Zotov, Vsevolod was prince of Kiev in 1206, 1207 and from 1210 until 1214 (*O Chernigovskikh knyazyakh*, no. 30, p. 273).

[4] The Hypatian Chronicle (PSRL 1, cols. 726-7). The chronicle places this entry under the year 1208. However, there is some controversy among historians concerning the correct date of the execution of the Igorevichi; see Zotov, *O Chernigovskikh knyazyakh*, pp. 276-7.

[5] See above p. 73. The fact that Daniil chose to flee to Hungary in 1235 is noteworthy. After the death of Mstislav Mstislavich in 1228, Daniil became Hungary's chief rival for the throne of Galich. It appears that with the accession of a new king in Hungary, and with the loss of his ally Vladimir Ryurikovich, Daniil was forced to seek the aid of his former enemy against the Ol'govichi.

[6] Only one source claims that another Ol'govich besides Mikhail challenged Daniil for control over Galich. According to Długosz, Izyaslav Vladimirovich, the senior Igorevich and Mikhail's close ally, contested the throne after the death of Prince Andrew in the winter of 1233/4 (*Historiae Polonicae*, col. 633).

defending it against Daniil.[7] Since he had championed Hungary's claim to southwest Rus' in 1226,[8] his death deprived the king of the agent who had successfully challenged Daniil for control over the region. Understandably the king did not wish to lose the commercial benefits he derived from his ties with Galicia. More important, he hoped to prevent Daniil from strengthening his position by unifying Galicia and Volyn'. Consequently, the Hungarians not only tolerated but even welcomed Mikhail's arrival in Galich, not because he championed their interests, but because he could be used as a weapon against Daniil.[9]

A second death, and more significant, which weighted the scales in favour of Mikhail's occupation of Galich was that of the king of Hungary, Andrew II, on 21 September 1235.[10] There had been much unrest in the country during his reign so that his death proved to be of great moment both for revitalizing the internal government of Hungary and the office of monarch. In 1222 the nobles had formulated their *Magna Carta* in the form of the Golden Bull with which they restricted the authority of the king.[11] Surprisingly, the leader of the nobility opposed to King Andrew's policies had been none other than the king's own son, and the future king, Béla. Therefore, when Béla IV succeeded his father to the throne in October 1235, he tried to institute reforms which would restore to the king a degree of his former power.[12] His primary concern after taking office was to consolidate his authority among the nobles at home rather than in the district of Galicia. Mikhail took advantage of this period of internal instability in Hungary; he occupied Galich at the time of, or shortly after, the coronation of Béla IV.[13]

---

[7] The Hypatian Chronicle (PSRL 2, col. 771). The chronicle has this information under 1234. According to the account Daniil waited nine weeks for the ice to form so that he could attack Galich. A short time afterwards, Prince Andrew died in the town and the Galicians sent for Daniil to be their prince. Therefore, these events occurred during the winter of 1233/4 since, in the following winter, Daniil and Vladimir Ryurikovich attacked Mikhail in Chernigov.

[8] B. Hóman, *Magyar Történet*, vol. 1 (Budapest, 1935), p. 436.

[9] It appears that Mikhail and the king of Hungary reached some working agreement at this time, for the chronicle records that in the following year, 1236, when Daniil attacked Mikhail and Rostislav in Galich, the latter were aided by the Hungarians; see the Hypatian Chronicle (PSRL 2, col. 776).

[10] B. Hóman, *Geschichte des Ungarischen Mittelalters*, vol. 2 (Berlin, 1943), p. 105.

[11] C. A. Macartney, *Hungary, A Short History* (Edinburgh, 1962), p. 26.

[12] Macartney points out that Béla IV threw several bellicose nobles into prison and also sent out commissioners to check the legitimacy of his father's donations of land (ibid. pp. 31-2).

[13] See above p. 79.

Another reason which prompted Mikhail to occupy Galich was the fact that his victory deprived Daniil of the support which the Rostislavichi and Vladimir Ryurikovich had been able to offer him. As long as the latter had been grand prince his troops and the location of Kiev between the principalities of Chernigov and Galicia had deterred Mikhail from attacking the latter. But Mikhail destroyed the effectiveness of the buffer zone by sacking Kiev and by defeating the Rostislavichi. He undermined their morale by capturing their senior prince and he inflicted further losses upon their already depleted manpower.[14] Therefore, Mikhail not only eliminated Vladimir as his most dangerous rival but, at the same time, ensured that there was no longer any prince in southern or southwest Rus' powerful enough to give Daniil effective assistance against the Ol'govichi.

Mikhail's victory also weakened the support which Daniil had previously received from the boyars of southwest Rus'. When he fled to Galich from Torchesk he found them in an ugly mood. The chronicle explains that the reason for their discontent was the conduct of his younger brother Vasil'ko who had departed with the spoils of the campaign without distributing them among the other participants.[15] One reason why the boyars were able to present such strong opposition against Daniil was that many of those boyars who had supported him were captured or killed by the Ol'govichi and the Polovtsy.[16] By eliminating the core of Daniil's supporters the Ol'govichi strengthened the position of the boyars who favoured Mikhail's rule in Galich.

Mikhail, therefore, was also encouraged to occupy the town by the support which he received from what might be described as the Ol'govichi fifth column in Galicia.[17] In 1234 certain "unfaithful Galicians" and the "princes of Bolokhov" marched against the town of Kamenets, a major citadel of the Romanovichi on the eastern border of their principality, but

[14] See above pp. 72-73.
[15] The Hypatian Chronicle (PSRL 2, col. 774). Solv'ev suggests that the boyars rebelled against Daniil for another reason. When Daniil dispatched Vasil'ko his brother to defend the town of Vladimir he gave the latter all his troops. When the boyars realized that Daniil was left without soldiers they rose against him (*Istoriya*, book 2, p. 134).
[16] The account of the battle states that along with Vladimir Ryurikovich, Daniil's *voevoda* Miroslav and many other boyars were also taken prisoner (PSRL 2, col. 774). No doubt, the boyars who were captured by the Ol'govichi were those supporting Daniil's rule.
[17] Evidence of internal support in Galich for the Ol'govichi goes back as early as 1206. At that time the boyars invited the Igorevichi to be their princes (PSRL 2, col. 719; the Laurentian Chronicle, PSRL 1, col. 427; concerning the dating, see Berezhkov, *Khronologiya*, pp. 99-100).

were captured by Daniil. Later Mikhail and his ally Izyaslav Vladmiro-vich demanded that he release these their "brothers."[18] It was probably these same "unfaithful Galicians" who turned against Daniil at the battle near Torchesk and it was also they who later complained against Vasil'ko and drove Daniil out of Galich.[19]

Two boyars in particular, Grigory Vasil'evich and Dobroslav Sud'ich, are singled out by the chronicler. They appear to have been the guiding lights among that group of "unfaithful Galicians" who fomented unrest in southwest Rus' and who ultimately forced Daniil to flee to Hungary. For example, the chronicle explains that in the spring of 1235 Grand Prince Vladimir and Daniil's *voevoda* Miroslav were captured by the Polovtsy because the boyar Grigory Vasil'evich, along with certain other boyars of the Molibogovich family, betrayed him.[20] Later, this same Grigory became the major-domo (i.e., *dvorskiy*, the steward who managed the prince's household and landed estates and took part in administrative and judicial activities) to Mikhail's son Rostislav in Galich and defended the town against Daniil.[21] In 1241 Grigory is singled out again; on this occasion he was one of the two malefactors who caused untold havoc

---

[18] The Hypatian Chronicle (PSRL 2, cols. 774-5). The chronicle has this information under 1235. However, it states that the "princes of Bolokhov" were brought to Daniil when he was still in Vladimir. As we have seen, he occupied Galich after the death of Prince Andrew during the winter of 1233/4, therefore, the attack on Kamenets must have occurred prior to that time, in 1233. Since Mikhail and Izyaslav Vladimirovich sent threatening messages to Daniil in the summer, this probably happened after Izyaslav had initiated the rivalry between the Ol'govichi and the Romanovichi by attacking Tikhoml' (PSRL 2, col. 770).

[19] The Hypatian Chronicle gives the names of various boyars who opposed Daniil during the late 1220s and the early 1230s and who probably supported Mikhail in 1235. These were: (1) Sudislav who backed Prince Andrew until the latter's death in the winter of 1233/4 (PSRL 2, col. 771); under 1228, when Mikhail attacked Kamenets, the chronicler explains that Prince Andrew was in Galich with Sudislav and they were at peace with Mikhail (PSRL 2, col. 753); (2) Zhiroslav who in 1226 fled to Mikhail's ally Izyaslav Vladimirovich (PSRL 2, cols. 747-750); (3) the boyars of the Molibogovich family who plotted to kill Daniil in 1230, but twenty-eight of them were captured and later released (PSRL 2, cols. 762-763); they also betrayed Daniil at Torchesk (PSRL 2, col. 774); (4) Filip who, in 1230, plotted to kill Daniil with the boyars of the Molibogovich family (PSRL 2, col. 762); (5) the boyar Klimyata from Golyye Gory who deserted Daniil in 1231 (PSRL 2, col. 765); (6) the boyars of the Arbuzovich family who were attacked by Daniil in 1232 (PSRL 2, col. 770); (7) Dobroslav Sud'ich who conspired against Daniil at Torchesk in 1235, as well as (8) Grigory Vasil'evich, (9) the boyar Zbyslav and (10) Boris of Mezhibozh'e (PSRL 2, col. 774). The "princes of Bolokhov" were also Daniil's enemies (PSRL 2, col. 767, s.a. 1231; col. 774, s.a. 1235).

[20] PSRL 2, col. 774. Concerning the Molibogovich family of boyars, see Pashuto, *Ocherki*, p. 144.

[21] The Hypatian Chronicle (PSRL 2, col. 777); see below p. 105.

throughout the lands of Galicia when Daniil was absent from Rus'.[22] The other boyar was Dobroslav Sud'ich. The chronicler states that he had occupied the prince's throne and plundered the whole land. Dobroslav also had conspired against Daniil previously, in 1235, just as Grigory had done. After Daniil fled to Galich from Torchesk, Dobroslav and one Zbyslav advised a certain Boris of Mezhibozh'e to inform Daniil that Izyaslav Vladimirovich and the Polovtsy had departed from Torchesk and were marching against his town of Vladimir in Volyn'. But Daniil realized that this was a ruse, and that the boyars merely wished to lure him out of Galich on a false pretence.[23] Although the chronicle does not state whom Dobroslav and his cohorts intended to invite to replace Daniil, there is little doubt that it was they who later asked Mikhail to rule in Galich.[24]

Mikhail, however, was not the only Ol'govich who deprived Daniil of what the latter considered to be his patrimony. It appears that Izyaslav Vladimirovich, Mikhail's comrade-in-arms, occupied the town of Kamenets on the Khomora river on the eastern border of Volyn'. This was obviously an important town. As we have seen, in order to undermine Daniil's authority in Volyn', Mikhail and Vladimir Ryurikovich had attacked Kamenets in 1228 and, five years later, the "unfaithful Galicians" and the "princes of Bolkhov" also had besieged it. However, it has been noted that in 1239 Mikhail and his wife were in the town when it was attacked by Yaroslav Vsevolodovich, grand prince of Vladimir in Rostov-Suzdal'. Mikhail's presence in Kamenets indicates that it was in the hands of a friend, but the latter could not have been Daniil since, as we shall see, he was at war with Mikhail. It is significant, therefore, that a year later when Baty attacked Kamenets, the chronicler refers to it as "Izyaslav's Kamenets."[25] To judge from this information, the ally whom Mikhail was visiting in 1239 was Izyaslav Vladimirovich. Even though the chronicle

[22] PSRL 2, cols. 789-91; see below p. 116.

[23] PSRL 2, col. 774.

[24] The boyars of Galich no doubt invited Mikhail to become their prince in the traditional manner. This is implied later in the confession made by them to Daniil after he drove Rostislav Mikhaylovich from Galich. At that time, they came to beg Daniil's forgiveness and admitted that they had sinned against him by supporting another prince (PSRL 2, col. 778).

[25] "Каменцю Изяславлю," the Hypatian Chronicle (PSRL 2, col. 786); see also the Novgorod Fourth Chronicle (PSRL 4, p. 227), the Ermolinskiy Chronicle (PSRL 23, pp. 77-78), the Nikon Chronicle (PSRL 10, p. 117). Some sources, however, state that he came "to Kamenets the town of Izyaslav" ("Каменцю, граду Изяславлю"), e.g., the Sofiyskiy First Chronicle (PSRL 5, p. 220), the svod of 1479 (PSRL 25, p. 131) and the Nikon Chronicle (PSRL 10, p. 117).

gives no indication when Kàmenets changed hands from Daniil to Izyaslav, it can be assumed that the latter gained control of it soon after he and Mikhail defeated Daniil in 1235. After the victory Mikhail took Galich from Daniil. Izyaslav also must have been given a share in the spoils. The price which Daniil had to pay him was the town of Kamenets.[26]

By reaffirming the authority of the Ol'govichi over southern and southwest Rus', Mikhail made them potentially, if not in fact, the strongest political force in the land. But before the Ol'govichi could rest on their laurels, they had to consolidate their hold over the newly-won territory. This was not an easy task because the boyars, whose sustained support was mandatory for control over Galicia, had the reputation of vacillating in their allegiance from prince to prince. What is more, since the faction loyal to Daniil had not been destroyed, it continued to threaten Mikhail's authority. Therefore, he resolved to remain in Galich until he eliminated the danger to his rule presented by the Romanovichi and their supporters. As was to be expected, his occupation of the town did not go uncontested for long. The chronicler explains that when winter set in Vasil'ko marched against Galich with the Poles and Daniil came from Hungary and joined them. They waged war but, being unable to reach Galich, they returned home.[27]

For the next three years, 1236 to 1238, the Ol'govichi prevented the Romanovichi from regaining control over Galich. After the latter failed to take the town in the winter of 1235/6, Mikhail and Izyaslav Vladimirovich summoned the Poles, the Rous'[28] (Роусь – the inhabitants of Rus'), and the Polovtsy to their aid. Prince Conrad of Mazovia, Mikhail's uncle, "pitched camp on the spot where the town of Kholm now stands" and sent his troops to pillage the lands of Volyn'. Vasil'ko confronted the Poles and captured many of them. Meanwhile, Mikhail, who wished to join forces with his ally, Conrad, was waiting for Izyaslav

---

[26] For a detailed analysis of this question, see Dimnik, "Kamenec," pp. 31-33.

[27] Under the year 1234 the Hypatian Chronicle states that when winter set in Vasil'ko Romanovich, with the aid of the Poles, marched against Galicia. Daniil came from Hungary and joined his brother in the campaign. However, as the princes were not able to reach Galich, they returned to Volyn' (PSRL 2, col. 774). Since Daniil was in Hungary for the coronation of Béla IV on 14 October 1235, the winter referred to cannot be 1234/5, but must be 1235/6.

[28] The chronicler, as a rule, uses the term Роусь to single out the forces of Kievan Rus' in contrast to those of the Polovtsy, the Poles, the Hungarians and the Tatars, e.g., PSRL 2, col. 707, s.a. 1202; cols. 725-6, s.a. 1208; col. 730, s.a. 1211; cols. 740-5, s.a. 1224; cols. 755-7, s.a. 1229 and elsewhere.

to come with the Polovtsy. When the latter arrived they refused to march
against Daniil; instead, they pillaged the lands of Galicia and returned to
the steppe. After Mikhail received word of their betrayal he retreated to
Galich and Conrad escaped to Poland.[29]

In the spring of 1236, a year after they had defeated Daniil and
taken two important towns from him, Mikhail and Izyaslav wished to
consolidate their position. To judge from the account, Mikhail's most
important achievement towards this end was to conclude an alliance with
his uncle, Prince Conrad of Mazovia, whose lands were located northwest
of Volyn'. Mikhail, no doubt, had maintained friendly relations with his
uncle prior to this. However, it was not until 1236, according to chronicle
information, that he and the Poles concluded a military agreement. By his
action Conrad broke the alliance which he had formed with Daniil in
1229. At that time he had asked the latter to come to his aid[30] and, later,
the Poles assisted Daniil in his struggle against the Hungarians.[31]
Consequently, it is important to note that in 1236 Mikhail had the support
of not only the Hungarians, as we shall see, but also of the Poles.

The chronicler gives no reasons for Conrad's change of policy. No
doubt he was influenced, to some extent, by his blood relation to Mikhail;
but his main motive must have been political since his action weakened
the military strength of Daniil. As we have seen, in 1235 Mikhail had
deprived the former of Vladimir Ryurikovich's support. A year later,
Daniil lost his last ally when Conrad deserted him and, like the
Hungarians, came to Mikhail's assistance. Thus Mikhail successfully
isolated Daniil from his allies both by his victory in 1235 and by his
diplomacy in the following year.

After forming an alliance with the Poles, Mikhail and Izyaslav attacked
the lands of Volyn'. They were assisted not only by the Poles but also by
the Rous' (Роусь) and the Polovtsy. The Rous', for the most part, were the
boyars from Galicia and the "princes of Bolkhov." Mikhail may have
conscripted help also from the lands of Kiev which, prior to 1235, had

---

[29] PSRL 2, col. 775. The chronicle has several entries under the year 1235 concerning
encounters between the Ol'govichi and the Romanovichi in southwest Rus'. However, its
dating is not correct. Since it has no information for southwest Rus' under 1236 and 1237
(under the latter year it gives only the Tatar invasion of Ryazan' and Rostov-Suzdal'), and
given that the information under 1238 is for the years 1239 and 1241, it appears that the
accounts under 1235 describe events which occurred as late as 1238 and, perhaps, even
1239.

[30] PSRL 2, cols. 754, 757.

[31] PSRL 2, col. 761, s.a. 1229.

been under the command of Vladimir Ryurikovich and the Rostislavichi. According to the account, Izyaslav brought the Polovtsy from the steppe just as he had done in the previous year. However, they were capricious in their loyalty to the Ol'govichi since they also had strong ties of allegiance to Daniil. As we have seen, in 1228 they had pillaged the lands of southwest Rus' after Daniil persuaded them to betray their allies the Ol'govichi and the Rostislavichi when the latter attacked him in Kamenets. Similarly, in 1236, not wishing to attack Daniil, they betrayed the Ol'govichi and, after pillaging the lands of Galicia, returned to the steppe. Their perfidy saved Daniil from suffering further losses for it put an end to Mikhail's campaign forcing him to return to Galich.

In the summer, the Romanovichi retaliated and attacked Mikhail and his son Rostislav in Galich. The Ol'govichi barricaded themselves in the town and, since they also had many Hungarians helping them, the two brothers were not able to take it. They, therefore, diverted their attack against Zvenigorod, an important town north of Galich. But, failing to capture it also, they pillaged the district around it. Then in the autumn the Ol'govichi and the Romanovichi concluded peace. Later, under the year 1235, there is another brief entry which apparently refers to the same campaign. It states that Mikhail sued for peace when Daniil attacked Galich and gave him the town of Peremyshl'.[32]

It is significant that Mikhail had the backing of the Hungarians in 1236. As we have seen, Béla IV, who was crowned king in October of the previous year, refused to give Daniil assistance. In a way similar to his father, he continued to oppose Daniil's claim to Galich. Therefore, after the death of Prince Andrew in the winter of 1233/4, and given that he was not in a position to control Galich directly owing to internal unrest in Hungary, Béla IV concluded an alliance with the Ol'govichi to restrain Daniil's expansionism. His agreement strengthened Hungary's ties with the Ol'govichi. The latter had been on friendly terms with the Hungarians when Prince Andrew ruled in Galich in the late 1220s.[33] Since there is no chronicle evidence to suggest that they provided military assistance to each other prior to 1235, their arrangement must have been commercial in nature. It was Béla IV, apparently, who concluded the military alliance. Therefore, in 1236 the Ol'govichi and the Hungarians successfully

---

[32] PSRL 2, col. 776.

[33] In 1228 when the Ol'govichi and the Rostislavichi attacked Daniil in Kamenets, Prince Andrew was ruling in Galich. The chronicler explains that the Ol'govichi and the Rostislavichi were at peace with Prince Andrew (PSRL 2, col. 753).

repulsed Daniil's attack on Galich, concluded peace with him and gave him the town of Peremyshl'. The truce, however, merely gave Daniil an opportunity to attack Mikhail on another front.

In 1236, as we have seen, Mikhail's successes over Daniil forced the latter to conclude an unprecedented alliance with Grand Prince Yury of Rostov-Suzdal'. They coerced Vladimir Ryurikovich into leaving Kiev and appointed Yaroslav Vsevolodovich as grand prince. Daniil and Yury agreed to support Yaroslav in this venture in order to undermine Mikhail's control over southern and southwest Rus'. They wished, no doubt, to restore the buffer zone between the principalities of Chernigov and Galicia which had existed under the Rostislavichi until 1235. Although Yaroslav was not able to assert his control over Kiev and, apparently, remained there only for a short period of time, the stratagem demonstrated the vulnerability of Mikhail's hold over it. The latter realized that it was more urgent for him to be in Kiev than in Galich for it became clear that, if he wished to maintain his authority over Galicia, he must first establish his rule over southern Rus'. Therefore, in 1236, Mikhail replaced Yaroslav Vsevolodovich as grand prince of Kiev and appointed his son Rostislav commander in Galich.

When Mikhail became grand prince, to judge from the account, the Ol'govichi took Peremyshl' from Daniil once again.[34] After that, the chronicler explains, the two princes continued to alternate between being at peace and at war with each other. According to this information Mikhail's rule in Kiev was uneventful; his main concern was to help Rostislav maintain their hold over Galicia. In this they had much success. Although in 1236 they had lost Peremyshl', which was the second most important town in Galicia, they took it back from Daniil in the following year when Mikhail was grand prince. This victory established the authority of the Ol'govichi over most, if not all, of Galicia since they and their supporters controlled the important towns of Galich, Peremyshl' and Zvenigorod.[35] Therefore, despite their repeated attacks on Galicia after

[34] PSRL 2, col. 777.

[35] As we have seen, Mikhail appointed his son Rostislav to rule in Galich in 1236 and in the following year the Ol'govichi took Peremyshl' from Daniil. It has also bee noted that Daniil attempted to take Zvenigorod from the Ol'govichi, in 1236 but failed. However, there is some uncertainty concerning the important town of Yaroslavl' located north of Peremyshl' on the San river. In 1231 Daniil's supporters defended it against the Hungarians (PSRL 2, cols. 764-5). The town is not mentioned again until 1245 at which time Rostislav Mikhaylovich attempted to take it from the Romanovichi (see below, p. 124). Unfortunately, the chronicle fails to mention whether or not the Ol'govichi established their control over it in the 1230s.

1235, the Romanovichi were not able to take it from the Ol'govichi until either 1238 or 1239.

At that time Rostislav led a campaign against the Lithuanians taking with him all his "boyars and cavalry." Daniil's supporters in Galich, recognizing their opportunity, informed Daniil, who was in Kholm, of Rostislav's absence. Daniil jumped at the advantage and marched against the town. The citizens came out to meet him and were persuaded to accept him as their prince. However, Bishop Artemy and the major-domo Grigory Vasil'evich, who had been left in command of the town by Rostislav, remained faithful to their prince and would not allow Daniil to enter. Eventually, when they realized that their resistance was futile in the face of Daniil's troops and internal opposition in the town, they grudgingly succumbed to the pressure. Daniil entered the town without bloodshed and hung his banner over the "German Gates" as a sign of victory. When Rostislav was informed of this change of fortune he fled to Hungary. But the boyars who had accompanied him came back to Galich and begged Daniil for clemency. They pleaded guilty admitting that they had chosen to support a rival prince. However, they promised to be faithful to him and he pardoned them.[36]

The chronicler does not explain why Rostislav led a campaign against the Lithuanians since neither the Ol'govichi nor the Galicians had been involved in any hostilities with them. However, it is known that during this time Daniil was on friendly terms with the Lithuanians and incited them to attack the Poles. To judge from the account, after Daniil had concluded peace with Mikhail in the autumn of 1236, he sent the Lithuanians under Prince Mendog against Conrad in Mazovia.[37] Since the latter had helped the Ol'govichi attack Volyn' he, no doubt, asked them for assistance against the Lithuanians. Consequently, the purpose of Rostislav's campaign probably was to punish the Lithuanians for their attack on Poland and to weaken the alliance between them and Daniil. It was a major military operation since Rostislav took his entire *druzhina*, the cavalry and all the boyars of Galicia into the field of battle. The chronicle fails to mention, however, whether the outcome was successful.

---

[36] The Hypatian Chronicle (PSRL 2, cols. 777-8). It is difficult to determine the exact date on which Daniil replaced Rostislav in Galich. The chronicle gives this information as the last entry under the year 1235. However, Daniil obviously succeeded Rostislav some time after Mikhail returned to Kiev in 1236 and before the winter of 1239/40 since, at that time, Mikhail fled to Hungary just as his son had done before him (PSRL 2, col. 782). As we shall see, the event probably occurred after the Tatar invasion of Rus' in the winter of 1237/8; see below, p. 107.

[37] PSRL 2, col. 776.

Daniil took advantage of Rostislav's absence to occupy Galich. The latter had left it in the hands of Bishop Artemy and the major-domo Grigory Vasil'evich. Significantly, it was not Daniil's superior military strength which enabled him to occupy the town but the rebellion of its citizens against the Ol'govichi. Two observations can be made concerning Daniil's return to Galich. First, it is important to note that it was the townspeople who plotted against Rostislav and not the boyars. As we have seen, he had taken all the boyars with him on the campaign. The chronicle also fails to mention that any boyars opposed the Ol'govichi after 1235. This is an important omission in view of the fact that, after the beginning of the thirteenth century, the boyars had been at the centre of all political intrigues in Galicia and, invariably, rival factions had challenged the prince in power. The obvious inference which can be made from the chronicler's silence concerning the lack of boyar conspiracies is that the Ol'govichi successfully quashed all boyar opposition. This is supported by the chronicler's description of Rostislav's flight after Daniil occupied Galich. He explains that after Rostislav heard of the town's surrender he fled to Hungary. However, the boyars who had accompanied him came to Daniil and, falling on their knees, begged for mercy. They confessed that they had sinned against him by supporting another prince but now they pledged their allegiance to him.[38]

The second observation which can be made concerning Daniil's return to Galich is that Bishop Artemy and the major-domo Grigory had the support of foreign troops. According to the account, Daniil, after entering the town, hung his banner over the "German Gates" as a sign of victory. They, no doubt, were the entrance to the foreign quarter which contained the residences of not only the merchants and the artisans but also of the foreign soldiers. In 1236, as we have seen, Hungarian troops had helped Mikhail defend Galich against Daniil. Apparently, it was they who remained in the town after Rostislav departed with his cavalry and all the boyars. The bishop and Grigory must have had soldiers under their command when Daniil arrived since they prevented him from entering the town. The fact that the townspeople, who had invited Daniil to come, were not able to open the gates suggests that the latter were guarded by the Hungarians. Therefore, Daniil's action of hanging his banner over the "German Gates" as a sign of victory is evidence that the Ol'govichi and the Hungarians were still working together against him.

[38] PSRL 2, col. 778.

The chronicler gives no explanation why Rostislav fled to Hungary rather than to his father in Kiev. It has been noted that the Ol'govichi and the Hungarians were allies and that the latter had helped Rostislav defend Galich. To be sure, he probably was accompanied to Hungary by fleeing Hungarian soldiers. However, a more important reason for his decision must have been the Tatar invasion. Although there is no chronicle evidence to confirm this assumption, it seems that Daniil occupied Galich after the principalities of Ryazan' and Rostov-Suzdal' had been devastated during the winter of 1237/8. This observation is supported by the fact that the Ol'govichi, on this occasion, made no attempt to regain control over Galich, instead, Rostislav fled to Hungary. In view of the inevitable Tatar attack on Chernigov and Kiev, Rostislav realized that his father would not deploy to Galicia troops which were needed for the defence of southern Rus'. Therefore, if he wished to obtain assistance against Daniil, Rostislav's only alternative was to go to King Béla IV.

After Rostislav's flight to Hungary, the conflict for Galicia was suspended temporarily, at least from the standpoint of the Ol'govichi. The Tatar invasion of Rus' forced Mikhail to turn his attention to the defence of his lands. These were not subjected to the full force of the Tatar onslaught until October of the following year when Chernigov fell.[39] As we have seen, after the Tatars sacked the town they concluded peace with various princes in Rus' – Vladimir Ryurikovich of Smolensk, Daniil of Volyn' and Mikhail's cousin Mstislav Glebovich of Chernigov. However, as the chronicles point out in some detail, Baty failed to come to any agreement with Grand Prince Mikhail in Kiev. He alone of all the senior princes rejected the khan's offer and, consequently, in the winter of 1239/40 was forced to flee to Hungary just as his son had done before him.[40]

Mikhail was required to seek assistance not only against the Tatars but also against his domestic enemies. It is noteworthy that, as grand prince of Kiev, he not only failed to obtain support from other princes of Rus' against the Tatars but, as we have seen, several of the princes attacked him during the critical years of 1239 and 1240.[41] In the face of this twofold

[39] The first time that the Tatars attacked the principality of Chernigov had been in the spring of 1238 when they ravaged its northeast periphery around the region of the town of Kozel'sk (PSRL 2, cols. 780-1).

[40] See above, pp. 86-87.

[41] It has been noted that even after the lands of Rostov-Suzdal' had been devastated in 1238 and after the sack of southern Pereyaslavl' on 3 March 1239, Yaroslav Vsevolodovich attacked Mikhail in Kamenets. As we have seen, Daniil also occupied Galich after the Tatar invasion of Rus'. Later, after Mikhail fled to Hungary, Rostislav Mstislavich of Smolensk occupied Kiev and then Daniil took it from him.

opposition Mikhail's only recourse was to seek aid from a foreign power. He attempted to persuade Béla IV to give his daughter in marriage to his son Rostislav. However, given Mikhail's plight, Béla IV saw little advantage to himself in such a commitment and rejected the proposal. His refusal quashed Mikhail's last hope of recouping some of the military strength which he had lost when Chernigov capitulated to the Tatars and when Galich was taken from him by Daniil. To add insult to injury, the king drove out Mikhail and his son from Hungary. They went to Mikhail's uncle, Conrad, prince of Mazovia.[42]

Unable to form an alliance in Hungary, Mikhail was left with no alternative but to become reconciled with Daniil. His loss of Galich, the devastation of Chernigov, his flight from Kiev and its subsequent occupation by Daniil changed the political relationship which had existed between him and Daniil in 1235. At that time Mikhail's victory had forced Daniil to flee to Hungary in search of assistance. The Tatar invasion reversed their roles and now Mikhail was the fugitive.

In 1240, therefore, Daniil gained the upper hand in their negotiations; he not only controlled Kiev and Galich (thus effectively challenging Mikhail's control over southern and southwest Rus'), but he also had Mikhail's wife in "custody."[43] This left Mikhail with little bargaining power. From Poland he sent envoys to his brother-in-law and sued for peace. He admitted that he had acted unjustly on various occasions and that he had broken his promises to Daniil. He sought to justify his behaviour by explaining that whenever he wanted to be at peace with Daniil the "unfaithful Galicians" had not allowed it. But now Mikhail was prepared to swear an oath not to conspire against him in the future. Daniil, welcoming his offer of peace, returned his wife, agreed to hand over Kiev and gave his son Rostislav the town of Lutsk, east of Vladimir in the principality of Volyn'.[44]

The chronicler does not explain why Daniil returned Kiev so readily; he did so presumably on the understanding that Mikhail would not contest the throne of Galich in the future. This can be inferred from the fact that Daniil wished to compensate Rostislav for his loss of Galich with

---

[42] The Hypatian Chronicle (PSRL 2, col. 783). The chronicle has this entry under the year 1238. However, it has been noted that Mikhail fled to Hungary in the winter of 1239/40. King Béla's rebuttal of Mikhail's request does not mean that he was more favourably disposed to Daniil at this time. Before Kiev was sacked, Daniil himself travelled to Hungary to ask the king for his daughter's hand in marriage for his son Lev. Béla rejected Daniil's suit as well (PSRL 2, col. 787; see also col. 809, s.a. 1250).

[43] See above pp. 83-84.

[44] PSRL 2, col. 783.

the important town of Lutsk in his own principality of Volyn'.[45] Mikhail
had no alternative but to accept the terms unconditionally; however,
he did not return to Kiev but became Daniil's guest and lived in his
principality.[46] Daniil, to be sure, made the most of the momentary
advantage which derived from the fact that his lands had not been ravaged
yet by the Tatars.

Daniil's conduct not only shows that he enjoyed an advantage over
Mikhail, but also suggests that his lands were safe from Tatar invasion, at
least in the immediate future. As we have seen, it was "fear of the Tatars"
that dissuaded Mikhail from returning to Kiev in 1240. But Daniil did not
show the same apprehension; he did not even fortify his lands against the
threat of an invasion.[47] At the time when a renewed Tatar attack appeared
imminent (at least to Mikhail), namely, after the fall of Chernigov and
southern Pereyaslavl', and in the face of the persistent Tatar advance
westward, Daniil left his principality leaderless in order to go to Hungary.
His visit, unlike Mikhail's, to judge from chronicle information, did not
have a note of urgency in it. Having been informed, no doubt, that
Mikhail had failed to obtain assistance and to form a marriage alliance
with the king, he wished to try his luck and propose a marriage between
his son Lev and Béla's daughter. Daniil had reason to be more optimistic
in this venture than Mikhail had been, since, unlike the latter, he was
negotiating from a position of power. Such an alliance with King Béla IV
would have been a significant victory for Daniil.

While Daniil was in Hungary the Tatars besieged Kiev; as we have
seen, it fell on 6 December 1240. Although they captured Daniil's *voevoda*
Dmitry who had been wounded during the attack, the chronicler explains
that they spared his life "because of his bravery." When Baty was
informed that Daniil was in Hungary he set out toward Volyn'. On the
way he captured the towns of Kolodyazhen and Kamenets but failed to
take Kremenets and Danilov. He took Vladimir by storm and devastated
Galich as well as many other towns. Finally, Dmitry counselled Baty to

[45] This is the first time that an Ol'govich was given control over the town of Lutsk.
However, Oleg Svyatoslavich's nephew, Svyatoslav Davidovich, ruled in the town at the
end of the eleventh century; see Zotov, *O Chernigovskikh knyazyakh*, p. 281, no. 8.

[46] Since Mikhail could not return to Kiev "for fear of the Tatars," Daniil allowed him
and Rostislav to live in the lands of Volyn' (PSRL 2, col. 783). However, there is no
chronicle information to suggest that they stayed in Lutsk. To judge from subsequent
information, Mikhail was accompanied on his peregrinations not only by Rostislav but by
all his family (see below, p. 113).

[47] Five years later, in 1245, the Galicians expressed regret for the fact that he had not
fortified their lands (PSRL 2, cols. 805-6).

move on to Hungary. He warned the khan that if he remained in the land of Rus' the Tatars would not be allowed to return home because it was powerful and it would rise up against him. Dmitry advised Baty in this manner, says the chronicler, because he saw that the people of Rus' were perishing under the Tatar onslaught. He points out that Baty "heeded Dmitry's warning." However, news of the disaster did not reach Daniil while he was in Hungary. His suit having been rejected by Béla IV, he returned to Volyn'. Only when he met fugitives fleeing before the advancing enemy did he learn of the calamity which had befallen his principality. Since he had a small *druzhina* accompanying him he could not pass through the land of Rus' and so he returned to Hungary.[48]

The episode concerning Dmitry's relations with the Tatars is enigmatic; it appears that the chronicler attempted to whitewash the *voevoda*'s complicity with the enemy. He claims that after the Tatars captured Kiev they did not kill Dmitry "because of his bravery." This explanation is not convincing since no other commander or prince who opposed the Tatars was spared for his courage. For example, the princes of Ryazan' and Rostov-Suzdal' who defended their towns were killed.[49] More important is the manner in which the Tatars treated Prince Vasil'ko Konstantinovich of Rostov. After capturing him, they attempted to persuade him to "capitulate to their terms and to fight with them" ("быти въ их воли. и воєвати с ними"). When Vasil'ko adamantly refused to have any dealings with them they killed him.[50] This episode suggests that the Tatars spared the commanders and princes of Rus' not if the latter fought bravely but if they capitulated to their terms and became their allies. This is supported by chronicle information given under 1239. As we have seen, at that time three princes came to terms with the Tatars, namely Vladimir Ryurikovich, Daniil Romanovich and Mstislav Glebovich. Significantly, they were not killed by the Tatars. Therefore, when the chronicler states that Dmitry was not put to death "because of his bravery," it is more correct to assume that, unlike Vasil'ko, he capitulated to the Tatar demands and agreed to cooperate with them. Or, what was more likely the case, he acted in accord with the agreement which Daniil had concluded with the Tatars in the previous year.

Furthermore, the fact that Dmitry accompanied the Tatars after they departed from Kiev suggests that he was of service to them. Since he was

---

[48] PSRL 2, cols. 784-7.
[49] PSRL 1, cols. 460-67.
[50] PSRL 1, cols. 465-6.

Daniil's *voevoda* there can be little doubt that they used his military expertise to pillage southern and southwest Rus'. According to the account, the Tatars sacked Kolodyazhen and Kamenets on their march to Volyn'. Then, when they came upon the towns of Kremenets and Danilov, which were Daniil's towns in the principality of Volyn', the chronicler explains that Baty "saw" that he could not take them; it appears that he did not even attack the towns. It is difficult to imagine that the fortifications of two small towns would have deterred Baty from attacking them in view of the fact that he had the whole Tatar army at his disposal. No doubt the real reason for his action was that he had concluded an agreement with Daniil. This is supported by the information which states that after capturing Kiev Baty devastated Kolodyazhen which was also in the principality of Kiev, and razed Kamenets which, as we have seen, was ruled by Mikhail's ally Izyaslav Vladimirovich. Baty's destruction of towns on his march westward appears to have been selective.

It is surprising that the chronicler gives the names of only two towns captured by the Tatars in lands ruled by Daniil, namely, Vladimir[51] and Galich. However, he does conclude his account, rather lamely, by stating that the Tatars destroyed "innumerable other towns."[52] This statement also is not convincing. It is difficult to believe that the chronicler, who was no doubt a native of Volyn', would have failed to give the names of other important towns if they had been destroyed.[53] There can be little doubt that the Tatars pillaged the principalities of Volyn' and Galicia in order to obtain provisions. However, there appears to be no evidence to suggest that they destroyed "innumerable other towns." Furthermore, if we can believe the chronicler's testimony, in view of the fact that Dmitry was in a position to give counsel to Baty, he must have advised the Tatars

---

[51] It appears that by 1241 Daniil no longer considered Vladimir to be his capital. As we have seen, he was residing in Kholm northwest of Vladimir in 1238 or 1239 when the inhabitants of Galich informed him that Rostislav had gone on a campaign (PSRL 2, col. 777). When Daniil returned to Volyn' in 1241 after the Tatars invaded Poland, he did not go to Vladimir but to Kholm which "God had spared from the godless Tatars" (PSRL 2, cols. 788-9, s.a. 1240).

[52] "град многы. имже нѣс числа" (PSRL 2, col. 786).

[53] Later when Daniil returned to Volyn' from Poland he passed through the town of Berestya (Brest) which had been devastated by the Tatars (PSRL 2, col. 788). This was a northern outpost of the principality of Volyn', and although Daniil claimed the town to be his patrimony, it had been under the control of the Poles in the past (PSRL 2, col. 720, s.a. 1204; col. 732, s.a. 1213). By the late 1220s and the early 1230s Berestya and its districts were subjected to repeated attacks from the Yatvyagi, a Lithuanian tribe living north of Volyn' (PSRL 2, col. 754, s.a. 1229; col. 776, s.a. 1235). The Tatars probably attacked Berestya during the course of their invasion of Poland and after they had released Dmitry.

to Daniil's advantage. This observation is supported by the chronicler's attempts to exonerate Dmitry. Since he does not condemn the *voevoda* for his complicity with the enemy, it may be concluded that he helped the Tatars having Daniil's interests in mind. Dmitry, no doubt, gave Baty advice intended to weaken Daniil's enemies in Rus'. More important, he attempted, apparently with considerable success, to spare the lands of Volyn' from the same fate which had befallen the principalities of Chernigov and Kiev since Daniil himself, who was in Hungary, could not direct the defence of his lands.

It is unimaginable that Daniil would have been so careless as to leave his lands both without having reinforced them and leaderless if he had been expecting a Tatar invasion. And yet, his apparent negligence and failure to keep in touch with developments in Rus' at a time when the whole country was under siege were no doubt deliberate. Only one reason could have induced him to act so confidently and to feel secure in his position, namely – that he was safe from attack. Daniil must have been given some assurance of immunity by the Tatars in 1239 when he made peace with them.[54]

By trusting the Tatars, Daniil, unlike Mikhail, miscalculated; Kiev fell and soon after the Tatars went on to pillage his principality of Volyn'. On this occasion not only were Mikhail and his son forced to abandon Volyn' and flee to Conrad in Mazovia for the second time,[55] but Daniil himself had to seek sanctuary. He returned to Hungary where he left his son in the hands of Galician boyars. The chronicler explains that "he knew their unfaithfulness and that is why he did not take him [Lev] with him." Daniil then fled to Mazovia, to Conrad's son, Bolesław, who gave him the town of Vyshegorod. He remained there until the Tatars departed from the lands of Rus'.[56] Consequently, the Tatars, who had given Daniil a temporary advantage over Mikhail when they razed Chernigov in the autumn of 1239, nullified that advantage when they invaded Volyn' and forced him to flee. The military and diplomatic struggle for Galich between Mikhail and Daniil – now both fugitives in Poland – fell into abeyance for a time.

To judge from this information, Daniil, before he fled to Poland, took a precautionary measure to secure the loyalty of certain Galician boyars

[54] See above p. 85.
[55] The Hypatian Chronicle (PSRL 2, cols. 783-4). The chronicle has this information under the year 1238. However, since Kiev fell on 6 December 1240, Mikhail and his son must have departed from Volyn' at the end of 1240 or the beginning of 1241.
[56] PSRL 2, cols. 787-8.

who had fled to Hungary before the advancing Tatars. Being aware of their unfaithfulness, he gave them his son for safekeeping as a pledge. The tactic worked for, after the Tatars departed from Volyn', Lev returned to his father from Hungary with the Galician boyars.[57] It is also interesting to note that from Hungary Daniil fled to Bolesław and not to the latter's father, Conrad, with whom Mikhail was staying. As we have seen, Daniil had sent the Lithuanians under Prince Mendog to attack Conrad's lands and the two were, apparently, still at war in 1241. Mikhail, however, had maintained the alliance which he had concluded with Conrad in 1236, to judge from the fact that the latter offered him asylum.

Mikhail and his son were forced to flee even from their sanctuary in Poland. When the Tatars drew near, he fled to what the chronicle calls "the land of Wrocław" (i.e., Breslau in Silesia) and arrived at a "German" town called "Sereda" (presumably Środa, north of Wrocław, also in Silesia). But before he could enter the town the Germans sallied out, plundered his goods and killed many of his retinue including his granddaughter.[58] The chronicle concludes that Mikhail was able to return to Conrad in Mazovia only after the Tatars had engaged in battle with Henry II the Pious, duke of Silesia,[59] and departed from Poland.[60]

Mikhail and his son returned to Rus' after April 1241.[61] He went to Vladimir in Volyn' and then passed through the town of Pinsk on his way to Kiev.[62] Thus Mikhail followed the Pripyat' river system which was the

---

[57] PSRL 2, col. 789, s.a. 1240.

[58] This child's death later became the subject of a local legend concerning the death of a Tatar princess; see S. N. Palauzova, *Rostislav Mikhaylovich', russkiy udel'nyy knyaz' na dunae v XIII veke* (Saint Petersburg, 1851), p. 13, n. 10 and A. V. Florovsky, *Chekhi i vostochnye slavyane*, vol. 1 (Prague, 1935), pp. 207-8. This is the only chronicle reference made during Mikhail's lifetime which suggests that he had more than one son. Since Rostislav was not yet married and the child could not have been his, she must have been the daughter of another son. Although Mikhail had two daughters, at the time they were both in the principality of Rostov-Suzdal' – one the wife of the former prince of Rostov, Vasil'ko, who was killed by the Tatars in 1238, and the other a nun in Suzdal' (see above p. 23). After the account of Mikhail's death in 1246 the Ermolinskiy Chronicle lists four of his sons excluding Rostislav (PSRL 23, p. 81); see Zotov, *O Chernigovskikh knyazyakh*, pp. 284-7.

[59] The battle took place at Liegnitz 9 April 1241. A second Tatar army moved into Hungary and confronted Béla IV at Mohi on the Sajó river; see the Hypatian Chronicle (PSRL 2, cols. 786-7). This battle occurred on 11 April 1241 (*Magyarország Története*, vol. 1 [Budapest, 1967], p. 81).

[60] The Hypatian Chronicle (PSRL 2, col. 784).

[61] The Hypatian Chronicle misplaces Mikhail's return to Rus' under the year 1240 (PSRL 2, col. 788). Since he was still in Poland after the battle of Liegnitz in April 1241, he must have returned to Rus' after that date.

[62] PSRL 2, cols. 788-9.

traditional route connecting Poland with Kiev. Although he travelled
through Pinsk this need not be interpreted to mean that Mikhail went
there from political motives or that Rostislav Vladimirovich, prince of
Pinsk, was his ally.[63] But it appears that Daniil expressed some concern
over Mikhail's visit and over the relationship which he thought existed
between Mikhail and Rostislav Vladimirovich. Daniil had good reason to
be suspicious of the two princes since, as has already been seen,[64] it
was chiefly owing to Rostislav's instigation that Mikhail and Vladimir
Ryurikovich had attacked Daniil in Kamenets in 1228. The chronicler
was relieved to observe that Rostislav elected to visit Daniil in Kholm,
where the latter was staying, as proof that he was not conspiring against
him. But Mikhail, in the chronicler's opinion, slighted Daniil by not
reporting to him personally.[65] Instead, Mikhail merely sent an envoy to
Volyn';[66] after that he returned to Kiev and his son assumed command of
Chernigov.[67]

According to the traditional course of lateral succession among the
Ol'govichi, Rostislav Mikhaylovich was not in line to rule in Chernigov in
1241. His uncle, Mstislav Glebovich, who had defended the town against
the Tatars, was senior to him. The fact that Rostislav superseded him
suggests either that he was dead by this time, or as was probably the case,
that Mikhail deliberately broke the traditional order of precedence and
debarred Mstislav from the line of succession. It is important to remember
that, contrary to the wishes of Mikhail, the former had concluded a peace
agreement with the Tatars after the fall of Chernigov. Disillusioned with

[63] Rostislav Vladimirovich was presumably the son of Vladimir of Pinsk who was
prince of that town in 1204 (PSRL 2, col. 720). To judge from the behaviour of the princes
of Volyn', "Bolokhov" and Chernigov, Rostislav probably fled from his principality in the
face of the Tatar invasion. The chronicle only implies that he returned to Pinsk at the same
time as Mikhail (PSRL 2, cols. 788-9). However, the seventeenth-century Gustinskiy
Chronicle states that Rostislav Vladimirovich was one of the princes who "returned to the
Rus'sian land" the same year as Daniil and Mikhail (PSRL 2, 1843 edition, p. 340).

[64] See above pp. 60-61.

[65] PSRL 2, col. 789. According to the chronicle, Daniil sought refuge with Bolesław the
son of Conrad of Mazovia, while the Tatars were ravaging Volyn'. After they departed he
returned home from Poland (PSRL 2, cols. 787-8). It appears that Daniil returned to Volyn'
before Mikhail.

[66] The chronicle entry reads: "[Михаил] проиде. землю его и и пославъ. посла иде
въ Киевъ" (PSRL 2, col. 789). G. E. Perfecky translates this passage to read: "He crossed
[Danilo's] land without even sending a courier [to him], went to Kiev,..." (The Hypatian
Codex Part Two: The Galician-Volynian Chronicle [Munich, 1973], p. 50). Solv'ev was also
of the opinion that Mikhail did not let Daniil know he passed through Volyn' (Istoriya,
book 2, p. 171).

[67] The Hypatian Chronicle (PSRL 2, cols. 788-9).

Mstislav's capitulation, Mikhail expressed his displeasure by replacing him on the throne of Chernigov with his own son.

The fact that Rostislav returned to Chernigov rather than to Lutsk, which had been promised to him by his uncle Daniil in 1240, suggests that Mikhail no longer felt bound by the oath made to Daniil. By not accepting Lutsk, the Ol'govichi in effect declared their intention of renewing their fight for Galich. However, after Mikhail returned to Kiev he, personally, did not take an active part in the affairs of Galicia. Instead his son, who now assumed the position of the second senior prince among the Ol'govichi, became the main agent in the southwest, and there can be no doubt that in this he had Mikhail's full support. After their return to Rus' the Ol'govichi did not have long to wait before they were given an opportunity to renew their struggle for Galicia.

Even though the princes of Chernigov and the princes of Volyn' had been forced to temporize during the invasion, the opposing boyar factions in Galich had not remained inactive. Finding themselves without a prince while Daniil was a fugitive abroad, the boyars appropriated his functions. The supporters of the Ol'govichi attained the upper hand in the self-styled rule. Their task was made easier since boyars who supported Daniil, as we have seen, had fled to Hungary where they were holding his son as a pledge. Consequently, the boyar Dobroslav Sud'ich assumed the role of prince.[68] In his new capacity he distributed Galician territory to the boyars of Chernigov rather than to the boyars of Galicia, thus strengthening the Ol'govichi faction in southwest Rus'.[69] Contrary to Daniil's wish, Dobroslav also confiscated the town of Bakota on the Dnestr river and the Poniz'e district around it which comprised the southern periphery of the territory of Galicia.[70] He thereby gained control over the town of Kolomyya on the Prut river whose rich salt resources were very important to the princes for financing their armies.[71] Dobroslav no doubt

---

[68] Concerning Dobroslav's activities, see above pp. 99-100.

[69] Dobroslav probably gave grants of land to fugitive boyars from Chernigov who fled at the time of the destruction of Chernigov in 1239.

[70] The southern district of the principality, or the Poniz'e, comprised a series of towns – Kalius, Ushitsa, Bakota, Onut, Vasiliev, Kolomyya – which formed a protective border against the incursions of nomads from the steppe. Although incorporated into the principality of Galicia, the towns did not have a strong affiliation with its central government. In the twelfth century the region was called the "Galician borderland" (*Galichskaya ukrayna*), but in the thirteenth century it became known as the Poniz'e. See Map no. 4; P. A. Rappoport, "Voennoe zodchestvo zapadnorusskikh zemel' x-xiv vv.," *Materialy i issledovaniya po arkheologii sssr*, no. 140 (Leningrad, 1967), p. 177.

[71] The Hypatian Chronicle (psrl 2, col. 790).

diverted much of this salt to Chernigov; indeed, Daniil condemned him for cutting off his salt supply.[72]

Grigory Vasil'evich,[73] the former major-domo of Rostislav Mikhaylo-vich in Galich, was the other boyar who stirred up unrest against Daniil at this time. He attempted to appropriate that section of the town of Peremyshl' which was on the left bank of the San river[74] and which presumably belonged to Daniil's supporters. In this way, during the years 1240 and 1241, Daniil's control over Galicia was undermined consider-ably through the anarchy instigated by Dobroslav and Grigory. The anonymous chronicler emphasizes the strong anti-Daniil sentiments shared by the two boyars by stressing that even when they were at odds with each other, Dobroslav and Grigory were in agreement on one point: they did not wish to obey Daniil but sought to "deliver his land to another prince."[75] Although the chronicler does not name this "other prince" it was no doubt an Ol'govich. Daniil retaliated by throwing both boyars into prison. But his action, rather than quelling the unrest in Galicia, increased his problem; it served as a cue for the Ol'govichi to intervene directly once more in the politics of southwest Rus'.

Despite the losses inflicted upon the princes of Rus' by the Tatars, the damage was not sufficient to deter them from pursuing their former domestic rivalries. After Daniil regained control over Bakota, the centre of the Poniz'e region, by imprisoning Dobroslav, Rostislav Mikhaylovich attempted to repossess it for the Ol'govichi. He was driven off by Daniil's "chancellor" (*pechatnik*) Kirill and withdrew to Chernigov.[76] It is note-

---

[72] PSRL 2, col. 789. The chronicle places all this information under the year 1240. However, the boyars of Galicia probably established their control over the territory when Daniil fled to Poland after the invasion of his principality in the early part of 1241.

[73] Concerning Grigory's activities, see above pp. 99-100.

[74] Grigory sought to appropriate "горноую страноу Перемышльскоую" (PSRL 2, col. 789). According to V. Dal' "горная страна," in general, is the higher or hilly bank of a river; this is also the left bank (*Tolkovyy slovar'*, vol. 2 [Moscow, 1956], under "Лугъ," p. 271). Perfecky translated this prase to read "the hilly region of Peremyshl'" (*The Galician-Volynian Chronicle*, p. 50).

[75] The Hypatian Chronicle (PSRL 2, cols. 790-1).

[76] The chronicle states that Rostislav gathered the "princes of Bolokhov" and "the remainder of the Galicians" and marched on Bakota (PSRL 2, col. 791). The entry is placed under the year 1241. In all probability the event occurred soon after Daniil imprisoned Dobroslav and Grigory. Consequently, Rostislav marched on the Poniz'e in the second half of 1241. Some historians have suggested that *Pechatnik* Kirill was the same man who became metropolitan in the early 1240s, but their arguments are not conclusive. See, for example, J. T. Fuhrmann, "Metropolitan Cyril II (1242-1281) and the Politics of Accomodation," *Jahrbücher für Geschichte Osteuropas*, Neue Folge, Band 24 (Wiesbaden, 1976), pp. 161-3.

worthy that on this occasion Rostislav sought to regain Bakota rather than Galich. The Ol'govichi had probably derived considerable benefit from Bakota during the period of Dobroslav's rule, especially in view of the economic importance of the salt resources of Kolomyya.[77] Rostislav was accompanied on his campaign by "the remainder of the Galicians" and by the "princes of Bolokhov." This "remainder" probably comprised those boyars from Galicia who were opposed to Daniil's rule and who, having escaped his punitive measure after his return from Poland, fled to the Ol'govichi for assistance.

Presumably Daniil had not taken any disciplinary action against the "princes of Bolokhov" when he punished Dobroslav and Grigory and all the other recalcitrant boyars of Galicia. However, he took severe measures against them after he was told that they had attacked Galicia with the Ol'govichi. The Hypatian Chronicle describes Daniil's retaliation against the "princes of Bolokhov" in the following manner. After he discovered that they had helped Rostislav attack Bakota he raided their lands, set their towns on fire and dug up their walls. He took much booty and razed their towns. At the same time Daniil's "chancellor" Kirill came (from Bakota?)[78] with his infantry and cavalry and sacked one of the towns[79] and from there went on to pillage the "Bolokhov" lands.[80]

---

[77] Galicia appears to have been the chief purveyor of salt for most of Rus' to judge from information given for the eleventh century. At that time, when the princes of Galicia "prevented merchants [гость] from leaving Galicia and prohibited boats from departing from Peremyshl', there was no salt to be had throughout the land of Rus'" (see D. Abramovich, *Kievo-Pecherskiy Paterik* [Kiev, 1930], pp. 151-2). The importance of the Galician salt trade is reflected further in the size of its caravans. Under the year 1164, the Hypatian Chronicle states that when the Dnestr river flooded its banks it claimed the lives of over 300 men who had brought salt from the town of Udech (presumably, in the Poniz'e region) (PSRL 2, col. 524).

[78] The "Bolokhov" towns named are "Деревичь Гоубинъ. и Кобоудъ. Коудинъ городѣць. Божьскыи Дадьковъ." Daniil probably pillaged these towns before Rostislav and the "princes of Bolokhov" were able to withdraw from the Poniz'e. The apparent ease with which Daniil razed their towns suggests that the princes had not yet returned from the campaign. It appears that Kirill, who defended Bakota against Rostislav (PSRL 2, col. 791), came to help Daniil after he repelled Rostislav's attack.

[79] I.e., "Дадьковъ град." In this instance the town is called "Дадьковъ град" whereas in the reference before it is spoke of as "Божьскыи Дадьковъ." This suggests that "Dyad'ko" was probably a boyar or a prince and that his town, Bozh'skyy, was the one sacked by Kirill.

[80] This account helps to establish the location of the "Bolokhov" lands. They were situated in the southwest corner of the principality of Kiev, bordering on the principalities of Volyn' and Galicia. The "Bolokhov" towns enumerated by the chronicler were located to the north and east of the town of Mezhibozh'e which is located on the upper reaches of the Southern Bug river. The southern boundary of the "Bolokhov" lands was probably the

The chronicler goes on to explain that the Tatars had not plundered
these lands because they wanted the "princes of Bolokhov" to supply their
army with wheat and millet. Daniil despised the princes for placing their
hopes on the Tatars. He was also incensed with them because at the time
of the invasion, when they fled from their lands, he had saved them from
Bolesław, prince of Mazovia. The latter had challenged them for seeking
sanctuary in his lands because, explains the chronicler, they were
independent princes and not Daniil's protégés. They, however, assured
Bolesław that they would be his vassals but at the same time asked the
Romanovichi to help them. The princes of Volyn' were willing even to go
to war against Bolesław on behalf of their countrymen. But this was not
necessary since Vasil'ko managed to appease Bolesław with many gifts
and to persuade him to set the princes free. And now, the chronicler
concludes, because "they did not remember the benevolence of the
Romanovichi, God took revenge on them so that nothing remained in
their towns and everything was plundered."[81]

The account of Daniil's punitive action against the "princes of
Bolokhov" gives the most detailed definition of their political status to be
found anywhere in the sources. It refers to them as autonomous princes
who were politically independent of Daniil. Although they had opposed
him in the past[82] these princes solicited his aid when they were fugitives in
Poland. To judge from the fact that he helped them in their plight Daniil
desired to cultivate their friendship. However, they did not consider
their plea for aid in Poland to have been a commitment of unreserved
allegiance to him. As soon as circumstances permitted, that is, when they

---

natural border provided by the Southern Bug river. This view is supported by the fact that
the first "Bolokhov" town which Kirill apparently encountered when he came north from
Bakota was Bozh'skyy (i.e., "Дадьковъ градъ"). This town, according to Solov'ev, was
Buzhsk which was probably situated on the shores of the river Buzhok; the latter flows
into the Southern Bug river at the town of Mezhibozh'e (*Istoriya*, book 1, p. 711, n. 242).
According to the same chronicle entry, the "Bolokhov" lands were not devastated by the
Tatars when they advanced west from Kiev. However, the invaders destroyed the towns
of Kolodyazhen and Kamenets; although they did not attack them, they passed by
Kremenets and Danilov; see the Hypatian Chronicle (PSRL 2, col. 786). It may be assumed,
therefore, that these towns formed a line north of the "Bolokhov" lands. See Map no. 4
and P. A. Rappoport, "Goroda Bolokhovskoy zemli," *Kratie Soobshcheniya o dokladakh i
polevykh issledovaniyakh instituta istorii material'noy kul'tury*, vol. 57 (Moscow, 1955),
pp. 52-9.

[81] The Hypatian Chronicle (PSRL 2, cols. 791-3).

[82] It has been noted that the "princes of Bolokhov" allied themselves with the boyars of
Galicia not only when they attacked Bakota in 1241, but also earlier, in 1233, when they
attacked Daniil's town of Kamenets (see above pp. 98-99).

returned home safely from Poland, they turned against him and renewed their former ties with the Ol'govichi.[83] Daniil retaliated by ravaging their lands in the hope of curtailing their striking power and undermining their autonomy.[84] His action gained for him a temporary respite from the incursions of the "princes of Bolokhov";[85] however, it did not prevent Rostislav Mikhaylovich from reviving his quest for control over Galich.

The Hypatian Chronicle relates that, after failing to take Bakota, Rostislav and the boyar Volodislav marched on Galich and occupied it, whereupon Rostislav appointed Volodislav to the post of *tysyatskiy*. When Daniil and Vasil'ko learnt that Galich had been taken, they marched against Rostislav. He was unable to withstand their attack and fled from the town accompanied by Bishop Artemy of Galich and by other townsmen. While the Romanovichi were pursuing him they received word that the Tatars had withdrawn from Hungary and were returning through Galicia. This news, explains the chronicler, saved

---

[83] It is difficult to ascertain accurately the relationship of the "princes of Bolokhov" and the Ol'govichi. Much has been written, and various theories have been formulated, based on the same scraps of evidence, about "Bolokhov," the "болоховцы" and the "princes of Bolokhov." Concerning this literature see V. V. Mavrodin, "Nekotorye momenty iz istorii razlozheniya rodovogo stroya na teritorii Drevney Rusi," *Uchenye zapiski*, vol. xix (Leningrad, 1939), pp. 165-74. For the purpose of this discussion suffice it to point out that, as we have seen, Mikhail and Izyaslav Vladimirovich called the "princes of Bolokhov" their "brothers." It is noteworthy that in 1146 Izyaslav Mstislavich, a grandson of Vladimir *Monomakh* (see Baumgarten, *Généalogies*, Table V, no. 23, pp. 22-3), gave Mikhail's grandfather, Svyatoslav Vsevolodovich the towns of "Buzhsk and Mezhibozh'e, five towns [in all]" ("Боужьскыи и Межибожье пять городовъ"); see the Hypatian Chronicle (PSRL 2, cols. 329-30). Solov'ev claims that the towns given to Svyatoslav Vsevolodovich were Buzhsk, Mezhibozh'e, Kotel'nitsa and two others. Kotel'nitsa was located on the river Guyva, west of Kamenets (*Istoriya*, book 1, p. 711, n. 242). See Map no. 4. It is therefore possible that the relationship between the Ol'govichi and the lands of "Bolokhov" stems from 1146.

[84] To judge from archeological evidence found on the sites of two "Bolokhov" towns – Gubin (Goubin) and Kudin – Daniil's punitive measures were severe. This evidence confirms the chronicle information that the inner ramparts of mounds (defensively the most important earthworks of the towns) were dug up. The significant lack of human skeletons on the sites suggests that, rather than killing off the inhabitants, Daniil probably resettled them onto his own lands. Furthermore, the absence of traces of fire on the "Bolokhov" lands shows that Daniil did not wish to destroy the rich agricultural lands; see Rappoport, "Goroda Bolokhovskoy zemli," p. 59.

[85] It appears that Daniil's severe measures taken against the "princes of Bolokhov" were not sufficient to deter the latter from taking hostile action against him in the future. This is suggested by information given in the Hypatian Chronicle under the year 1257 when the "Bolokhov" lands are mentioned for the last time. In that year, Daniil once again ordered the "Bolokhov" lands to be devastated; after this all the "болоховцы" came to him, presumably to acknowledge him as their prince (PSRL 2, col. 838).

Rostislav from the princes of Volyn' but some of his boyars were captured.[86]

After driving out Mikhail's son from Galich, Daniil attempted to restore order in the principality. Presumably, he tried to extirpate all troublesome Ol'govichi elements. He directed his attention to the Poniz'e region, chiefly to the towns of Bakota and Kalius.[87] This suggests that the salt supply was at issue again. The chronicler also considered it worth mentioning that Daniil took special punitive action against the important town of Peremyshl', where the local opposition had been spearheaded by the bishop and by Rostislav's ally, a certain Prince Konstantin of Ryazan'.[88]

The fact that the bishops of Galich and Peremyshl', the only two sees in the principality,[89] both supported the Ol'govichi suggests that they had a

[86] PSRL 2, col. 793. Khan Ugedei died on 11 December 1241 (B. Spuler, *Die Goldene Horde. Die Mongolen in Russland, 1223-1502* [Wiesbaden, 1965], p. 24). Baty received the news in Europe towards the end of March 1242 at which time he decided to return east. Rostislav's flight from Galich must have occurred, therefore, after March 1242. The Hypatian Chronicle misplaces the information under 1243 (PSRL 2, col. 794).

[87] PSRL 2, col. 793.

[88] PSRL 2, cols. 793-4. This is the only reference to Konstantin prince of Ryazan'. Presumably he survived the Tatar invasion and escaped to Chernigov where he joined Rostislav. Although this is a rare reference to contacts between the princes of Ryazan' and Chernigov, such events must have been frequent. Lack of information concerning these contacts is due to the fact, no doubt, that it was destroyed. Evidence that ties existed between the two principalities is found also, for example, in literary accounts. According to the "Tale of the Destruction of Ryazan' by Baty," a certain "grandee" (*velmozh*) Eupaty Kolovrat and a certain Prince Ingvar Ingorevich were visiting in Chernigov when they were informed that Ryazan' had been attacked by the Tatars; see "Povest' o razorenii Ryazani Batyem," *A Historical Russian Reader: A Selection of Texts from the xiith. to the xviith. Centuries*, J. Fennell and D. Obolensky eds. (Oxford, 1969), pp. 80-81.

[89] It appears that there were two bishoprics in the principality of Galicia during the first half of the thirteenth century, one in Galich and one in Peremyshl'. According to Tatishchev, the latter was the older of the two sees (*Istoriya*, vol. 3, p. 60). This is understandable since in the tenth century, at the time of the Christianization of Rus' under Prince Vladimir, Peremyshl' was the capital of Galicia. Galich did not become the capital until the reign of Vladimir Volodarevich, a descendant of Vladimir the eldest son of Yaroslav "the Wise," who ruled in it from 1141 until 1153. Presumably, the ecclesiastical centre of the principality was also moved from Peremyshl' to Galich during his reign. Bishop Koz'ma, who was appointed bishop in 1157, is the first bishop of Galich mentioned in the sources (Tatishchev, *Istoriya*, vol. 3, p. 60). The only other reference to the see of Galich is that made in connection with Bishop Artemy, who gave his support to the Ol'govichi in the years 1235 and 1241; see the Hypatian Chronicle (PSRL 2, cols. 777 and 793). Despite its seniority, the bishopric of Peremyshl' is not mentioned until 1220 when Archbishop Antony of Novgorod was sent there as bishop; see the Novgorod First Chronicle (NPL, pp. 60, 261). The only other reference to it is made, under the year 1241, when the bishop led the local opposition to Daniil. (Concerning the two bishoprics, see E. Golubinsky, *Istoriya russkoy tserkvi*, vol. 1, part 1 [Moscow, 1901], pp. 691-5; 698-9.)

special grievance against Daniil. Surprisingly, their main fear was not his desire to curry favour with the Hungarians even though this would increase the influence of the Roman Catholic Church in Galicia. As we have seen, they supported the Ol'govichi who had concluded an alliance with Béla ıv and who had brought Hungarians to defend Galich. Although there is no chronicle evidence, it may be assumed that Daniil either confiscated lands belonging to the Church or restricted its authority while consolidating his control over the region. Perhaps he even attempted to subordinate the sees in Galicia to the bishopric of Vladimir in Volyn'. There can be little doubt that Daniil was interested in manipulating the government of the Church. This is testified to by the fact that after the sack of Kiev, when he was in Kholm, he was accompanied by "Metropolitan Kirill" whom, it appears, he had appointed to the post.[90] Consequently the two bishops, wishing to protect their independence and to strengthen their ties with the metropolitan, turned for support to Mikhail who was the grand prince of Kiev, the political and ecclesiastical centre in Rus'. However, despite their unified action, Daniil defeated the bishops and reasserted his rule over Galicia by 1242.

Soon after he overcame the internal opposition in southwest Rus', Daniil was confronted by the Tatars. While he was in Kholm one of his spies from the Polovtsy informed him that Baty was returning from Hungary and had sent two "commanders" (*bogatyrya*) "to find" him. Daniil barricaded Kholm and went to his brother Vasil'ko.[91] This information is significant. It shows not only that Baty knew of Daniil but, more important, that the former expressed a special interest in him since he sent two commanders to Volyn'. It would seem that their mission exclusively was to search for Daniil in view of the fact that they did not destroy any towns. Unfortunately, the chronicler does not explain why Baty wished "to find" him. As we have seen, in 1239 Daniil had been one of the three princes who concluded peace with the invaders. However, he alone was not attacked.[92] No doubt, he concluded his agreement through the envoys sent to him by Baty. The terms accepted by Daniil and the other two princes must have required them not only to swear allegiance

---

[90] PSRL 2, col. 794, s.a. 1243. Concerning Metropolitan Kirill ııı, see E. Golubinsky, *Istoriya russkoy tserkvi*, vol. 2, part 1 [Moscow, 1900], pp. 50-89.

[91] PSRL 2, col. 794, s.a. 1243.

[92] It has been noted that the two other princes who concluded peace were Vladimir Ryurikovich of Smolensk and Mstislav Glebovich of Chernigov. It appears that Smolensk was attacked when the Tatars retreated from the lands of Novgorod in the winter of 1237/8 and, as it has been noted, Chernigov was sacked in the autumn of 1239.

and to capitulate to the khan but also to supply troops. Since the Tatar
armies had not reached Volyn' in 1239, Daniil, presumably, did not
honour his agreement at that time. Two years later, when they came to
Volyn', he was in Hungary. Consequently, when Baty returned from
Hungary, he sent troops to Kholm to "remind" Daniil of his obligation.
But Daniil hid because he was forewarned of their arrival and avoided a
confrontation with the enemy once again. However, soon after the Tatars
departed, Rostislav, who had fled to Hungary, returned once again to
challenge Daniil for Galicia.

When Rostislav arrived at Béla's court in 1242, the king, on this
occasion, was more receptive to his suit and gave Rostislav his daughter in
marriage.[93] No reason is given as to why the king chose to marry his
daughter to the prince this time after having refused him in 1240.
However, the defeat inflicted upon the Hungarian armies by the Tatars at
Mohi no doubt influenced him in reversing his former decision. In 1240,
when Grand Prince Mikhail had proposed this union to the king, the
principality of Chernigov had been sacked by the Tatars but Hungary still
remained untouched; by 1242 the Tatars had ravaged Hungary as well,
and Béla's predicament was similar to that of the Ol'govichi. Mikhail's
son, who was heir apparent to the throne of Chernigov and Daniil's chief
rival for the throne of Galich, could prove to be an excellent agent for
Hungary. Through the marriage Béla IV hoped to acquire an ally who
would eventually control the buffer zone between Hungary and the
Tatars.[94]

When Mikhail was informed of his son's marriage he set off for
Hungary. The king and Rostislav, however, "did not welcome him with
due honour." Angered by his son's behaviour Mikhail returned to
Chernigov.[95] No explanation is given for Rostislav's disrespectful conduct.

---

[93] PSRL 2, col. 794. It has been noted that Rostislav probably fled to Hungary after
March 1242. However, the date of his marriage has not been preserved. Since the king
apparently had no objection to the marriage on this occasion, it probably took place soon
after Rostislav arrived in Hungary.

[94] Macartney points out that after the Tatars devastated Hungary, the king organized a
completely new defence system based on chains of fortresses. Furthermore, "in the south
and east Hungary was surrounded by a ring of 'Bánáts' or client states embracing Bosnia
and north Serbia, Severin, Cumania (in the later Wallachia) and Galicia" (*Hungary*,
pp. 33-4).

[95] The Hypatian Chronicle (PSRL 2, col. 795). Although the chronicle has this
information under the year 1245, it is unlikely that it took Mikhail almost two years to
find out about his son's marriage. He was probably informed soon after the event and
would have departed for Hungary at once. The account states that Mikhail "fled to
Hungary" but it does not say whether he "fled" from Kiev or from Chernigov. However,

However, Mikhail obviously considered it to be tantamount to treason, for the estrangement between him and his son became so severe that this was the last occasion on which they met. There is no chronicle evidence to suggest that Rostislav returned to Chernigov. He lived out his life in the kingdom of Hungary where his father-in-law honoured him with various titles.[96]

When Mikhail returned to Chernigov he left not only his son in Hungary but also his last hope of ever regaining control over southwest Rus'. Rostislav, who had championed the policy of the Ol'govichi in Galicia since 1236, ceased to represent their interests when he married King Béla's daughter.[97] By becoming the king's son-in-law, he entered not only a marriage relationship but also a political alliance; he became the agent of Hungary's expansionism in southwest Rus'. Although the king considered himself to be the official sovereign of Galicia, he appointed Rostislav as his lieutenant in the principality.[98] Consequently, Rostislav's defection effectively terminated Mikhail's involvement in southwest Rus'.

Various agents were instrumental in undermining Mikhail's hold over Galicia; the most important were the Tatars. In 1239 they inflicted untold

---

the fact that on returning from Hungary he went to Chernigov suggests that Kiev was already in the hands of Yaroslav Vsevolodovich. Mikhail must have returned, therefore, in 1243 or soon after. Yaroslav Vsevolodovich went to Saray in the winter of 1242/3 and probably returned to Rus' early in 1243. For the dating of his visit to Saray, see Berezhkov, *Khronologiya*, p. 271.

[96] See Florovsky, *Chekhi i vostochniye slavyane*, vol. 1, pp. 240-1.

[97] It appears that Rostislav's defection to Hungary was taken very seriously by the Ol'govichi. To judge from the only chronicle list of Mikhail's sons (this is found in the Ermolinskiy Chronicle after the account of Mikhail's death in 1246), Rostislav's name was deleted from the genealogical charts of the Ol'govichi. The chronicle fails to list him as Mikhail's son; instead it records the names of four other sons and gives Roman as the firstborn (PSRL 23, p. 81). Zotov observes, with some perplexity, that the *Lyubetksiy sinodik* not only fails to include Rostislav as one of the princes who ruled in Chernigov, but completely omits him from the register of princes. Therefore, concludes Zotov, it is doubtful whether Rostislav ever ruled in Chernigov (*O Chernigovskikh knyazyakh*, pp. 194-5). On the contrary, the Hypatian Chronicle leaves no doubt when it states that Rostislav went to Chernigov in 1241 as prince (PSRL 2, col. 789). The reason why he is omitted from the register in the *sinodik* was, as has been suggested, the same as his omission from the genealogy in the Ermolinskiy Chronicle, namely, the fact that he defected to Hungary.

[98] According to Hungarian sources, Béla's full title was "King of Hungary, Dalmatia, Croatia, Bosnia (Rama), Serbia, Galicia, Vladimir (Lodomeria) and Cumania" (*Codex diplomaticus Hungariae ecclesiasticus ac civilis*, ed. G. Fejér, book 4, vol. 1 [Budae, 1829], p. 577). In a Fragment of 1245 in which King Béla extols the exploits of a certain Master Lawrence, the king refers to "our beloved son-in-law Rostislav (Ratislao) prince of Galicia" (ibid. p. 396).

damage to his resources by ravaging his patrimony of Chernigov. By concluding peace agreements with the other families of princes they isolated him from any support he may have desired to obtain from his fellow princes. The following year they razed Kiev depriving him of its resources. Then in 1243 Baty appointed Yaroslav Vsevolodovich grand prince of Vladimir, senior prince of Rus' and grand prince of Kiev. Daniil of Volyn' was also instrumental in weakening Mikhail's hold over Galicia. He not only replaced Rostislav in Galich in the late 1230s but also drove him out, once and for all, in 1242; on both occasions he forced Rostislav to flee to Hungary. Daniil, therefore, was instrumental in his defection. After Rostislav's second flight from Galich Daniil extirpated the fractious boyars who had supported the Ol'govichi in southwest Rus'.

However, it was Rostislav's unexpected decision to join Hungary which terminated Mikhail's involvement in Galicia. His son's betrayal came as a triple blow: it deprived him of his most experienced agent in southwest Rus'; it robbed him of the much needed alliance with Béla IV; and it encouraged the king to renew Hungary's claim to Galicia. Needless to say, Mikhail also must have experienced great personal grief at the loss of his son. Thus, over the course of four years, from the time the Tatars invaded Rus' in the winter of 1237/8 until Rostislav's defection in 1242, Mikhail's authority in Galicia was weakened so effectively by the Tatars, by Daniil and finally by his own son that he found himself powerless against his enemies.

Although Daniil was freed of Mikhail's opposition to his rule in Galich he still had Rostislav to contend with, but, now as the agent of Hungary. With the aid of the king's army he made two unsuccessful attempts to recover possession of Galicia. His first attack came soon after his father returned to Chernigov.[99] In 1245 he conducted his second campaign against the Romanovichi, with the help of Hungarian and Polish forces.[100] He besieged the town of Yaroslavl' on the San river north of Peremyshl', but his army was annihilated by the combined troops of the Romanovichi and the Polovtsy. Many of the Hungarians and Poles were captured, and Daniil ordered a number of the former to be executed including the Hungarian general whom he killed with his own hands. The boyar

[99] The Hypatian Chronicle (PSRL 2, col. 797). Since this entry is placed under the same year as the information concerning Mikhail's visit to Hungary, the attack probably occurred soon after.

[100] PSRL 2, col. 800. The chronicle misplaces this information under the year 1249. See below, n. 105.

Volodislav Yur'evich of Galich was also captured and executed,[101] but Rostislav escaped and fled to Hungary. Daniil won this resounding victory on the eve of the feat of Saints Florus and Laurus, that is, 17 August 1245.[102]

The battle at Yaroslavl' terminated the rivalry between Rostislav and Daniil for control over Galicia. By his peremptory and dramatic execution of so many of the enemy prisoners Daniil made it obvious, both to the boyars of Galicia and to the Hungarians, that he was determined to hold on to Galich at all costs. His measures achieved the desired result. The execution of the boyar Volodislav eliminated the last effective opposition to his rule in Galich itself, and the liquidation of Hungarian prisoners clearly discouraged King Béla IV from renewing hostilities.[103] Following Rostislav's defeat at Yaroslavl' in 1245, neither the Hungarians nor the Ol'govichi were able to regain possession of the principality. Daniil became the undisputed claimant in Rus' to the throne of Galich.

His victory, however, did not automatically ensure for him suzerainty over Galicia. According to the Hypatian Chronicle, one of the Tatar commanders named Moguchey sent a missive to Daniil, demanding that he "hand over Galich."[104] But Daniil did not wish to surrender "half of his patrimony." He therefore resolved to visit Khan Baty in person and set off on the feast of St. Dmitry, 26 October 1245.[105] On his way to Saray, Khan

---

[101] According to chronicle information, Volodislav oscillated in his allegiance to Daniil and to Rostislav. In 1229 he fought for Daniil (PSRL 2, col. 759). In 1231, on one occasion he is called a traitor to Daniil (PSRL 2, col. 764), and on another he is dispatched by the prince to command his forces (PSRL 2, col. 766). In 1241, however, he helped Rostislav regain control over Galich from Daniil (PSRL 2, col. 793) and in the final battle of 1245 he again sided with Rostislav. But on this occasion Daniil acted decisively. There is no previous chronicle record of Daniil executing his enemies whether they be the "princes of Bolokhov" or Galicians.

[102] PSRL 2, cols. 804-5.

[103] After the Tatar devastation of Hungary it would appear that Béla's chief objective was to repair the damage. According to Macartney, the invasion, followed by plague and starvation, cost Hungary about half of its total population (*Hungary*, p. 33). Apparently the king considered further losses such as those incurred at Yaroslavl' to be too high a price to pay at this time for control over Galicia. Instead he sought to form a marriage alliance with Daniil; see the Hypatian Chronicle (PSRL 2, col. 809).

[104] "да и Галичь" (PSRL 2, cols. 805-6); concerning this text, see Pashuto, *Ocherki*, p. 235 and Hrushevsky, *Istoriia*, vol. 3, p. 159.

[105] Probably the feast of St. Dmitry of Salonica, 26 October 1245. This date is corroborated by the account of the monk John de Plano Carpini who visited Khan Baty soon after Daniil. The monk departed from Lyons on 16 April 1245. En route he visited Germany, Bohemia and Poland. In Poland he met Vasil'ko Romanovich and was informed by the latter that his brother Daniil was visiting the khan at that time. After staying with Vasil'ko in Volyn', the monk passed through the town of Danilov, where,

Baty's capital, he stopped at the monastery of St. Michael the Archangel near Kiev. From there he proceeded to Baty's camp on the Volga river and spent twenty-five days as the guest of the khan. The visit proved to be successful; he was granted the "patent" (*yarlyk*) to rule both in Volyn' and Galicia.[106]

When Daniil received the khan's mandate to rule in Galicia, any aspirations that Mikhail still may have entertained of regaining southwest Rus' were dashed once and for all. Just as Yaroslav Vsevolodovich grand prince of Vladimir kowtowed to the khan and had been given a patent to rule in Kiev, so, too, in 1245 Daniil was given Galich. By that year, therefore, Mikhail had been deprived not only of the two principalities through the machinations of the Tatars, but his rule in his own patrimony now lay in the balance, since he had not gone yet to the khan to receive his patent. By the beginning of 1246, three years after Baty had made Yaroslav Vsevolodovich prince of Kiev, Mikhail alone of all the major princes of Rus' had not made the mandatory pilgrimage to Saray to obtain his *yarlyk*. Since he stood the chance of losing Chernigov if he did not embark upon this dangerous and humiliating mission, he resigned himself to the inevitable and set out. However, Mikhail's sojourn at Baty's court was not to be as fortunate as those of Yaroslav and Daniil had been.

* *
*

Mikhail, like his father and grandfather before him, attempted to establish the control of the Ol'govichi over Galicia. He had more success than his predecessors. In 1235 he judged, for various reasons, that the time was propitious for him to occupy Galich. First, the king of Hungary had died and his successor, Béla IV, was preoccupied with consolidating his authority over the country. Second, the victory of Mikhail and Izyaslav Vladimirovich over the Romanovichi and the Rostislavichi near Torchesk was a strong stimulus to the authority of the Ol'govichi because they defeated, at one fell swoop, their main rivals for control over southern and southwest Rus'. The final factor was the support which Mikhail was given in Galicia. After defeating Daniil he won the allegiance

---

being on the point of death, he was transported on a cart through intense cold and deep snow (John de Plano Carpini, *The Journey of Friar John of Pian de Carpini to the Court of Kuyuk Khan 1245-47 as narrated by himself*, ed. and trans., W. W. Rockhill [London, 1900], pp. 1-4). If the friar was in Danilov in the winter of 1245/6, Daniil must have departed some time after his victory at Yaroslavl' on 17 August and before the winter. The date 26 October 1245 is, therefore, most likely the correct one.

[106] The Hypatian Chronicle (PSRL 2, cols. 805-8). Daniil probably returned to Volyn' at the beginning of 1246.

of not only the majority of the boyars but also of the bishops of Galich and Peremyshl'. Given these reasons, the Ol'govichi followed up their victory over the Romanovichi by occupying both Galich, the capital town in Galicia, and Kamenets which was a stronghold of the Romanovichi on the easter border of Volyn'.

The Ol'govichi also achieved diplomatic as well as military victories over the Romanovichi. After they occupied Galich and Kamenets, Mikhail and Izyaslav attempted to consolidate their position by forming military alliances with Daniil's western neighbours. In 1236, Mikhail concluded an agreement with his uncle Conrad of Mazovia who had supported Daniil in the past. Similarly, he won the assistance of King Béla IV and used Hungarian troops to defend Galich against Daniil. Consequently, Mikhail not only deprived Daniil of his ally Vladimir Ryurikovich in southern Rus', but through diplomacy he also isolated Daniil from his foreign neighbours.

Daniil was forced to look for new allies. His desperation is illustrated by the fact that in 1236 he reached an agreement, for the first time, with the princes of Rostov-Suzdal'; they were the only family in Rus' sufficiently strong to challenge the Ol'govichi. Despite their alliance, Daniil and the Vsevolodovichi failed to take Kiev from Mikhail. Daniil also turned to the Lithuanians and to the Polovtsy for help. He instigated the former to attack Mikhail's ally Prince Conrad in Poland, and the Polovtsy, because of their allegiance to Daniil, betrayed the Ol'govichi on at least two occasions. However, Daniil's most effective support came from the townsmen of Galich. In 1234 he occupied the town after the death of Prince Andrew of Hungary, because the Galicians asked him to be their prince. Similarly, in the late 1230s, while Rostislav was away from Galich on a campaign, the townspeople invited Daniil to occupy the town during his absence. Their betrayal was the immediate cause for Daniil's return to Galich. In the long run, however, it was the Tatars who enabled him to remain there as prince.

The Tatar invasion of Rus' in the winter of 1237/8 was the most important reason why Mikhail failed to maintain his hold over southwest Rus'. After he occupied Galich in 1235 the Romanovichi were not able to regain it, first because he had the support of the local boyars and bishops and second because he could draw on resources both from Kiev where he became grand prince and from Chernigov his patrimony. It was not until Rostislav's absence from Galich sometime in 1238 that Daniil was able to occupy the town successfully. At that time the Ol'govichi made no attempt to drive him out because the Tatars had devastated Ryazan' and the lands of Rostov-Suzdal' and were preparing to invade southern Rus'. Daniil realized, therefore, that in the light of this threat to Mikhail's lands Rostislav could no longer rely on obtaining support from his father. The latter could not send to Galich troops which were needed to defend southern Rus'.

Although Mikhail attempted to strengthen his lands against the expected Tatar attack, he received no help from the other princes. As we have seen, Daniil took advantage of Mikhail's plight by occupying Galich and his ally Yaroslav Vsevolodovich, grand prince of Vladimir in Rostov-Suzdal', attacked Mikhail in Kamenets which Daniil also had lost to the Ol'govichi. If Mikhail had any hope of conscripting support from the other princes of southern Rus' it was completely shattered in 1239 when the Tatars concluded peace with three important princes. After that, in the last resort, Mikhail fled to Hungary to seek aid. When Béla IV refused to give him troops Mikhail fled to Prince Conrad in Poland.

Meanwhile, Daniil, having concluded peace with the Tatars, strengthened his position, at least for a time. Considering himself to be safe from Tatar attack, he occupied Kiev after Mikhail had fled to Hungary in the winter of 1239/40. Later he imposed his terms on the former who was a fugitive in Poland: Daniil agreed to return Kiev and Mikhail's wife whom he was holding captive, provided Mikhail renounce his claim to Galich. Control over the town, clearly, was Daniil's major concern. It is significant that, even after the Tatar invasion, Daniil was not confident that he could take Galich from the Ol'govichi.

Although Daniil was in a position to make demands from Mikhail during the years 1240 and 1241, the latter was not without support in Galicia. To be sure, after the Tatars invaded Volyn', Mikhail probably held the upper hand in southwest Rus'. The boyars who remained in Galich during the invasion of the region were, for the most part, supporters of the Ol'govichi since many of the boyars who backed Daniil had gone to Hungary. At the same time, boyars who fled from their estates in Chernigov to Galicia were given new lands by Mikhail's supporters. Consequently, even while Mikhail and Daniil were fugitives in Poland, the Ol'govichi fortified their position in southwest Rus'. But by 1242, despite the strength of the local opposition, Daniil suppressed it and drove out Rostislav from Galich for the last time.

Daniil's victory was significant not only because it gave him Galich but also because it was the occasion of Rostislav's defection to Hungary. The loss of his son was a fatal blow to Mikhail's policy. When Rostislav defected Béla IV broke his alliance with Mikhail and renewed his own claim to Galich. Rostislav's betrayal also undermined the unity of the Ol'govichi which already had suffered a severe setback in 1239. At that time Mikhail's cousin Mstislav Glebovich, the next in seniority after him and prince of Chernigov, acted contrary to his wishes by concluding peace with the Tatars. Following Mstislav's insubordination Mikhail broke the traditional order of succession and appointed his son to replace Mstislav as prince of Chernigov; in this way he hoped to re-establish the solidarity of the Ol'govichi. However, some three years later, Rostislav himself deserted his father and further weakened the unity of the family. In spite of the dissension among the Ol'govichi and despite having lost Galich, Mikhail still refused to acknowledge the overlordship of the Tatars.

His policy in Galicia suffered its ultimate blow in 1245. In that year Daniil won a resounding victory at Yaroslavl' where he defeated Rostislav and his Hungarian and Polish troops, and executed boyars who had supported the Ol'govichi in southwest Rus'. Daniil consolidated his authority over the region by going to Saray and receiving from Baty a patent to rule in Galich. His action quashed any hope Mikhail may have had of returning to the town. Seeing that he was completely at the mercy of the Tatars who had devastated his patrimony, had given Kiev to Yaroslav Vsevolodovich and had appointed Daniil to rule in Galich, Mikhail was aware that he might lose even Chernigov if he did not obtain a *yarlyk* from the khan. Therefore, he decided to go to Saray.

4

Mikhail's Death

Mikhail's trip to Saray and his execution (the latter was looked upon as a martyrdom by the Orthodox Church) became the subject of extensive writing. Only a few chronicles give brief factual entries recording his death. Most of the sources, instead, incorporate lengthy Church narratives of his martyrdom; in these his death is placed in a religious context and the few known facts are embellished with hagiographic *topoi*. For example, the oldest chronicle which contains such a narrative is the *Komissionnyy spisok* of the Novgorod First Chronicle. It begins its account with a brief historical description of the Tatar invasion, Mikhail's flight to Hungary, his return to Chernigov and his resolve to obey Baty's command to visit Saray. From this point on the narrative is laden with pious *topoi*. It explains that in preparation for the journey Mikhail is first warned of the perils which await him and after receiving spiritual counsel from his priest he also receives his blessing. When the prince and his boyar Fedor arrive in Saray they are presented to Baty and ordered to observe the usual ritual of purification and to bow to an idol. Mikhail refuses to comply with this command even though it is demanded of him in turn by Baty's sorcerers, by the latter's courtier Eldega and by his own grandson Boris Vasil'kovich of Rostov who came with him to Saray. As a symbolic gesture of his defiance and of his resolve to cast off the honours of this world, Mikhail flings his cloak at his tempters. After the Tatars execute him and his boyar Fedor a certain Doman beheads them. Their bodies are thrown away to be ravaged by dogs, but as a sign of divine favour they remain unmolested. In confirmation that the new martyrs have entered their eternal reward, God sends pillars of fire (a sign not uncommon to *Vitae* literature), which hover over their corpses.[1] Most other chronicles present variations of this narrative and, rarely, a new item of information.[2]

---

[1] NPL., s.a. 1245, pp. 298-303. This *spisok* also has a brief chronicle entry but the older *Sinodal'nyy spisok* of this source has no information concerning Mikhail's death.

[2] The narrative in the Sofiyskiy First Chronicle is almost identical with the above. However, it gives the name of Mikhail's priest – "Ivan"; it also calls his executioner

The Church narratives are of greater value as examples of medieval hagiographic literature and religious thought than as aids for establishing the historical circumstances surrounding Mikhail's death. Since they base their accounts on a comparatively few laconic details provided by the sources, it is necessary to turn to the latter in order to discover, if possible, the reasons for Mikhail's execution.

Following is the information concerning Mikhail's trip to Saray. According to the Hypatian Chronicle, which has the most detailed account, he set off from Chernigov and went to Baty to ask for permission to rule his principality. But before he was given the *yarlyk* Mikhail was ordered by the khan to worship according to the laws of his ancestors. The prince replied that God had delivered him and his lands into Baty's hands because of his sins; therefore, he would bow to the khan and pay him due homage. But Mikhail refused to worship according to the laws of Baty's ancestors since that was blasphemy before God. On hearing the rebuff Baty became enraged "like a wild beast" and peremptorily commanded that Mikhail be executed. The "lawless and godless Doman of Putivl'" killed the prince and his boyar Fedor who had accompanied him to Saray. Both men "died a martyr's death and received the crown [of glory] from Christ [who is] God."[3] Another source, the Laurentian Chronicle, adds that Mikhail was also accompanied by his grandson Boris Vasil'kovich of Rostov; the execution took place on 20 September 1246 on the feast of the martyr St. Eustace.[4]

Apart from the chronicle versions of Mikhail's death there is another source which gives added information. This is the description written by a

---

Doman a "Сѣверянинъ" (PSRL 5, s.a. 1245, pp. 230-5; the Novgorod Fourth Chronicle does not have a narrative account). The *svod* of 1479, although it has a shorter narrative, repeats the Sofiyskiy First Chronicle version (PSRL 25, pp. 136-9). The Ermolinskiy Chronicle presents a severely abbreviated account (PSRL 23, p. 81), and the L'vov Chronicle has merely a short entry (PSRL 20, p. 161). The Nikon Chronicle deviated the most from the account given by the Novgorod First Chronicle. Its introduction is more extensive and contains unique information. It states that after the Tatars sent envoys to Mikhail a second time he killed them and fled to Hungary. Although the Tatars pursued him they were unable to catch him. The narrator of this account appears to have been less interested in the historical events surrounding Mikhail's execution than in the exposition of the defence of his faith. The latter, therefore, engages in lengthy polemics with Baty's courtier Eldega and discourse eloquently – and he is told so by the latter – on his beliefs (PSRL 10, pp. 130-3).

[3] PSRL 2, col. 795. The chronicle misplaces the information under the year 1245 and fails to give a date for the event.

[4] PSRL 1, col. 471; cf. the Novgorod First Chronicle (NPL, p. 298; the *Komissionnyy spisok* has both a short chronicle entry and a narrative account, however, they give conflicting dates for the event, 18 September and 20 September respectively). Concerning the date of Mikhail's death, see below n. 7.

contemporary of the event, friar John de Plano Carpini.[5] His account is
important because, as an independent source and one not written in Rus',
it verifies the information presented in the chronicles. The friar begins his
narrative by describing how the Tatars made an idol of their first emperor,
Chingis Khan, and put it in a place of honour by the tent of the khan; they
bowed to it at noon, as to a god. Certain "illustrious per§onages" who had
been subjugated by the Tatars were compelled to do likewise. As an
example of this, the friar points out the occasion on which they insisted
that a prince of Rus', Mikhail of Chernigov, worship the idol.[6] First, as
was the custom, they made him walk between two fires. Then they
demanded that he bow to the idol of Chingis Khan at noon; but the prince
refused. He replied that, although it was fitting for him to bow to Baty and
to his servants, he would not bow to an image made of a dead man. This
was not the practice of Christians. After Mikhail persistently refused to
comply with the khan's command, Baty sent a message to him through
the "son of Yaroslav Vsevolodovich" informing him that if he did not
obey he would be executed. Despite the threat, Mikhail remained resolute.
True to his word Baty sent one of his bodyguards who kicked at Mikhail's
heart with his heel until he expired. Meanwhile, "one of Mikhail's
soldiers" (i.e., Fedor) who was looking on counselled him to persevere in
the faith. The Tatars cut off his head with a knife and then beheaded "the
soldier" who had encouraged him.[7]

---

[5] As we have seen, the Franciscan friar John de Plano Carpini, accompanied by Friar
Benedict of Poland, was sent by Pope Innocent IV to Mongolia in the hope of converting
the Tatars. The friar departed from Lyons in April 1245 and arrived in Baty's camp in
Saray in April 1246; however, it was not until his return journey from Karakorum (from
where he departed in the middle of November 1246) that he was informed of Mikhail's
execution; see G. Vernadsky, *The Mongols and Russia*, pp. 62-4.

[6] Carpini writes that according to his knowledge, the Tatars did not compel anyone to
deny his faith by bowing to this idol, that is, except for Mikhail Vsevolodovich; see A. I.
Malein ed., *Istoriya Mongalov* (Saint Petersburg, 1911), p. 8.

[7] Ibid. Unfortunately the friar does not record the date of Mikhail's death. The
chronicles are not in agreement as to whether it occurred in 1245 (the Hypatian
Chronicle, PSRL 2, col. 795 and the Novgorod First Chronicle, NPL, p. 298) or in 1246 (the
Laurentian Chronicle, PSRL 1, col. 471). Berezhkov investigates the problem of dating at
length but inconclusively (*Khronologiya*, pp. 111-2). Despite the inconsistency among the
chronicle dates, most historians who have postulated a date agree on 1246 (Karamzin,
Istoriya, vol. 4, p. 9, n. 38; Zotov, *O Chernigovskikh knyazyakh*, p. 279; Solov'ev, *Istoriya*,
book 2, p. 191; Golubinsky, *Istoriya russkoy tserkvi*, vol. 2, part 1, p. 47; Baumgarten,
Généalogies, Table IV, p. 19, no. 51 [he mistakenly gives the day as 30 September];
Nasonov, *Mongoly i Rus'*, p. 26).

It is noteworthy that in its account of Daniil Romanovich's visit to Saray the
Hypatian Chronicle states that when he arrived at the khan's court he met a certain
Sangor, Yaroslav Vsevolodovich's man (PSRL 2, col. 807). Similarly, John de Plano Carpini

Although the official cause of Mikhail's undoing was his refusal to observe a Tatar religious ritual, no doubt, the real motive for his execution was political. It has been noted that, as far as Carpini knew, Mikhail was the only foreign ruler whom the Tatars peremptorily commanded to worship the idol of Chingis Khan. Friar Benedict, the Pole who accompanied Carpini on his journey, explains that the friars were also asked to worship the idol but after they refused to do so the Tatars did not remain adamant in their demand. The friars were nevertheless obliged to bow their heads to it.[8] Given these observations, Baty's reason for insisting that Mikhail worship the idol becomes clear; similar to other Christians, he expected the prince to refuse and this would give the khan a pretext for executing him.[9]

To judge from the accounts of the two friars, Carpini and Benedict, Baty's command to Mikhail was out of the ordinary; the obeisance demanded from him was more formal than, and of a different nature to, that which was customarily expected of the princes of Rus'.[10] By placing

---

writes that when he arrived in Saray he met a son of Yaroslav Vsevolodovich who was accompanied by a soldier named Sangor (Malein, *Istoriya Mongalov*, p. 61). It was apparently this same son of Yaroslav Vsevolodovich who informed Mikhail that he would be put to death (ibid. p. 8). Finally, the Laurentian Chronicle states that in 1246 Svyatoslav and Ivan (the brothers of Yaroslav Vsevolodovich) and their nephews (presumably including this "son of Yaroslav") returned to their lands in Rus'. Immediately following this information the chronicle records Mikhail's visit and death (PSRL 1, col. 471). To judge from this sequence of events it would appear that Mikhail's death occurred while Yaroslav's son and the soldier Sangor were in Saray, that is, between the winter of 1245/6 (when they were seen by Daniil and Carpini) and some time in 1246 (before they returned to Rostov-Suzdal'). The chronicle account of Daniil's visit to Saray does not suggest that he had any knowledge of Mikhail's death. It may be presumed, therefore, that Mikhail was killed after Daniil returned home. However, since Daniil did not depart from Volyn' for Saray until 26 October 1245 (see above p. 125), and since Mikhail was killed in the month of September, the year of his death must have been 1246.

[8] See below, note 10.

[9] Malein, *Istoriya Mongalov*, p. 34.

[10] It appears that all visitors had to bow to the idol of Chingis Khan before they entered Baty's tent. Friar Benedict, the Pole who accompanied Carpini, explains how the friars were confronted with this obligation. "Beyond the fires there was a cart with a golden statue of the emperor, which it is likewise customary to worship. But the Friars refusing positively to worship it, were nevertheless obliged to bow their heads [before it]." (W. W. Rockhill ed., *The Journey of Friar John of Pian de Carpini to the Court of Kuyuk Khan 1245-47 as narrated by himself* [London, 1900], p. 35). Carpini himself admitted that "they [the Tatars] led us into the dwelling [of the khan], after having made a bow" (ibid. p. 10). The chronicles written in Rus' testify that the princes of Rus' were required to do the same. The Hypatian Chronicle states that when Daniil arrived in Saray he met Yaroslav's man Sangor. The latter informed him that Yaroslav had worshipped a "bush" (коуст) and that Daniil would be required to do the same. Strangely enough, after explaining how Daniil was spared the "Tatar's godless devilry and sorcery," the chronicler

this unusual obligation on Mikhail, one which was made only on those whom Carpini calls "illustrious personages" subject to the khan, the Tatars acknowledged Mikhail's pre-eminence in Rus'. However, the nature of their demand also shows that they wished to destroy his political effectiveness. On the one hand, if he agreed to perform the extraordinary ritual of submission, that is, to worship the golden idol at noon, he would lose face in the eyes of his countrymen as well as incur the anthema of the Orthodox Church. On the other hand, his refusal would be looked upon as political insubordination by the Tatars and would give them a legitimate pretext for executing him. The fact that Baty resorted to using this extreme measure to confirm Mikhail's allegiance shows that, in 1246, he still considered the former to be a major obstacle to Tatar rule in Rus'.

Although the chronicle does not say why the Tatars mistrusted Mikhail, reasons for their scepticism are not difficult to find. First and foremost, Mikhail was grand prince of Kiev when they invaded Rus' and this made him *de facto* their chief opponent.[11] Mikhail fortified the khan's suspicions of him by refusing to cooperate. This can be seen from his action in 1239 when, as grand prince of Kiev, he refused to listen to two embassies sent to him by Baty even though the princes of Chernigov, Smolensk and Volyn' had come to terms with the Tatars. On the second of these occasions he even had the envoys put to death.[12] Nor would his

---

says that Daniil "bowed according to their custom" ("поклонисѧ по обьчаю ихъ") and entered Baty's tent (PSRL 2, col. 807); cf. the seventeenth-century Gustinskiy Chronicle (PSRL 2, 1843 edition, p. 340). It appears that the princes of Rus' accepted as a matter of course this Tatar ritual which required them both to walk between two fires and to bow to the idol of Chingis Khan. Their willingless to comply with this demand is also emphasized in the narrative account of Mikhail's death. The version found in the *Komissionnyy spisok* of the Novgorod First Chronicle records how Boris Vasil'kovich, prince of Rostov, beseeched Mikhail, his grandfather, to obey the khan's order. The boyars of Rostov also pleaded with him and they all promised to perform the required "penance" ("епитемию") for him (NPL, p. 301).

[11] Reports found in other sources suggest that the Tatars considered Mikhail the last major political and military obstacle to be eliminated before they could effectively overrun the lands of Rus'. For example, the "*Poslanie Spiridona-Savvy*," apparently written during the reign of Vasily III (1505-33) (see R. P. Dmitrieva, *Skazanie o knyazyakh Vladimirskikh* [Moscow-Leningrad, 1955], p. 110), describes how, after the death of Mikhail of Chernigov and his boyar Fedor, the Ishmaelites (i.e., Tatars) "spilled out over the whole land" and "flew over it like birds through the air." They "butchered some Christians with their swords" and "others they led away into captivity"; those who survived the onslaught died of starvation (ibid. p. 166). Similar sentiments are found also in copies of the "Rodoslovie velikikh knyazey litovskago knyazhestva," "Zapadnorusskie letopisi" (PSRL 17 [Saint Petersburg, 1907], s.a. 1328, cols. 413-4; s.a. 1327, col. 603), and elsewhere.

[12] Golubinsky points out that, according to Carpini, it was customary for the Tatars never to conclude peace with anyone who had killed their envoys or maltreated them.

attempt to form an alliance with King Béla IV have been welcomed by the khan. Finally, Mikhail was the last senior prince of Rus' to visit Saray and acknowledge Baty as his overlord. His procrastination was unlikely to foster unquestioning trust on the part of the khan. Consequently, when he arrived in Saray in 1246, he was not given a *yarlyk* even for Chernigov his patrimony. Instead, he was executed in retribution for all his acts of defiance to the invaders.[13] Even though the Tatars camouflaged Mikhail's death behind a façade of religious controversy, Baty's motive for liquidating the grand prince of Kiev was, without a doubt, political.

Golubinsky suggests, therefore, the fact that Mikhail had the Tatar envoys put to death in 1239 may have been the reason why Baty had him executed (*Istoriya russkoy tserkvi*, vol. 2, part 1, p. 45).

[13] Nasonov was of the opinion that Yaroslav Vsevolodovich was implicated in Mikhail's death (*Mongoly i Rus'*, p. 27). It is possible that Yaroslav desired the permanent removal of Mikhail (although the chronicles give no suggestion of this), but it is difficult to find substantial evidence for his complicity. Nasonov bases his argument on the fact that the "son of Yaroslav" conveyed the verdict of death to Mikhail (ibid.). Sending Yaroslav's son on such an errand would not have been an empty gesture on the part of Baty. However, this is not sufficient proof to implicate Yaroslav in the execution (Yaroslav himself was in Karakorum at that time and died in the same month as Mikhail, 30 September); see the Laurentian Chronicle (PSRL 1, col. 471). It has been noted that both Yaroslav and Daniil had visited Baty by 1245, and that each one received a *yarlyk*. Mikhail, who had not yet visited the khan, was an embarrassment to the ambitions of these princes; (it will be remembered that Daniil and the Vsevolodovichi had formed a coalition against Mikhail in 1236). To be sure, Daniil had a stronger and more immediate motive for eliminating Mikhail as a result of their rivalry over Galicia. Daniil's determination to quash all opposition to him was made evident after his victory at Yaroslavl' in 1245. As we have seen, at that time he took the unprecedented measure of putting to death his chief opponents so as to secure control over Galicia: there can be little doubt that he also desired to remove his chief rival in Rus' – Mikhail.

Conclusion

Historians have underrated the political significance of Mikhail Vsevolodovich and the Ol'govichi in the history of Kievan Rus' during the first half of the thirteenth century. Various contentions made by them are disputable or incorrect – that the chief political centres in Rus' were the lands of Galicia-Volyn' and Rostov-Suzdal'; that the principality of Chernigov had become decentralized with only nominal ties of allegiance between its princes; that the Ol'govichi had become too weak to be of any significance in the politics of Rus'; and that Mikhail was more interested in obtaining control over Galich than Kiev.

The lands of Galicia-Volyn' and Rostov-Suzdal' were not the only centres of power in Rus' at the time of the Tatar invasion in the winter of 1237/8 even though they had been extremely strong at the beginning of the thirteenth century. At that time Roman Mstislavich became prince of Galicia as well as Volyn' thereby establishing his control over the largest principalities in west and southwest Rus'. However, his empire crumbled after his premature death in 1205. Similarly, Vsevolod Yur'evich of Vladimir assumed control over northern and northeast Rus' giving the princes of Rostov-Suzdal' an unprecedented sphere of influence over much of the land. His death in 1212 and the ensuing rivalry among his sons for the title of grand prince brought about a fragmentation of his authority also. The decline of both these powers left the Ol'govichi of Chernigov and the Rostislavichi of Smolensk in contention not only for control over southern Rus' but also for supremacy over the other families of princes. The Rostislavichi were the first to succeed by occupying Kiev and Galich. They established their pre-eminence for a decade, from 1212 until 1223, under Grand Prince Mstislav Romanovich. Then, after his death at the Kalka battle, the princes of Chernigov asserted their control under the leadership of Mikhail Vsevolodovich.

In 1235, Mikhail succeeded in destroying the last vestige of supremacy held by the Rostislavichi by defeating them and their allies, the Romanovichi of Volyn', and gaining control over Kiev. At the same time, the Ol'govichi inflicted a severe setback on the ambitions of Daniil Romanovich by occupying Galich and Kamenets. After this Mikhail ruled as grand prince of Kiev until the Tatars invaded Rus'; it was they rather than a rival prince who deprived him of the title of grand prince. Consequently, during the first half of the thirteenth century, supreme political power among the families of princes did not remain localized in one or two principalities but fluctuated from family to family. After 1212, it was the Rostislavichi who held the upper hand, and then in 1235 the Ol'govichi superseded them by establishing their authority over both the lands of Kiev and Galicia.

The principality of Chernigov was not decentralized nor were there merely nominal ties of allegiance between its princes as has been suggested. The success with which the Ol'govichi asserted their authority over their rivals bespeaks a well organized family structure. It is noteworthy that, prior to the Tatar invasion, there was only one instance in the first half of the thirteenth century, in 1226, when the internal order of the Ol'govichi was disrupted, and that after fifty years of concord. A family which was able to adhere so successfully to the tradition of lateral succession must have functioned on a closely knit system of allegiance. The chronicles not only refer to the princes of Chernigov as "brothers" who lived in concord, but give two important examples of their cooperation during Mikhail's reign. When the latter became grand prince of Kiev his cousin, and next in seniority, Mstislav Glebovich, automatically became prince of Chernigov and defended it against the Tatars in 1239. More important was the support proffered to Mikhail by Izyaslav Vladimirovich, the senior prince of the Igorevichi, princes of a cadet branch of the Ol'govichi. Izyaslav helped Mikhail assert his control over Galicia.

Historians also have argued that the prince of Chernigov had become too weak to be of any political significance in Rus' during the first half of the thirteenth century. This, as we have seen, does not appear to be a correct evaluation of the available source material. Not only was the prince of Chernigov the chief rival of the Vsevolodovichi for control over Novgorod in the late 1220s, but he also defeated the Rostislavichi in Kiev and the Romanovichi in Galich in 1235. What is more, Mikhail's success over his rivals was so overwhelming that the Romanovichi and the Vsevolodovichi – his only remaining viable opponents in the land but living in the two diametrically most distant principalities in southwest and northeast Rus' – had to form an alliance between them against the Ol'govichi, an action unprecedented in the thirteenth century. Even so, they failed to take Kiev from the princes of Chernigov.

Finally, the historian Hrushevsky argued that Mikhail was more interested in obtaining control over Galich than Kiev. This does not appear to be a correct analysis of Mikhail's policy. Rather, following the tradition of his father and grandfather, Mikhail attempted to secure the hegemony of the Ol'govichi over *all* southern and southwest Rus'. Significantly, when he initiated his expansionist policy in 1231, his aggression was directed first against Grand Prince Vladimir Ryurikovich of Kiev. By 1235, Mikhail was able to break the hold of the Rostislavichi over the "golden throne" and to make them ineffectual rivals of his authority in southern Rus'; only then did he proceed to Galich against the Romanovichi in order to establish his rule there. Furthermore, had Mikhail been more interested in Galich than in Kiev, as Hrushevsky suggested, he need not have come to the latter in 1236 after Yaroslav Vsevolodovich vacated it. Mikhail's occupation of Kiev is strong evidence that his primary objective was to secure his hold over the "golden throne" especially in view of the fact that, once in Kiev, he never returned to Galich as prince. His action supports the observation that Kiev, as well as being the ecclesiastical centre and a major emporium, was still the focus of political activity in Rus'. Finally, given the geographical position of Chernigov in relation to Galich, it would have been very difficult for the Ol'govichi to maintain their influence over the latter, without controlling the intervening principality of Kiev. From this point of view also, Kiev was of greater importance than Galich, for without it Galich was lost.

To neglect, as historians have done, the activities of the Ol'govichi, and especially of Mikhail Vsevolodovich, during the first half of the thirteenth century is a cardinal omission. It gives the historian a false picture of the period. Not only were the Ol'govichi a component part of this picture, but they were one of its most important elements. Their activities extended to Novgorod in the north and to Galicia in the southwest and, consequently, they were the only family of princes whose policy was, so to speak, "all-Rus'sian." The Vsevolodovichi and the Romanovichi confined their interests to the regions of northern and southwest Rus' respectively. Mikhail's activity, therefore, was more in tune with the traditional policy of the grand prince of Kiev in that he attempted to maintain Kiev as the political, commercial and ecclesiastical centre, one whose influence extended to all the regions of Rus'. Since his ambitions encroached upon the interests of both the Vsevolodovichi and the Romanovichi, he pre-vented them from becoming too parochial in their outlooks; they were forced to keep a watchful eye on southern Rus' and his expansionist activities there. In 1235, his successes compelled them to relegate their regional activities to the background and to occupy Kiev in an abortive attempt to weaken his authority.

Although the Vsevolodovichi and the Romanovichi failed to destroy the pre-eminence of the Ol'govichi, their task was accomplished for them by the Tatars. The destruction of Chernigov, the sack of Kiev and, finally, the execution of Mikhail in Saray freed the Vsevolodovichi and the Romanovichi of the one internal threat to their autonomy. After Mikhail's death, and under the overlordship of the Tatars, they concentrated their energies on Novgorod and Galich thus bifurcating the lands of Rus' into two separate spheres of interest. Meanwhile, the principality of Kiev with its symbolic "golden throne," which had served as the unifying element for the families of princes in Kievan Rus' until the Tatar invasion, in effect, became a political vacuum to be filled, eventually, by the Lithuanians.

Epilogue

The peers of Mikhail Vsevolodovich must have looked upon his execution as the ultimate failure which could befall a prince, but the Orthodox Church in Rus' regarded it as a victory over paganism, a triumph which won for him a martyr's crown and eternal salvation. Had he not died defending the faith, later generations would have remembered him merely as the grand prince who defended Rus' at the time of the Tatar invasion in 1237/8. But, by the fact that he was beheaded because, as an Orthodox Christian, he refused to bow to a golden idol of Chingis Khan, he became the first martyr of Kievan Rus'; this distinction won for him universal renown.[1] He was a perdurable reminder to the faithful of Tatar

---

[1] Prince Mikhail was the first "martyr" of Rus' in the traditionally accepted meaning of the term, that is, "one who undergoes [the] penalty of death for persistence in [his] Christian faith or obedience to [the] law of the Church" (*The Concise Oxford Dictionary*). The Orthodox Church, however, has another category of "martyr" called "passion-sufferer" (*strastoterpets*). Although this term is used generally to apply to all martyrs, it refers specifically to those Christians who suffered a violent death at the hands of their fellow Christians as victims of perfidy and treachery; consequently, the fact that they were Christians was not the primary reason for their death. Examples of *strastoterptsy* are Saints Boris and Gleb who were killed by their older brother Svyatopolk in 1015 during the course of a power struggle for control over Kiev (see E. Golubinsky, *Istoriya kanonizatsii svyatykh v Russkoy tserkvi* [Moscow, 1903], pp. 43-9); similarly, Prince Igor' Ol'govich of Chernigov who was killed by the citizens of Kiev for political reasons in 1147 was later venerated as a saint (ibid. p. 58). Other princes, contemporaries of Mikhail Vsevolodovich, were killed by the Tatars in the winter of 1237/8 while defending their principalities; they were also canonized but do not fall into the category of martyr: for example, Vasil'ko Konstantinovich of Rostov (Mikhail's son-in-law), Grand Prince Yury Vsevolodovich of Vladimir (Mikhail's brother-in-law) and Merkury of Smolensk (ibid. pp. 140-1). It is interesting to note that Yaroslav Vsevolodovich, Mikhail's chief rival in northern Rus', was apparently poisoned by the Tatars on his return journey from their capital Karakorum and died ten days after Mikhail on 30 September 1246; see the Laurentian Chronicle (PSRL 1, col. 471), and Nasonov, *Mongoly i Rus'*, p. 32. But the Church never elevated him to the status of martyr or saint. There is an entry in the Laurentian Chronicle, under the year 1229, which states that a certain Avraamy was martyred by the Volga Bulgars and in the following year buried in a monastery in Vladimir. However, the chronicler explains, he was not a native of Rus' (PSRL 1, col. 452; Golubinsky, *Istoriya kanonizatsii*, p. 62). For a detailed discussion of the two groups of canonized princes, i.e. those venerated for religious reasons and those venerated for secular reasons, see M. Cherniavsky, "Saintly Princes and Princely Saints," *Tsar and People* (New Haven: Yale University Press, 1961), pp. 5-43.

tyranny; more important, he was a paragon of Orthodoxy in the face of pagan persecution.

The cult of Mikhail and his boyar Fedor, or "The Miracle-Workers of Chernigov" as they were known,[2] soon rivalled that of the most illustrious saints of Kievan Rus' – St. Ol'ga, St. Vladimir (the Christianizer of Rus'), his sons the *strastoterptsy* Boris and Gleb (the first canonized saints of Rus') and the monks Antony and Feodosy (the founders of the Monastery of the Caves in Kiev). Unfortunately, little is known about the initial period of the cult of Saints Mikhail and Fedor. Soon after their martyrdom they became venerated locally, but this practice was not confined merely to Chernigov. There is reason to believe that several centres, independently of each other, commemorated the memory of the former grand prince of Kiev. Thus in southern Rus', as well as Chernigov, he was venerated in Pereyaslavl' where he had undergone a cure as a child. In some places Mikhail was worshipped as a local saint because of his former political involvement – in Kiev and Novgorod for example. His reign in Galicia had been supported by the bishops of Galich and Peremyshl'. They, no doubt, commemorated his martyrdom in these towns.

Mikhail's relatives, as we shall see, were also instrumental in promulgating his cult. His daughter Maria, the princess of Rostov, conscientiously strove to preserve the memory of her father in her own principality. His other daughter Feodula became the nun Evfrosinia in Suzdal'; according to her "Life" (*Zhitie*), she took an active part in her father's martyrdom and this belief was preserved in local tradition. These towns, as well as others, became the centres of local worship of Saints Mikhail and Fedor and gradually turned into focal points for the dissemination of their cult.

There has survived what appears to be a reference to the original promulgation of the feast of "The Miracle-Workers of Chernigov." According to one source, a few years after Mikhail's martyrdom his daughter Maria (who married Prince Vasil'ko Konstantinovich of Rostov in 1227) and her two sons Boris and Gleb built a church in his honour; they "arranged to celebrate the feast on 20 September ... on the day they [Mikhail and Fedor] suffered for Christ."[3] Thus Mikhail's feast was

---

[2] Both, chronicle narrative accounts and Church religious literature, almost always speak of Mikhail in the company of his boyar Fedor. In Church narrative literature they are frequently referred to as "The Miracle-Workers of Chernigov" (*Chernigovskie chudotvortsy*) or "The Martyrs of Chernigov" (*Chernigovskie strastoterptsy*).

[3] Serebryansky, *Zhitiya*, Texts, p. 51; see also p. 111. As for miracles – a prerequisite for canonization – only three associated with the saints have been recorded. The first occurred immediately after their martyrdom. According to the narrative account found

entered into the Church calendar in Rostov soon after his execution, and before 1271, the year of Maria's death.[4] Similarly, even though there is no record of it, we may assume that Mikhail's widow and his sons instituted the commemoration of his feast in the principality of Chernigov, perhaps on the occasion of, or soon after, the translation of his relics from Saray.

To judge from various sources, the cult of the two martyrs burgeoned and soon assumed national dimensions. In the years 1547 and 1549 Metropolitan Makary (1542-63) convoked two Church councils in Moscow for the specific purpose of canonizing the saints of Kievan Rus' and Muscovy. His intention was not so much to name new saints as to affirm the canonical position of those who were already venerated locally. The councils either elevated the feasts of local saints to national status or, in some instances, merely confirmed already existing cults. Significantly, no mention was made of the traditionally established feasts of national saints such as St. Ol'ga, St. Vladimir, Saints Boris and Gleb, Saints Antony and Feodosy and Saints Mikhail and Fedor.[5] The national status of Mikhail's feast was confirmed ten years after the first council, in 1557, when Tsar Ivan IV sent a list of princes of Rus' to the Patriarch of Constantinople requesting that "these, the most worthy of saints," be commemorated in Church services (*molebnekh*), namely, St. Vladimir, Saints Boris and Gleb, St. Mikhail of Chernigov and others.[6] Some ten years after this request the tsar and the metropolitan ordered that the relics of "The Miracle-Workers of Chernigov" be brought to Moscow. On this occasion, the Church instituted a second feast to honour the event.[7]

The momentous occasion of the translation of their relics serves as uncontestable proof of the popularity which their cult had attained by the

---

in the Novgorod First Chronicle, after their heads were cut off "God glorified His new martyrs" by sending pillars of fire which hovered over their bodies (NPL, p. 303). The other miracles were recorded in the "Life" of his daughter St. Evfrosinia: Mikhail and Fedor appeared to her in her sleep immediately after their martyrdom and proclaimed to her the good news of their glorification; just before her death the two saints appeared to her again (Georgievsky, "Zhitie," pp. 168 and 170). The veracity of these accounts is questionable since the nature of the miracles described falls more readily into the category of literary *topoi*. However, even though records of miracles performed through the intercession of the two martyrs are not available, there can be little doubt that miracles did occur given the fact that Saints Mikhail and Fedor are sometimes called "The Miracle-Workers of Chernigov."

[4] Serebryansky, *Zhitiya*, p. 111; Baumgarten, *Généalogies*, Table XII, no. 2, p. 54.
[5] Golubinsky, *Istoriya kanonizatsii*, pp. 99-104.
[6] Ibid. p. 565.
[7] Makary, Mitropolit Moskovskiy, *Istoriya russkoy tserkvi*, vol. 8 (Saint Petersburg, 1898), p. 32.

middle of the sixteenth century. It was not a matter of small import that Mikhail, a prince of southern Rus' and an Ol'govich, was honoured with the unique distinction of being buried in the Kremlin of Moscow – the royal repository of the princes of Muscovy, the descendants of Vladimir *Monomakh* and the traditional rivals of the princes of Chernigov. However, before Mikhail's and Fedor's remains arrived in their final resting place they underwent a long odyssey.

Initially, the bodies of "The Miracle-Workers of Chernigov" were brought from Saray to Chernigov where they were placed in the Cathedral of the Transfiguration. They were entombed in a side-chapel dedicated to their honour to the right of the main altar.[8] Over three hundred years later, in the 1570s, their relics were translated to Moscow at the request of Tsar Ivan IV, Metropolitan Antony and the Church council;[9] they were brought to the capital on 14 February.[10] The metropolitan, the bishops and the faithful of the city came out in solemn procession to meet "The Martyrs of Chernigov" and carried them to their new repository, a cathedral built especially in their honour.[11]

The symbolism of this historic act had political as well as religious connotations. Even though the rivalry between the princely families of the Monomashichi and the Ol'govichi had become a memory by the middle of the sixteenth century, the transfer of Mikhail's relics from Chernigov to Moscow served to symbolize not only the disappearance of those

---

[8] Filaret, *Opisanie*, vol. 5, pp. 4-5, 10. According to Khavsky, the relics were first brought to Vladimir in Rostov-Suzdal' and then transferred to Chernigov where they were to remain for some 330 years (*Istoricheskoe issledovanie*, p. 51).

[9] There is some discrepancy among Church historians concerning the year in which the relics arrived in Moscow. Some say it was in 1578 (Makary, *Istoriya*, vol. 8, pp. 31-2; Barsukov, *Istochniki*, col. 374); Golubinsky says the date was 1575 (*Istoriya russkoy tserkvi*, vol. 2, part 1, p. 47); others give 1572 (Filaret, *Opisanie*, vol. 5, p. 5; Khavsky, *Istoricheskoe issledovanie*, p. 51; *Entsiklopedicheskiy slovar'*, F. A. Brokgauz and I. A. Efron [Saint Petersburg, 1890-1907], vol. XIXa, p. 487).

[10] Khavsky, *Istoricheskoe issledovanie*, p. 51; Makary, *Istoriya*, vol. 8, p. 32; Barsukov, *Istochniki*, col. 373; D. A. Eristov, *Slovar' istoricheskiy o svyatykh proslavlennykh v rossiyskoy tserkvi* (Saint Petersburg, 1836), p. 190. According to Filaret, part of the relics remained in Chernigov. In the last quarter of the nineteenth century they were kept in the sacristy of the archbishop's palace in the *Il'inskiy* Monastery in Chernigov (*Opisanie*, vol. 2, p. 47).

[11] Makary claims that this cathedral was located "below the pine forest beyond the river" (*Istoriya*, vol. 8, p. 32). Others believe that it was situated in the Kremlin: see Golubinsky, *Istoriya russkoy tserkvi*, vol. 2, part 1, p. 47; Eristov, *Slovar'*, p. 190. According to Khavsky the martyrs were buried near the *Tainitskiy* Tower. In 1681, when their church was undergoing repairs, they were transferred to the Cathedral of St. Michael the Archangel until 1683 (*Istoricheskoe issledovanie*, p. 51).

conflicts, but also the political continuity between Kievan Rus' and Muscovy. Furthermore, the remains of the great national saints – St. Ol'ga, St. Vladimir, Saints Boris and Gleb, Saints Antony and Feodosy – hidden for safekeeping before the advancing pagan hordes, were never recovered. Consequently, "The Miracle-Workers of Chernigov" also served as a tangible witness to the continuity of religious beliefs between pre-Tatar Rus' and post-Tatar Muscovy.

It is significant that Ivan IV acted in concord with the metropolitan in bringing the relics to Moscow. Just as, some three hundred years previously, Mikhail's martyrdom heralded the arrival of Tatar oppression, this unprecedented gesture signalled the beginning of a new era in the history of Muscovy. The relics were brought to Moscow by Ivan IV who defeated the Tatars of Kazan' and Astrakhan' in the early 1550s. These victories avenged Mikhail, the paragon of Orthodox resistance to the pagans. The tsar and the metropolitan no doubt wished to demonstrate their respect to Mikhail for his opposition to the Tatars by bringing his remains to the capital of the "new" Muscovy, one that was free from religious persecution. However, the cathedral built in honour of "The Miracle-Workers of Chernigov" in the middle of the sixteenth century was not to remain the permanent repository of their relics.

Some two hundred years later, on 25 August 1770, when the cathedral was demolished, their remains were transferred to the Cathedral of the Purification (*Sretenskiy sobor*).[12] But, four years later, on 21 November, they were moved once again, this time to their final abode, the Cathedral of St. Michael the Archangel (*Arkhangel'skiy sobor*). On this occasion they were entombed in a silver "shrine" (*raka*) cast by a certain Peter Robert. It had been commissioned by Empress Catherine II in gratitude to the saints for their intercession in helping her conclude peace with Turkey.[13] Finally, in 1812, after the Napoleonic invasion of Moscow at which time the silver shrine was apparently pillaged, the relics were placed in a bronze tomb[14] and soon after taken away from public view and placed

[12] Khavsky, *Istoricheskoe issledovanie*, p. 51; Eristov, *Slovar'*, p. 190; Golubinsky, *Istoriya russkoy tserkvi*, vol. 2, part 1, p. 47.

[13] Peace was concluded on 10 July 1774; on 14 October she requested Bishop Samuil of Krutitsy, later the metropolitan of Kiev, to transfer the relics from the *Sretenskiy sobor* to the Cathedral of St. Michael the Archangel. They were placed by the second column on the right side of the cathedral (Khavsky, *Istoricheskoe issledovanie*, pp. 51, 77-9). Catherine II ordered that her main achievements be recorded around the silver shrine; however, the year 1244 was erroneously inscribed on the tomb rather than 1246 (Eristov, *Slovar'*, p. 190).

[14] Khavsky, *Istoricheskoe issledovanie*, p. 51; *Entsiklopedicheskiy slovar'*, vol. XIXa, p. 487.

beneath the cathedral.[15] Thus, after almost six hundred years of peregrinations, "The Miracle-Workers of Chernigov" found their permanent home in the most illustrious repository in Russia. However, it did not take their sacred memory nearly as long to become ensconced in the religious beliefs of the faithful.

Saints Mikhail and Fedor, especially during the two centuries of Tatar domination immediately following their martyrdom, were invoked repeatedly by the people of Rus' and Muscovy against their pagan oppressors. Their popularity as intercessors is attested to by the fact that they were soon included in the official prayers of the Church. For example, they were among the saints named in the opening prayer before the liturgy in a "service-book" (*sluzhebnik*) written before the end of the fourteenth century or at the beginning of the fifteenth century in Novgorod.[16] The "rule" (*ustav*) of The Holy Trinity Monastery of Zagorsk, written in 1429, contains short liturgical hymns to be sung on the feast of Saints Mikhail and Fedor.[17] Most significant is the fact that over twenty copies of the "service" (*sluzhba*) written in their honour, dating from the fifteenth to the seventeenth centuries, were found preserved in various libraries of northern Russia.[18] Finally, according to the rule of 1621 from the Cathedral of the Assumption of the Mother of God in the Kremlin of Moscow, their feast was one of six celebrated with special solemnity in the month of September.[19]

To appreciate better the import of these samplings of early liturgical prayers in honour of the two martyrs it is necessary to keep in mind the nature of the Church's veneration of national saints prior to the appearance of printed service-books in the seventeenth century. According to the instructions accompanying the institution of the feast of St. Kornily Komel'skiy in 1600, it was to be commemorated with a "vesper service" (*vechernaya*), with "nocturnal singing" (*vsenoshchnoe penie*) and the liturgy, in the Cathedral of the Assumption of the Mother of God in Moscow as well as in the cathedral churches of all the metropolitanates, archbishoprics and bishoprics in the land.[20] Local parishes were excluded from this obligation owing to the fact, no doubt, that they did not have the necessary liturgical prayer-books. Since the latter contained only few

[15] Golubinsky, *Istoriya kanonizatsii*, p. 63.
[16] Makary, *Istoriya*, vol. 4 (Saint Petersburg, 1886), p. 264.
[17] Ibid.
[18] Barsukov, *Istochniki*, cols. 378-9.
[19] Golubinsky, *Istoriya russkoy tserkvi*, p. 412.
[20] Ibid. p. 226.

commemorations of Rus'sian saints in any case, the cathedral churches probably had separate copies of prayers, the liturgy and "Lives" of these saints. Thus, it is noteworthy not only that two such exemplars of prayers to Saints Mikhail and Fedor have survived in manuscripts from the end of the fourteenth century and the beginning of the fifteenth century, but that there are also over twenty copies of the special service in their honour preserved from the fifteenth to the seventeenth centuries.[21] The national dimensions of their feast are attested to not only by Orthodox liturgical services but also by the tsar's observance of the cult.

There is evidence that various sovereigns cultivated a devotion to "The Martyrs of Chernigov." It has already been noted that Tsar Ivan iv had a special reverence for them since he ordered that their relics be transferred to the capital in the 1570s. However, there is written testimony of his devotion even prior to that event. For example, in 1552, before he invaded Kazan', the tsar beseeched God to come to his aid and to intercede on behalf of all the "miracle-workers" of the Church, including the "great martyrs Prince Mikhail of Chernigov and his boyar Fedor."[22] At the same time, on the eve of the tsar's ultimate victory over the Tatars, a victorious icon was painted in his honour, entitled "The Blessed Host" (*Blagoslovennoe voinstvo*). Ivan was portrayed entering the "heavenly Jerusalem" accompanied by all the "warrior-saints" of Rus', including Saints Mikhail and Fedor.[23] In 1557, as already noted, he sent a missive to the Patriarch of Constantinople requesting the latter to commemorate the sacred memory of the most venerated princes of Rus' including Mikhail of Chernigov. Other sources, under 1563, state that Ivan iv gave thanks to God for His many graces and for the many saints with whom He had blessed the land including Saints Mikhail and Fedor.[24]

Some one hundred years later they were still the objects of special devotion by the tsar. This is exemplified by one recorded instance from 1670. In that year, as Tsar Alexis i was not able to leave his residence on 20 September to venerate their remains in the cathedral built in their

---

[21] Concerning the various redactions and "copies" (*spiski*) of "Lives" still extant from various churches and monasteries of Russia, see below pp. 151-154.

[22] "Kazanskiy letopisets" (psrl 19 [Saint Petersburg, 1903], col. 412).

[23] See O. I. Podobedova, *Moskovskaya shkola zhivopisi pri Ivane iv* (Moscow, 1972), p. 26 and V. I. Antonova and N. E. Mneva, *Katalog drevnerusskoy zhivopisi*, vol. 2 (Moscow, 1963), pp. 129, 132-3.

[24] The Nikon Chronicle (psrl 13 [Saint Petersburg, 1904], pp. 360-1); the "Lebedevskaya letopis'" (psrl 29 [Moscow, 1965], pp. 314-5); the "Aleksandronevskaya letopis'" (rib, vol. 3, col. 126).

honour, he had the relics brought to his private chapel.[25] This suggests
that the tsars ordinarily venerated the two saints on their feast in the
cathedral where they lay entombed. Finally, it has been noted that
Catherine II invoked their intercession to help bring negotiations with
Turkey to a successful conclusion. Although the saints were venerated
officially through the liturgy of the Church and publicly by the rulers of
the country, their cult was reflected also in other ways in the religious life
of the faithful.

"The Miracle-Workers of Chernigov" became popular subjects of
Church art especially icons; iconographers were given detailed instructions for painting them. One "iconographers' handbook" (*ikonopisnyy
podlinnik*) gives the following directions. Mikhail's hair is light brown and
curly; his beard is similar to that of John the Precursor but has streaks of
gray. He wears a rose coloured (damask) fur coat and his upper garment is
sky-blue coloured with vermilion and white. His lower garment is sky-
blue and damask. He holds a cross in his right hand while his left hand
rests on his sword which is sheathed in its scabbard. Fedor, on the other
hand, has gray hair which is slightly curly around his ears; his beard is
longer than that of St. Athanasius and is also wider. He, like the prince, is
wearing a fur coat; his top garment is light blue and damask in colour, but
his lower garment is vermilion. In his hands, which are to be portrayed in
a praying position, he holds a church. However, in some icons, according
to the *podlinnik*, he holds a cross in one hand while the other rests on a
sheathed sword.[26]

Another handbook, the *Stroganovskiy ikonopisnyy litsevoy podlinnik*,
gives similar instructions under 20 September. However, it states that
Fedor holds a cross. In the illustration accompanying these instructions
the heads of both martyrs are surrounded with an aureole and Mikhail
also wears a crown. The two saints face each other with the prince
standing on the left. Their left hands rest on their sheathed swords while
both of them hold their right hand upraised.[27] The icons were often
decorated with gold, silver and precious stones.[28] Other icons commemo-

[25] Golubinsky, *Istoriya kanonizatsii*, p. 541; according to the monthly manuals
(*mesyatseslovy ustavov*) of 1682 and 1695, their feast continued to be celebrated with
festive solemnity in the Kremlin in the cathedral where their bodies lay preserved (ibid.
pp. 243-4).

[26] Barsukov, *Istochniki*, col. 373.

[27] See illustration no. 1; cf. illustration no. 2 and frontispiece.

[28] For example, in the eighteenth century, the Church of the Purification of Our Lord
in the convent dedicated to The Deposition of the Precious Robe of the Theotokos at
Blachernae in Suzdal' (i.e., the convent where Mikhail's daughter Feodula had been a

rate the transfer of their relics from Chernigov to Moscow and, as
noted above, the martyrs are also among the "warrior-saints" portrayed
accompanying Tsar Ivan ιν in the icon entitled "The Blessed Host"
(*Blagoslovennoe voinstvo*).[29]

Saints Mikhail and Fedor were also represented in religious miniature
painting. A series of miniatures portraying the saints has survived in the
form of illustrations for the account of the *Zhitie* of St. Evfrosinia
(Mikhail's daughter Feodula). Mikhail, and in some instances Fedor too,
appears in twelve miniatures; more than half depict him in various stages
of Evfrosinia's life before her betrothal. However, several of them are
associated with his martyrdom. One scene depicts Mikhail giving the
order to kill the Tatar envoys who came to him in Kiev. Another portrays
him and his boyar "exposing Baty's dishonesty." The miniature which
illustrates their martyrdom is divided into two scenes, an upper and a
lower. The top picture depicts Baty in his tent giving the order to kill the
two saints; the bottom scene shows Tatar soldiers executing the martyrs
in the centre of a black landscape. Baty is depicted standing in the
background, to one side, surrounded by his entourage. The last two
miniatures illustrate episodes occurring after the execution. In one, the
martyrs appear to Evfrosinia immediately after their martyrdom while, in
the other, they appear to her at a later date, as she lies dying on her bed.[30]
Aside from icons and miniatures, "The Martyrs of Chernigov" were
portrayed in frescoes and on various liturgical objects and vessels as, for
example, on the enamels of a chalice owned by the *Il'inskiy* Monastery in
Chernigov.[31]

The most monumental method used by the Orthodox faithful to
commemorate the memory of its miracle workers was, of course, in the
building of churches. Unfortunately, it is difficult to determine how many
churches were dedicated to Mikhail since most of them no doubt, were
built from wood and would have existed from only three to four
generations. However, as has been mentioned, a chapel was dedicated to
his honour by the people of Chernigov in the Cathedral of the Transfiguration, the most illustrious church in the principality. A record has

nun), had an icon of Saints Mikhail and Fedor. According to the inventory of the convent
made in 1771, the icon had two silver crowns mounted over the heads of the saints (see
"Arkhivnye materialy (opisi, gramoty, ukazy, i pr.), – prilozhenie k opisaniyu Rizpolo-
zhenskago monastyrya," *Trudy Vladimirskoy uchenoy arkhivnoy kommissii*, book 2
[Vladimir, 1900], p. 45).

[29] Podobedova, *Moskovskaya shkola*, p. 26; Antonova, *Katalog*, vol. 2, pp. 129, 132-3.
[30] Georgievsky, "Zhitie," pp. 154-70; see illustrations nos. 3 and 4.
[31] Filaret, *Opisanie*, vol. 2, p. 48.

Illustration No. 1. An example of an icon of Saints Mikhail and Fedor given for iconographers in the *Stroganovskiy ikonopisnyy litsevoy podlinnik* (see p. 147).

Illustration No. 2. Icon of Saints Mikhail and Fedor of unknown origin.

Illustration No. 3. Saints Mikhail and Fedor depicted "exposing Baty's dishonesty." Miniature No. 40 from the "Life" of St. Evfrosinia (see p. 148).

Illustration No. 4. Miniature with two scenes: the top scene depicts Baty giving the order to execute Saints Mikhail and Fedor; the bottom scene shows Tatar soldiers cutting off the heads of the martyrs. Miniature No. 42 from the "Life" of St. Evfrosinia (see p. 148).

also been preserved from 1691, which states that a certain *voevoda* of Chernigov built a wooden church in his honour but it was demolished in 1766 because of its age.[32] Some fifty years later, in 1805, a stone church was built in Mikhail's honour in the seminary of Chernigov thus demonstrating the continuing tradition of faithful veneration of two of the most illustrious saints of the city.[33] However, this devotion was not confined to the boundaries of the prince's own patrimony. It appears that even as late as the nineteenth century an "ancient stone chapel" stood preserved near southern Pereyaslavl' on the spot where, according to tradition, Mikhail was cured of an infirmity and where he later erected a cross.[34]

Churches were built in honour of Saints Mikhail and Fedor in northeast Rus' as well, and the chief centres appear to have been Rostov, Suzdal' and Moscow. As has been noted, Mikhail's daughter Maria, princess of Rostov, dedicated a church to his memory on the occasion of the promulgation of his feast.[35] It appears that the cult of Mikhail was also popular in Suzdal' especially in the convent dedicated to "The Deposition of the Precious Robe of the Theotokos at Blachernae" (*Rizpolozhenskiy monastyr'*) where his second daughter Feodula had been a nun. Information from the seventeenth century states that there was a chapel dedicated to Saints Mikhail and Fedor in the wooden church of "The Miraculous Apparition of the Mother of God" (*Znamenie Bogoroditsy*).[36] In the middle of the sixteenth century, a cathedral bearing the name of "The Miracle-Workers of Chernigov" was built in Moscow where their relics were laid to rest with due ceremony.[37] Records from the beginning of the seventeenth century state that a church dedicated to them was located "beyond the river";[38] according to one source it was still standing in 1915.[39]

The prince-martyr became the ideal, the champion, the model, the protector and intercessor for the faithful of the Orthodox Church. That

[32] M. E. Markov, "O dostopamyatonostyakh Chernigova," *Chteniya*, no. 1 (Moscow, 1847), p. 20; cf. Filaret, *Opisanie*, vol. 5, p. 67.

[33] Filaret, *Opisanie*, vol. 5, p. 67.

[34] I. P. Sakharov, *Zapiski dlya obozreniya russkikh drevnostey* (Saint Petersburg, 1851), p. 36, n. 65.

[35] Serebryansky, *Zhitiya*, Texts, p. 51; see also p. 111.

[36] See "Arkhivnye materialy," *Trudy Vladimirskoy uchenoy arkhivnoy kommissii*, book 2, p. 7.

[37] See above p. 143.

[38] Khavsky, *Drevnost' Moskvy*, p. 127, no. 311.

[39] According to M. Aleksandrovsky this church was located on the *Chernigovskiy pereulok* (*Ukazatel' Moskovskikh tserkvey* [Moscow, 1915], p. 17, no. 106).

Mikhail was the ideal and protector of soldiers is seen from the fact that, at the end of the seventeenth century, the resident soldiers and archers of the fortification in the "small upper town" in Chernigov requested their *voevoda* to build a church in his honour.[40] A similar incident shows that he was also venerated as the champion of the faith. In 1805, a chapel was built to Mikhail in the seminary of Chernigov, the centre of Orthodox faith and worship in the principality, the institution which produced the future proponents of the faith. He was also looked upon as the model to whom princes who had led saintly lives or those who had been martyred were compared. For example, Roman Ol'govich of Ryazan', killed by the Tatars on 19 July 1270, is compared to his relative Mikhail, with whom he now shared the crown of martyrdom.[41] Similarly, when Mikhail Yaroslavich of Tver' was executed by the Tatars in 1318, the chronicler praised him for winning the crown of martyrdom just as his namesake Mikhail of Chernigov had done before him.[42] Finally, in his *History of the Grand Prince of Moscow*, Prince Kurbsky described how various descendants of Mikhail Vsevolodovich killed by Tsar Ivan IV emulated his virtuous example.[43]

Church narrative literature, of course, was the most popular medium used by the faithful for extolling the sanctity of Prince Mikhail. There are two unique accounts. One narrative records an early episode in the prince's life. It describes a miraculous cure which he underwent as a boy through the intercession of the stylite Nikita of Pereyaslavl' in southern Rus'. The account is presented in the form of a triptych; it opens with a description of Mikhail's ailment and an explanation of how God allowed the youth to become afflicted with a malady which enfeebled him and for which he could not obtain a cure. When he was informed of the miraculous cures performed through the intercession of the stylite in Pereyaslavl', he set off to seek his aid. The second part of the narrative explains that before he reached the holy man Mikhail was subjected to three temptations in imitation of Christ's temptations by Satan. He reached Nikita only after successfully renouncing the devil who tempted him

[40] Markov, "O dostopamyatnostyakh Chernigova," p. 20.

[41] The Trinity Chronicle (TL, p. 330); "Simeonovskaya letopis'" (PSRL 18 [Saint Petersburg, 1913], p. 73).

[42] The *svod* of 1479 (PSRL 25, p. 165); see B. A. Kuchkin, *Povesti o Mikhaile Tverskom* (Moscow, 1974), p. 252.

[43] He mentions Petr Obolensky-Serebryany, Aleksandr Ivanovich Yaroslavov, Vladimir Konstantinovich Kurlyatev, Nikita Romanovich Odoevsky and Mikhail Ivanovich Vorotynsky, all descendants of Mikhail of Chernigov (J. L. I. Fennell ed., *Prince A. M. Kurbsky's History of Ivan IV* [Cambridge, 1965], pp. 182-5; 195-201).

under various guises. Finally, after he was cured, the prince ordered that a cross be erected on the site of the miracle as a reminder of God's loving kindness.[44]

The second unique account is a description of Mikhail's death given in the *Zhitie* of St. Evfrosinia. It explains that his daughter, a nun in Suzdal', played a salutary role in his martyrdom. When Evfrosinia was in her convent she was informed of her father's trial in Saray and that he was on the verge of succumbing to the khan's demands to worship the golden idol. Horrified lest her father weaken in his resolve, she wrote "books" (*knigi*) to him, endeavouring to dissuade him from capitulating to the pagan demands and entreating him to persevere in his faith. She pleaded that he refuse to listen to the "friend of the devil," Prince Boris Vasil'kovich of Rostov (her nephew), but heed the wise counsel of his boyar Fedor, who was a "philosopher's philosopher." Mikhail, the *Zhitie* explains, received his daughter's "books" in time and, inspired by her admonition, persevered in the faith and won the crown of glory.[45]

By far the most popular example of Church narrative literature concerning Mikhail was his "Life" – more correctly an explication of his martyrdom – describing his trip to Saray and his execution. Unfortunately, a detailed analysis of all available manuscript material has not yet been made. N. Serebryansky who has completed the most comprehensive study of these sources to date, surveyed over ninety copies of narrative accounts and divided them into four categories: brief Prologue[46] entries of Saints Mikhail and Fedor; short Prologue "Lives"; "disseminated Prologue narrative accounts" (*rasprostranennyya prolozhnyya skazaniya*) and the detailed "Life" written by the monk Pakhomy[47] with its variants.[48]

There are two versions of short Prologue entries: the older redaction which was also more widely used, and the late sixteenth-century

[44] "Kniga stepennaya" (PSRL 21, pp. 248-9); cf. "Mazurinskiy letopisets" (PSRL 31, p. 65).

[45] Georgievsky, "Zhitie," pp. 116-8.

[46] The Prologue was a collection of saints "Lives" arranged according to the days of the year. It was probably translated in the twelfth century from the original Greek into Slavic and soon enriched with new material – both translated and Slavic. As well as saints "Lives," it came to include individual moralizing tales, aphorisms, maxims, homilies by the Fathers of the Church and similar materials.

[47] Pakhomy Logofet was a Serbian monk and a professional scribe. He arrived in Novgorod around 1430 and was invited to The Holy Trinity Monastery in Zagorsk in 1440. He worked in Moscow between 1461 and 1462, and in the Monastery of the White Lake (Beloozero) between 1462 and 1463. He died at the age of seventy-six, before 1484.

[48] The following presentation of Church narrative accounts of Mikhail's *Zhitie* is a summary of the conclusions reached by Serebryansky (*Zhitiya*, pp. 108-41).

redaction of which there is only one copy. These entries which are relatively few, at best, contained sparse information concerning the martyrs. The older redaction was not written at the time of the martyrdom nor was it made by an eyewitness.[49] Although the two versions have no unique information, they serve to illustrate the nature of the literature written concerning "The Martyrs of Chernigov" from the fourteenth to the sixteenth century.

Serebryansky divides the copies of the short Prologue "Lives" into three redactions: the Rostov, the "all-Rus'sian" and the "unique." The Rostov redaction is of special interest because it is the first Church narrative account of Mikhail's martyrdom. It was commissioned by his daughter, Maria, the princess of Rostov, and her two sons, Boris and Gleb, in conjunction with the promulgation of Mikhail's feast and with the dedication of a church in his honour. The author was not an eye-witness but, apparently, obtained his information from such people as Prince Boris, Mikhail's grandson, who accompanied him to Saray. This account was written before the 1270s.[50]

The "disseminated Prologue narrative accounts" are those included in prayer-books and reading-books, written over a period of several centuries and located in various parts of the country. Copies of most of these "Lives" can be divided, according to Serebryansky, into four groups: the redaction attributed to the priest Andrey; the one purportedly written by Bishop Ioann of Chernigov,[51] or anonymous versions of it; revisions of Andrey's account; abbreviated versions of Bishop Ioann's narrative. Serebryansky believes that Andrey's account is probably the original version of the four redactions and served as the model for the others. It used the Rostov account of the short Prologue "Lives" as its source and was written as early as the second half of the thirteenth century. It is a matter of conjecture whether or not the priest Andrey was Mikhail's

---

[49] Similar to the Prologue entries, short notices announcing Mikhail's execution were also inserted into the chronicles. These were made by contemporaries of the event and preceded both the Church narrative accounts as well as the short Prologue entries; see for example, the Novgorod First Chronicle (NPL, *Komissionnyy spisok*, p. 298, s.a. 1245); the Laurentian Chronicle (PSRL 1, col. 471, s.a. 1246) and the Hypatian Chronicle (PSRL 2, col. 795, s.a. 1245).

[50] Serebryansky, *Zhitiya*, p. 111.

[51] There is no chronicle information concerning Bishop Ioann of Chernigov. However, the Laurentian Chronicle speaks of an *Igumen* Ioann. Under the year 1231, it records that Kirill was consecrated bishop in Kiev. Among the prelates who attended the ceremony was *Igumen* Ioann from Chernigov ("а от Чернигова Иоан. игуменъ") (PSRL 1, col. 457). It is possible that he became bishop of Chernigov at a later date.

spiritual director and accompanied him to Saray.[52] Nevertheless, there is evidence to suggest that Andrey's account may have been written not only in southern Rus' but in the principality of Chernigov.[53]

The last Church narrative of Mikhail's martyrdom, the detailed *Zhitie* written by the Serbian monk Pakhomy Logofet, became one of the most popular accounts during the sixteenth century.[54] Serebryansky divided the copies of this narrative into three versions: the *Solovetskiy*, the *Arkhivskiy* and the *Mineiniy*. Pakhomy probably wrote his account in Moscow, no doubt at the request of the metropolitan, some time in the middle of the fifteenth century. His *Zhitie* was copied most extensively during the sixteenth century when it was also incorporated into the "Book of Generations" (*Kniga stepennaya*),[55] and revised into a new redaction, the *Chudovskoe zhitie*. The latter is of special interest because its compiler added a "Lament" (*Plach*) of the princess, Mikhail's widow (the only redaction of all the Church narrative accounts to incorporate a lament); it also included unique information, apparently taken from oral tradition, concerning the invasion of northeast Rus' in 1237/8 and the death of Grand Prince Yury Vsevolodovich of Vladimir.[56] Since Pakhomy's

---

[52] This was not an unknown custom. When Prince Mikhail Yaroslavich of Tver' travelled to Saray where he was also executed, 22 November 1318, he was accompanied by his spiritual father (Serebryansky, *Zhitiya*, p. 115).

[53] Since Bishop Ioann's redaction is a reworking of Andrey's narrative, it is interesting to note that of the seven known copies of the former, the two oldest (from the fourteenth and the fifteenth century) are from western Rus'; one is from the Glukhov Monastery in the principality of Chernigov; the remaining copies (from the sixteenth and seventeenth century) are from various regions in the north. Thus, the chronological sequence of their appearance and their regional origins do not deny the possibility that Andrey's account was written in the principality of Chernigov. It was copied and revised by Bishop Ioann of Chernigov, and his redaction, in turn, was copied and disseminated to all parts of the country. The latter appears to have been an especially popular redaction to judge not only from the fact that copies have survived dating from the fourteenth century to the seventeenth century, but that it was also the redaction which was incorporated into most of the later chronicle compilations.

[54] I. Yablonsky states that he knew of sixty-nine copies of Pakhomy's "Life" of Mikhail (*Pakhomy Serb* [Saint Petersburg, 1908], pp. 104-5).

[55] "The Book of Generations of the Tsars' Genealogy" (*Kniga stepennaya tsarskogo rodosloviya*) (PSRL 21). This is an extensive revision of the chronicles. The work traces the genealogies of the princes from St. Ol'ga up to the reign of Tsar Ivan IV. It is called the book of "generations" (*stepenei*) because it is divided into seventeen generations. As well as historical information, the work contains new apocryphal materials derived from no longer extant sources and from oral tradition. Various passages include instructions, religious epistles and eulogies. Begun by Metropolitan Kiprian (1389-1406), it was concluded by Metropolitan Makary and published in two parts in Moscow in 1775.

[56] See above, Ch. 1, n. 73.

primary purpose for writing his account was to make stylistic revisions to existing narratives rather than to rework biographical data, his version has little historical value. However, it achieved immense popularity as a didactic narrative, especially during the sixteenth century.

Such is the *mélange* of known copies of Church narrative accounts of Mikhail's martyrdom.[57] The authors of the redactions did not, as a rule, incorporate chronicle information into their biographical data. This was due to the fact that the chronicles at their disposal either had little additional information or else the material they contained was not suitable for illustrating the life of the prince-martyr whom the narrator wished to depict as a model for the faithful.[58] The authors, instead, confined themselves to using material that was edifying rather than historically accurate. There is little doubt that they were successful in their task to judge from the number of surviving copies of Mikhail's "Life,"[59] collected from all parts of the country and from various centuries. As well as the Church narrative accounts of the *Zhitie*, "encomiums" (*pokhvaly*) have also survived. These followed closely the pattern of the narrative accounts but various passages were embellished with pious asides – didactic admonitions, prayers and invocations.[60]

It was the memory of Mikhail the prince-martyr rather than Mikhail the grand prince of Kiev which captivated the generations of Orthodox faithful after his execution. The people of Rus' and Muscovy, especially during the period of Tatar occupation, were not interested in preserving the memory of the grand prince's militant stand against Khan Baty, of his defiance of the invaders, or of his refusal to accept their overlordship until the last possible moment. Instead, the people were inspired by the martyr, so much so that he became the paragon of all believing Christians

[57] The texts of the various redactions are found in Serebryansky, *Zhitiya*, Texts, pp. 59-86. Narrative accounts of Mikhail's martyrdom are also found in various chronicles, see above pp. 130-131.

[58] Chronicles which contained little additional information were, for example, the Novgorod First Chronicle (NPL, p. 298, s.a. 1245) and the Laurentian Chronicle (PSRL 1, col. 471, s.a. 1246). Information which the author of the *Zhitie* would have found unsuitable is, for example, that found in the Hypatian Chronicle. It states that when Mikhail arrived in Hungary his son Rostislav and King Béla IV did not receive him with due honour; he became angry at his son and returned to Chernigov. From there he set off to Baty to ask for permission to rule in his own principality (PSRL 2, col. 795).

[59] Serebryansky lists over ninety copies of narrative accounts of Mikhail's "Life" which he consulted (*Zhitiya*, Texts, pp. 165-73, 179-81). He observes that, in comparing the Church narrative acounts written about Saints Boris and Gleb with those written about Saints Mikhail and Fedor, there were more redactions of the latter than of the former (ibid. p. 141).

[60] Barsukov, *Istochniki*, col. 378.

showing them how to become champions of their faith in the face of pagan oppression. Significantly, devotion to this defender of the faith did not wane after the Muscovites successfully cast off the Tatar yoke. Rather, his cult appears to have been revitalized during the middle of the sixteenth century when it received official approbation from both ecclesiastical and secular authorities; it remained an inherent component of the Orthodox religious tradition up to the beginning of the twentieth century. Ironically, therefore, the last grand prince of Kiev who, due to his execution, was judged to be a failure by his contemporaries, became a victorious champion of the Orthodox faith not only through the difficult centuries of the Tatar yoke, but into the twentieth century as well.[61]

---

[61] In 1913, the "Lives" of two saints – Prince Mikhail (and Fedor) and Father Irenarch the Hermit – were published in *The Russian Review* at the University of Liverpool. In their introduction to the translated "Lives" the editors (Bernard Pares, Maurice Baring and Samuel N. Harper) gave the following reasons for their selection.

> *The Lives of Saints* ... were for a long time not only the favourite but almost the only reading of the Russian peasant. They have a character of their own, which is in sequence both with the ancient *Annals* and with modern Russian literature.... We think that the national character of the Russian Church will be illustrated by the *Lives* of two Russian saints, of whom one, a layman [Mikhail] suffered martyrdom at the hands of the Tatars, and the other, a monk [Father Irenarch] ... combated the national and religious danger from the side of Poland. In each case it may be said that the Russian Church saved Russia.

See A. Zvegintsev, trans., "Two National Saints," *The Russian Review*, vol. 2, August, no. 3 (University of Liverpool, 1913), p. 21.

Table 1

The First Princes of Rus'

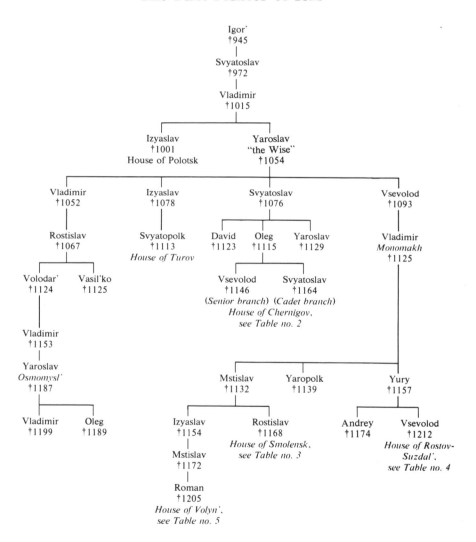

The generation after Ryurik to which a prince belongs is placed at the top of each column in roman numerals; d. = daughter of; p. = prince of; † = died; ∞ = married.

Table 2

Ol'govichi

(House of Chernigov)

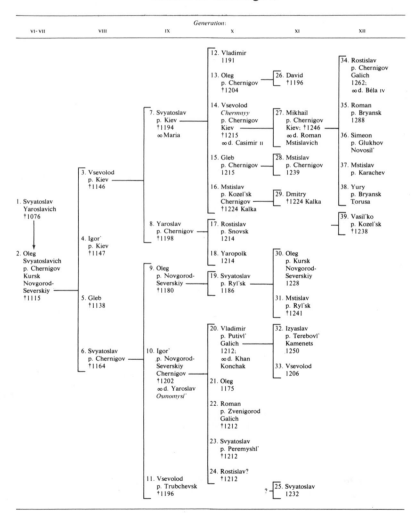

Table 3

Rostislavichi

(House of Smolensk)

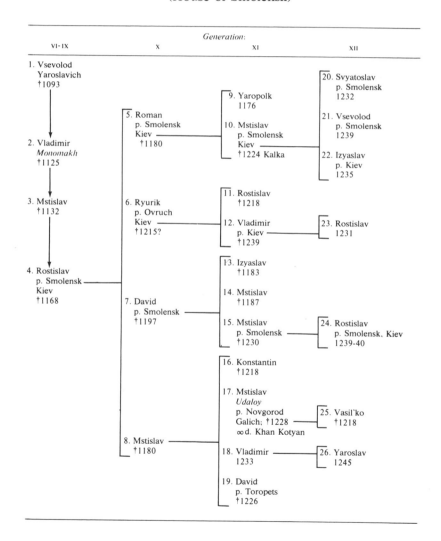

		Generation:	
VI-IX	X	XI	XII

1. Vsevolod Yaroslavich †1093

20. Svyatoslav p. Smolensk 1232

9. Yaropolk 1176

5. Roman p. Smolensk Kiev †1180

21. Vsevolod p. Smolensk 1239

10. Mstislav p. Smolensk Kiev †1224 Kalka

2. Vladimir *Monomakh* †1125

22. Izyaslav p. Kiev 1235

11. Rostislav †1218

3. Mstislav †1132

6. Ryurik p. Ovruch Kiev †1215?

12. Vladimir p. Kiev †1239

23. Rostislav 1231

13. Izyaslav †1183

4. Rostislav p. Smolensk Kiev †1168

14. Mstislav †1187

7. David p. Smolensk †1197

15. Mstislav p. Smolensk †1230

24. Rostislav p. Smolensk, Kiev 1239-40

16. Konstantin †1218

17. Mstislav *Udaloy* p. Novgorod Galich; †1228 ∞d. Khan Kotyan

25. Vasil'ko †1218

8. Mstislav †1180

18. Vladimir 1233

26. Yaroslav 1245

19. David p. Toropets †1226

Table 4

Vsevolodovichi

(House of Rostov-Suzdal')

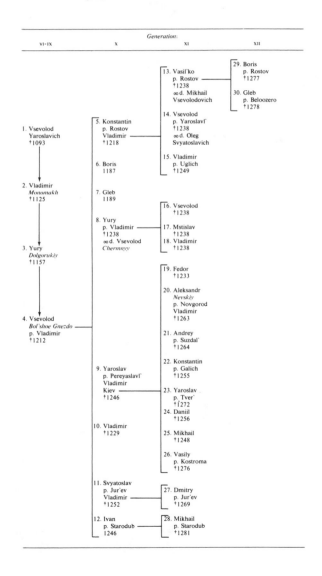

Generation:

VI-IX	X	XI	XII

1. Vsevolod Yaroslavich †1093

2. Vladimir *Monomakh* †1125

3. Yury *Dolgorukiy* †1157

4. Vsevolod *Bol'shoe Gnezdo* p. Vladimir †1212

5. Konstantin p. Rostov Vladimir †1218

6. Boris 1187

7. Gleb 1189

8. Yury p. Vladimir †1238 ∞ d. Vsevolod *Chermnyy*

9. Yaroslav p. Pereyaslavl' Vladimir Kiev †1246

10. Vladimir †1229

11. Svyatoslav p. Jur'ev Vladimir †1252

12. Ivan p. Starodub 1246

13. Vasil'ko p. Rostov †1238 ∞ d. Mikhail Vsevolodovich

14. Vsevolod p. Yaroslavl' †1238 ∞ d. Oleg Svyatoslavich

15. Vladimir p. Uglich †1249

16. Vsevolod †1238

17. Mstislav †1238

18. Vladimir †1238

19. Fedor †1233

20. Aleksandr *Nevskiy* p. Novgorod Vladimir †1263

21. Andrey p. Suzdal' †1264

22. Konstantin p. Galich †1255

23. Yaroslav p. Tver' †1272

24. Daniil †1256

25. Mikhail †1248

26. Vasily p. Kostroma †1276

27. Dmitry p. Jur'ev †1269

28. Mikhail p. Starodub †1281

29. Boris p. Rostov †1277

30. Gleb p. Beloozero †1278

Table 5

Princes of Volyn' and Galicia

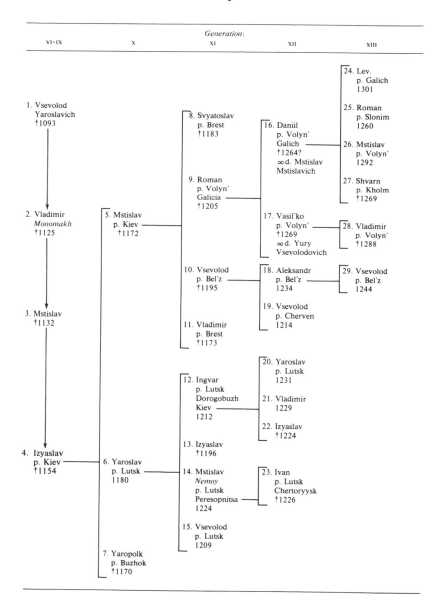

Generation:

VI-IX	X	XI	XII	XIII

Glossary

boyar – nobleman, landowner, senior advisor of the prince

chernye lyudi – common people (literally, "black people")

druzhina – bodyguard of the prince, detachment of troops

dvor – house, court, courtyard

dvorskiy – house-steward, major-domo, attendant in charge of the prince's residence, adviser of the prince

gramota – official document, law, deed

igumen – father superior of a monastery

izgoi – prince not eligible for the post of senior prince or of grand prince

kuny – pelt of marten, monetary unit

letopis' – chronicle, annals

men'shie lyudi – common people (literally, "lesser people")

posadnik – mayor

postrig – hair cutting ceremony initiating a young prince into civic life

prologue – a collection of saints' "Lives" arranged according to the days of the calendar

prostaya chad' – ordinary people, common people

sela – villages, lands

shurin – brother-in-law

sinodik – book into which the faithful inscribed the names of those deceased whom they wished to have commemorated in church services

sluzhba – service

sluzhebnik – church service-book

smerd – peasant

snem – congress, council

spisok – manuscript copy

starosta – elder, senior man, elected head

stol'nik – courtier

strastoterpets – martyr (literally, "passion-sufferer")

svet – congress, council

tysyatskiy – the town judge, police chief and military commander (literally, "one in charge of a thousand men")

udel – appanage

uezd – district, administrative unit of land

veche – popular assembly

velikiy knyaz' – grand prince

voevoda – military commander

volost' – district, area

yarlyk – charter, patent to rule in a principality or diocese given by the Tatars

Zhitie – "Life" of a saint

Chronological Table of Events

DR	Daniil Romanovich	RM Rostislav Mikhaylovich
IV	Izyaslav Vladimirovich	VR Vladimir Ryurikovich
MG	Mstislav Glebovich	YV Yaroslav Vsevolodovich
MV	Mikhail Vsevolodovich	

	Northern Rus'	Southern Rus'	Southwest Rus'
ca. 1179		—MV is born	
1186		—MV undergoes cure in southern Pereyaslavl'	
1205			—Roman Mstislavich of Galicia-Volyn' killed in Poland
1206		—MV appointed prince in southern Pereyaslavl'	—Igorevichi occupy Galich
ca. 1211		—MV marries daughter of Roman Mstislavich of Galicia-Volyn'	
1221	—Vsevolodovichi invited to rule in Novgorod		
1223		—MV attends *snem* in Kiev —MV fights at Kalka Battle —MV becomes prince of Chernigov —VR becomes grand prince of Kiev	
1224	—winter, MV helps Yury Vsevolodovich against Novgorod		
1225	—MV prince in Novgorod —YV prince in Novgorod	—MV returns to Chernigov	
1226		—MV has dispute with Oleg Svyatoslavich of Kursk	
1227	—MV's daughter Maria marries Vasil'ko Konstantinovich of Rostov		

	Northern Rus'	Southern Rus'	Southwest Rus'
1228			—the death of Mstislav Mstislavich "the Bold" —MV and VR attack DR in Kamenets
1229	—autumn, rains in Novgorod cause revolt —20 February, sons of YV flee from Novgorod —April, MV arrives in Novgorod: passes social reforms and demands that YV return Volok	—MV returns to Chernigov	
	—RM prince in Novgorod —YV revolts against Yury; crisis ends 7 September		
1230	—after 19 May, MV in Novgorod for *postrig* of his son RM	—MV returns to Chernigov —MV and VR send peace envoys to princes of Rostov-Suzdal'	
	—8 December, RM and *Posadnik* Vodovik flee to Torzhok	—Vodovik and his "brothers" flee to Chernigov —before 30 December, RM returns to Chernigov	
	—YV prince in Novgorod		—DR unifies lands of Volyn' by this date
1231		—6 April, *snem* in Kiev —MV attacks VR in Kiev and concludes truce	
	—winter, Vsevolodovichi and Novgorodians attack lands of Chernigov	—winter, *Posadnik* Vodovik dies in Chernigov	
1232		—MV terminates support of Novgorodians; they depart from Chernigov in March	
1233			—IV breaks truce between Ol'govichi and Rostislavichi;

Northern Rus'	Southern Rus'	Southwest Rus'
		he attacks lands of DR in Tikhoml'
		—the "unfaithful" Galicians and "the princes of Bolokhov" attack Kamenets
		—winter, Prince Andrew of Hungary dies in Galich; DR occupies the town
1234		—VR and DR form alliance against the Ol'govichi
	—winter, MV attacks VR in Kiev then withdraws to Chernigov	
1235	—6 January until 14 May, DR and VR besiege Chernigov unsuccessfully; they return to Kiev without peace	
	—MV, IV and the Polovtsy defeat VR and DR near Torchesk and sack Kiev	
	—Izyaslav Mstislavich prince in Kiev	
		—MV prince in Galich
		—IV prince in Kamenets
	—MG prince in Chernigov	
	—VR released for a ransom by the Polovtsy and returns to Kiev	
		—winter, Romanovichi fail to capture Galich
1236		—MV forms alliance with Béla IV of Hungary
		—MV forms alliance with Conrad of Mazovia
		—MV, IV, Poles, Роусь and the Polovtsy attack DR in Volyn'
		—Romanovichi attack the Ol'govichi and the Hungarians in Galich; autumn, they conclude a truce
—Yury Vsevolodovich and DR form an alliance against MV		
	—YV occupies Kiev; VR goes to Smolensk	

	Northern Rus'	Southern Rus'	Southwest Rus'
	−YV returns to Novgorod		−RM prince in Galich
		−MV grand prince of Kiev	
		−MG prince in Chernigov	
1237		−winter, Tatars invade Ryazan'	
1238	−Tatars invade Rostov-Suzdal' and kill Grand Prince Yury Vsevolodovich		
		−Tatars devastate Kozel'sk	
	−YV becomes grand prince in Vladimir		
	−Aleksandr Yaroslavich *Nevskiy* prince in Novgorod		
			−DR occupies Galich; RM flees to Hungary
1239		−3 March, Tatars sack southern Pereyaslavl'	
			−YV attacks Kamenets; MV escapes to Kiev
		−18 October, Tatars destroy Chernigov; MG escapes	
		−Tatars conclude peace with MG, VR and DR	
		−MV alone refuses to conclude peace with Tatars	
		−winter, MV flees to Hungary; he proposes marriage between his son RM and king's daughter	
		−death of VR?	
1240			−MV and his son RM flee to Conrad in Mazovia
		−Rostislav Mstislavich occupies Kiev	
		−DR occupies Kiev	
			−MV and DR conclude peace
			−MV and family live in Volyn'
			−DR goes to Hungary
		−6 December, Kiev falls; Dmitry is captured	
1241			−MV and son flee to Conrad in Mazovia
			−Tatars invade Volyn' and Galicia
			−DR flees to Poland
			−boyars in Galich assume functions of prince

	Northern Rus'	Southern Rus'	Southwest Rus'
			—MV flees to Silesia
			—after 9 April, MV returns to Poland
			—DR returns to Volyn'
		—MV returns to Rus'; he lives on an island below Kiev	
		—RM prince in Chernigov	
			—RM attacks Bakota in Poniz'e
1242			—RM occupies Galich
			—Romanovichi drive RM out of Galich
			—RM flees to Hungary after March
1242 or 1243			—RM marries daughter of Béla IV and defects to Hungary
1243	—YV goes to Saray; he is given a *yarlyk* and named grand prince of Kiev		
		—MV leaves Kiev and goes to Chernigov	
		—MV goes to Hungary, disowns son RM and returns to Chernigov	
			—RM attacks Galicia for Béla IV
1245			—17 August, RM defeated at Yaroslavl' by DR
			—26 October, DR departs for Saray
1246			—DR given patent by Baty and returns to Volyn'
		—MV goes to Saray; 20 September, he is executed with his boyar Fedor	
	—30 September, death of YV		

168

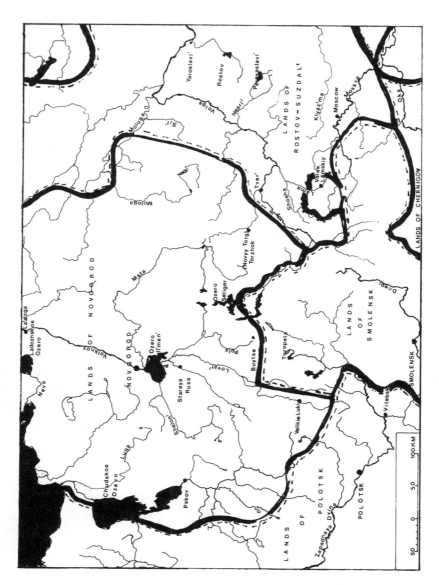

Map. 1. – The Lands of Novgorod.

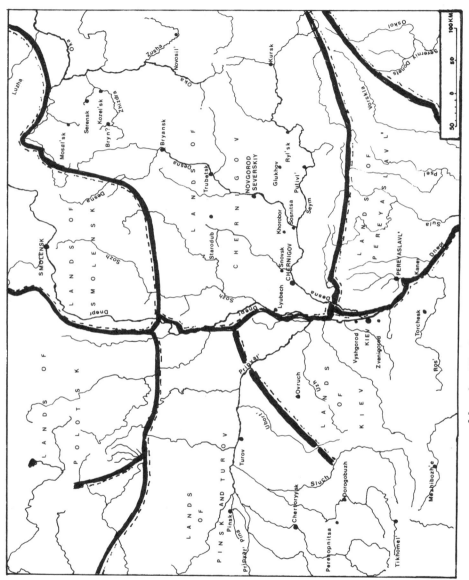

Map. 2. – The Lands of Kiev and Chernigov.

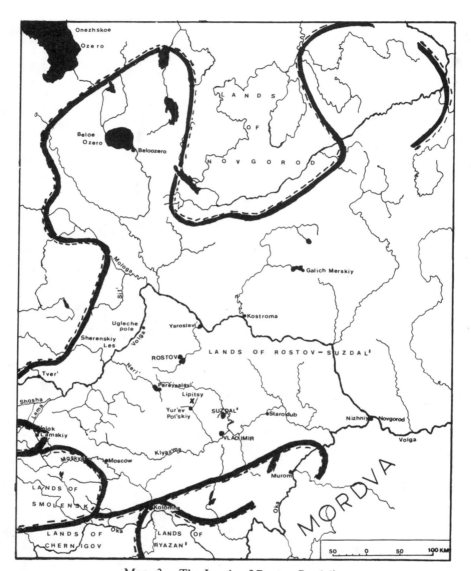

Map. 3. – The Lands of Rostov-Suzdal'.

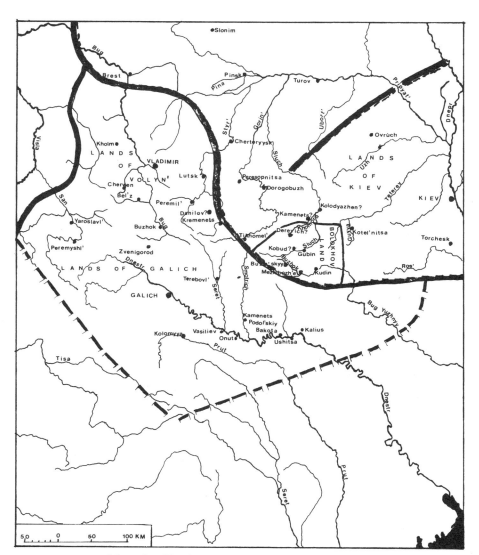

Map. 4. – The Lands of Volyn' and Galicia.

Selected Bibliography

Abramovich, D., *Kievo-Pecherskiy Paterik* (Kiev, 1930).

Acta Sanctorum, vol. 11 (Brussels, 1864).

Akty istoricheskie, 5 vols. (Saint Petersburg, 1841-1842).

Aleksandrovsky, M., *Ukazatel' Moskovskikh tserkvey* (Moscow, 1915).

"A narrative of Friar John de Pian de Carpine's mission derived from an oral statement of his companion Friar Benedict the Pole," in Rubruquis, William of, *The Journey of William of Rubruck to the Eastern Parts of the World 1253-55 as narrated by himself*, ed. and trans. W. W. Rockhill (London, 1900), pp. 33-39.

Antonova, V. I. and N. E. Mneva, *Katalog drevnerusskoy zhivopisi*, 2 vols. (Moscow, 1963).

"Arkivnye materialy (opisi, gramoty, ukazy, i pr.), – prilozhenie k opisaniyu Riz-polozhenskago monastyrya," *Trudy Vladimirskoy Uchenoy arkhivnoy kommissii*, book 2 (Vladimir, 1900).

Bagaley, D., *Istoriya Severskoy zemli do poloviny XIV stoletiya* (Kiev, 1882).

Barsov, N., *Materialy dlya istoriko-geograficheskago slovarya Rossii* (Vil'na, 1865).

Barsukov, N. P., *Istochniki russkoy agiografii* (Saint Petersburg, 1882).

Baumgarten, N. de, *Généalogies et mariages occidentaux des Rurikides Russes du xe au xiiie siècle* (*Orientalia Christiana*), vol. 9, no. 35 (Rome, 1927).

——, *Généalogies des branches régnantes des Rurikides du xiiie au xvie siècle* (*Orientalia Christiana*), vol. 35; no. 94 (Rome, 1934).

Beletsky, L. T., "Literaturnaya istoriya povesti o Merkurii Smolenskom," *Sbornik otdeleniya russkago yazyka i slovesnosti Rossiyskoy Akademii nauk*, vol. 99, no. 8 (Petrograd, 1922).

Berezhkov, N. G., *Khronologiya russkogo letopisaniya* (Moscow, 1963).

Bonnell, E., *Russisch-Liwländische Chronographie von der mitte neunten Jahrhunderts bis zum Jahre 1410* (Saint Petersburg, 1862).

Borzakovsky, V. S., *Istoriya Tverskago knyazhestva* (Saint Petersburg, 1876).

Brundage, I. A., trans., *The Chronicle of Henry of Livonia* (Madison, 1961).

Bryachevs'ky, M. Yu., "Kam'yanets'-podil'skiy, misto-muzey," *Ukrains'kiy istoricheskiy zhurnal*, no. 2 (Kiev, 1967), pp. 107-15.

Budovnits, I. U., *Obshchestvenno-politicheskaya mysl' Drevney Rusi* (Moscow, 1960).

Buganov, V. I., *Otechestvennaya istoriografiya russkogo letopisaniya* (Moscow, 1975).

The Cambridge History of Poland (Cambridge, 1950).

The Cambridge Medieval History, vol. 6 (Cambridge, 1968).

Cherniavsky, M., *Tsar and People, Studies in Russian Myths* (New Haven: Yale University Press, 1961).

Cherepanov, S. K., "K voprosu o yuzhnom istochnike Sofiyskoy ı i Novgorodskoy ıv letopisey," TODRL, vol. 30 (1976), pp. 279-83.

Cherepnin, L. V., "Letopisets Daniila Galitskogo," *Istoricheskie zapiski*, vol. 12 (1941), pp. 228-53.

——, *Russkie feodal'nye arkhivy xıv-xv vv.*, part 1 (Moscow-Leningrad, 1948).

——, "K voprosu o kharaktere i forme drevnerusskogo gosudarstva x- nachala xııı v.," *Istoricheskie zapiski*, vol. 89 (1972), pp. 353-408.

——, "Mongolo-tatary na Rusi (xııı v.)," *Tataro-mongoly v Azii i Evrope* (Moscow, 1970), pp. 179-203.

"Chernigovskie knyaz'ya," *Russkiy biograficheskiy slovar'*, vol. 22 (Saint Petersburg, 1905), pp. 231-67.

Codex diplomaticus Hungariae ecclesiasticus ac civilis, ed., G. Fejér, book 3, vol. 2 and book 4, vol. 1 (Budae, 1829).

Dal', V., *Tolkovyy slovar'*, 4 vols. (Moscow, 1956).

Danilevich, V. E., *Ocherk istorii Polotskoy zemli do kontsa xıv stoletiya* (Kiev, 1896). [Not available to me.]

Dawson, C., ed., *The Mongol Mission* (New York, 1955).

Denisov, L. I., *Pravoslavnye monastyri rossiyskoy imperii* (Moscow, 1908).

Dictionary of Russian historical terms from the eleventh century to 1917, compiled by S. G. Pushkarev (New Haven: Yale University Press, 1970).

Dimnik, M., "Russian Princes and their Identities in the First Half of the Thirteenth Century," *Mediaeval Studies*, vol. 40 (1978), pp. 157-189.

——, "The Siege of Chernigov in 1235," *Mediaeval Studies*, vol. 41 (1979), pp. 387-403.

——, "The Struggle for Control over Kiev in 1235 and 1236," *Canadian Slavonic Papers*, vol. 21, no. 1 (1979), pp. 28-44.

——, "Kamenec," *Russia Mediaevalis*, vol. 4 (1979), pp. 25-34.

Długosz, J., *Longini canonici Cracoviensis, Historiae Polonicae*, book 6 (Leipzig, 1711).

Dmitriev, L. A., "Syuzhetnoe povestvovanie v zhitiynykh pamyatnikakh kontsa xııı-xv v.," *Istoki russkoy belletristiki*, ed. Ya. S. Lur'e (Leningrad, 1970), pp. 208-62.

Dmitrieva, R. P., *Skazanie o knyazyakh Vladimirskikh* (Moscow-Leningrad, 1955).

——, *Bibliografiya russkago letopisaniya* (Moscow-Leningrad, 1962).

Dolgoruky, P., *Rossiyskaya rodoslovnaya kniga*, 4 vols. (Saint Petersburg, 1854-7).

Dovnar-Zapol'sky, M. V., *Ocherk istorii krivichskoy i dregovichskoy zemel' do kontsa xıı stoletiya* (Kiev, 1891). [Not available to me.]

Droblenkova, N. F., *Bibliografiya Sovetskikh Russkikh rabot po literature xi-xvii vv. 1917-57* (Moscow-Leningrad, 1961).
Dworzaczek, W., *Genealogia (Tablice)* (Warsaw, 1959).

Ekzemplyarsky, A. V., *Velikie i udel'nye knyaz'ya severnoy Rusi v tatarsky period s 1238 po 1505 g.*, 2 vols. (Saint Petersburg, 1889, 1891).
Entsiklopedicheskiy slovar', F. A. Brokgauz and I. A. Efron, ed. (Saint Petersburg, 1890-1907).
Epitome chronologica rerum Hungaricarum Transsilvanicarum et Illyricarum, ed. S. Katona, part 1 (Budae, 1796).
Eristov, D. A., *Slovar' istoricheskiy o svyatykh proslavlennykh v rossiyskoy tserkvi* (Saint Petersburg, 1836).
"Ermolinskaya letopis'," psrl 23 (Saint Petersburg, 1910).

Fedotov, G. P., *Svyatye Drevney Rusi (x-xvii st.)* (Paris, 1931).
Fennell, J. L. I., *The Emergence of Moscow 1304-59* (London, 1968).
——, "The struggle for power in north-east Russia, 1246-9: An investigation of the sources," *Oxford Slavonic Papers* (New Series), vol. 7 (1974), pp. 112-21.
——, "The Tale of the Murder of Michail of Tver'," *Studies in Slavic Linguistics and Poetics in Honor of Boris O. Unbegaun* (New York and London, 1968).
——, "The Tver' Uprising of 1327: a Study of the Sources," *Jahrbücher für Geschichte Osteuropas*, Heft 2 (1967).
——, "The Tale of the Death of Vasil'ko Konstantinovich; a Study of the Sources," *Osteuropa in Geschichte und Gegenwart, Festschrift für Gunther Stökl zum 60. Geburtstag* (Wien, 1977), pp. 34-46.
——, "The Tale of Baty's Invasion," *Russia Mediaevalis*, vol. 3 (1977), pp. 41-78.
——, ed., *Prince A. M. Kurbsky's History of Ivan iv* (Cambridge, 1965).
Filaret, archbishop of Chernigov (Gumilevsky, D. G.), *Obzor russkoy dukhovnoy literatury 862-1720* (Kharkov, 1859).
——, *Istoriko-statisticheskoe opisanie Chernigovskoy eparkhii*, 7 vols. (Chernigov, 1861-74).
——, *Russkie svyatye*, vol. 3, third edition (Saint Petersburg, 1882).
Florovsky, A. V., *Chekhi i vostochnye slavyane*, vol. 1 (Prague, 1935).
Fuhrmann, J. T., "Metropolitan Cyril ii (1242-1281) and the Politics of Accomodation," *Jahrbücher für Geschichte Osteuropas*, Neue Folge, Band 24 (Wiesbaden, 1976), pp. 161-172.

Georgievsky, V. T., "Zhitie pr. Evfrosinii Suzdal'skoy, s miniatyurami, po spisku xvii v.," *Trudy Vladimirskoy uchenoy arkhivnoy komissii*, book 1 (Vladimir, 1899).
——, "Suzdal'skiy Rizpolozhenskiy zhenskiy monastyr'," *Trudy Vladimirskoy uchenoy arkhivnoy komissii*, book 2 (Vladimir, 1900).

Golubinsky, E., *Istoriya russkoy tserkvi*, 2 vols. in four parts (Moscow, 1900-1911).

——, *Istoriya kanonizatsii svyatykh v Russkoy tserkvi*, second edition (Moscow, 1903); also in *Chteniya*, book 1 (Moscow, 1903).

Golubovsky, P. V., *Istoriya Severskoy zemli do poloviny XIV stoletiya* (Kiev, 1881).

——, *Istoriya Smolenskoy zemli do nachala XV st.* (Kiev, 1895).

Gramoty Velikogo Novgoroda i Pskova, gen. ed. S. N. Valk (Moscow-Leningrad, 1948).

"Gustinskaya letopis'," PSRL 2 (Saint Petersburg, 1843).

Historia critica regum Hungariae stirpis Arpadianae ex fide domesticorum et externorum scriptorum, ed. S. Katona, vol. 5 (Posonii et Cassoviae, 1783), vol. 6 (Budae, 1782).

Historia pragmatica Hungariae, ed. S. Katona, vol. 1 (Budae, 1782).

Hóman, B., *Magyar Történet*, vol. 1 (Budapest, 1935).

——, *Geschichte des Ungarischen Mittelalters*, vol. 2 (Berlin, 1943).

Hrushevsky, M., *Ocherk istorii Kievskoy zemli ot smerti Yaroslava do kontsa XIV stoletiya* (Kiev, 1891).

——, *Istoriia Ukrainy-Rusy*, 9 vols., second edition (L'vov, 1904-1931).

Ikonnikov, V. S., *Opyt' russkoy istoriografii*, vol. 2 (Kiev, 1908).

Ilovaysky, D., *Istoriya Ryazanskogo knyazhestva* (Moscow, 1858).

——, *Istoriya Rossii*, part 1: "Kievskiy period" (Moscow, 1876).

——, *Istoriya Rossii*, part 2: "Vladimirskiy period" (Moscow, 1880).

Immennoy i geograficheskiy ukazateli k Ipat'evskoy letopisi, compiled by L. L. Murav'eva and L. F. Kuz'mina (Moscow, 1975).

"Ipat'evskaya letopis'," PSRL 2 (Saint Petersburg, 1908).

"Izvestiya vengerskikh missionerov XII-XIV vv. o tatarakh i vostochnoy Evrope," ed. S. A. Anninsky, *Istoricheskiy arkhiv*, vol. 3 (Moscow-Leningrad, 1940), pp. 71-112.

Kamentseva, E. I., *Khronologiya* (Moscow, 1967).

——, and N. V. Ustyugov, *Russkaya metrologiya* (Moscow, 1965).

Karamzin, N. M., *Istoriya gosudarstva Rossiiskago*, 12 vols., third edition (Saint Petersburg, 1830-1831).

Karger, M. K., "Kiev i mongol'skoe zavoevanie," *Sovetskaya arkheologiya*, vol. 11 (Moscow-Leningrad, 1949), pp. 55-102.

——, "Drevnerusskiy gorod Izyaslavl' v svete arkheologicheskikh issledovaniy 1957-64 gg.," *I Mezhdunarodnyy kongress slavyanskoy arkheologii, Varshava 14-18, IX, 1965* (Warsaw, 1968), pp. 286-7.

Kartashev, A. V., *Ocherki po istorii russkoy tserkvi*, 2 vols. (Paris, 1959).

"Kazanskiy letopisets," PSRL 19 (Saint Petersburg, 1903).

Khavsky, P., *Istoricheskoe issledovanie o rodosloviyakh svyatago muchenika knyazya chernigovskago Mikhaila i rossiyskikh velikikh knyazey opochivayushchikh v Moskovskom Arhangelskom sobore* (Moscow, 1862).

——, *Drevnost' Moskvy ili ukazatel' istochnikov eya topografii i istorii*, third edition (Moscow, 1868).

Kholmogorov, V. I., "Dukhovnaya knyazya Vladimira Timofeevicha Dolgorukova (1633 goda yanvarya 1)," *Izvestiya russkago geneologicheskago obshchestva*, vypusk vtoroy (Saint Petersburg, 1903), pp. 17-25.

"Kholmogorskaya letopis'," PSRL 33 (Leningrad, 1977).

Klyuchevsky, V. O., *Drevnerusskiya zhitiya svyatykh kak istoricheskiy istochnik* (Moscow, 1871).

"Kniga stepennaya tsarskogo rodosloviya," PSRL 21, chast pervaya (Saint Petersburg, 1908).

Kochin, G. E., *Materialy dlya terminologicheskogo slovarya Drevney Rossii* (Moscow-Leningrad, 1937).

Korsakov, D., *Merya i Rostovskoe knyazhestvo* (Kazan', 1872).

Kostomarov, N. I., *Istoricheskiya monografii i issledovaniya*, vol. 1 (Saint Petersburg, 1863).

——, "Severnorusskiya narodopravstva," *Sobranie sochineniya*, book 3, vols. 7 and 8 (Saint Petersburg, 1904).

Kuchkin, B. A., *Povesti o Mikhaile Tverskom* (Moscow, 1974).

Kuza, A. V., "Novgorodskaya zemlya," *Drevnerusskie knyazhestva X-XIII vv.*, ed. L. G. Beskrovnyy (Moscow, 1975), pp. 144-201.

Kuz'min, A. G., "Ob istochnikovedcheskoy osnove 'Istorii Rossiyskoy' V. N. Tatishcheva," *Voprosy istorii*, part 9 (1963), pp. 214-8.

——, *Ryazanskoe letopisanie* (Moscow, 1965).

Kvashnin-Samarin, N., "Po povodu Lyubetskago sinodika," *Chteniya*, book 4 (Moscow, 1874).

"Lavrent'evskaya letopis'," PSRL 1, second edition (Leningrad, 1926).

"Lebedevskaya letopis'," PSRL 29 (Moscow, 1965).

Lederer, E., "Vengersko-Russkie otnosheniya i tataro-mongol'skoe nashestvie," *Mezhdunarodnye svyazi Rossii do XVII v.*, eds. A. A. Zimin and V. T. Pashuto (Moscow, 1961), pp. 181-202.

"Letopis' Avraamki," PSRL 16 (Saint Petersburg, 1889).

"Letopisets Pereyaslavlya-Suzdal'skogo," ed. M. A. Obolensky, VOIDR, book 9 (Moscow, 1851).

Levchenko, M. V., *Ocherki po istorii Russko-vizantiyskikh otnosheniy* (Moscow, 1956).

Likhachev, D. S., *Russkie letopisi i ikh kul'turno-istoricheskoe znachenie* (Moscow-Leningrad, 1947).

——, "Kogda bylo napisano 'Slovo o polku Igoreve'?" *Voprosy literatury*, no. 8 (Moscow, 1964), pp. 132-60.

Limonov, Yu. A., *Letopisanie Vladimiro-Suzdal'skoy Rusi* (Leningrad, 1967).

——, "Pol'skiy khronist Yan Dlugosh o Rossii," *Feodal'naya Rossiya vo vsemirno-istoricheskom protsesse* (Moscow, 1972), pp. 262-8.

Lunt, H. G., *Concise Dictionary of Old Russian (11th-17th Centuries)* (Munich, 1970).

Lur'e, Ya. S., "Iz istorii russkogo letopisaniya kontsa xv v.," TODRL, vol. 11 (1955), pp. 156-86.

——, "Obshcherusskiy svod-protograf Sofiyskoy I i Novgorodskoy IV letopisey," TODRL, vol. 28 (1974), pp. 114-39.

——, "Troitskaya letopis' i moskovskoe letopisanie XIV v.," *Vspomogatel'nye istoricheskie distsipliny*, vol. 6 (Leningrad, 1974), pp. 79-106.

——, "Moskovskiy svod 1479 g. i ego protograf," TODRL, vol. 30 (1976), pp. 95-113.

——, *Obshcherusskie letopisi XIV-XV vv.* (Leningrad, 1976).

"L'vovskaya letopis'," PSRL 20 (Saint Petersburg, 1910).

Lyaskoronsky, V. G., *Istoriya Pereyaslavl'skoy zemli s drevneyshikh vremen do poloviny XIII stoletiya* (Kiev, 1897).

Lyubavsky, M. K., *Ocherk istorii Litovsko-russkogo gosudarstva do Lyublinskoy unii vklyuchitel'no*, second edition (Moscow, 1915).

Macartney, C. A., *Hungary, A Short History* (Edinburgh, 1962).

——, "Hungary," *Encyclopaedia Britannica*, vol. 11 (London, 1963), pp. 901-4.

Magyarország Története, vol. 1 (Budapest, 1967).

Makary, Mitropolit Vserossiyskiy, *Velikiya Minei Chetii*, 14-24 September (Saint Petersburg, 1869), cols. 1298-1305.

Makary, Mitropolit Moskovskiy, *Istoriya russkoy tserkvi*, vols. 3, 4 and 8 (Saint Petersburg, 1888, 1886, 1898).

Markov, M. E., "O dostopamyatnostyakh Chernigova," *Chteniya*, no. 1 (Moscow, 1847).

Matthews, W. K., "The Latinisation of Cyrillic Characters," *The Slavonic and East European Review*, vol. 30, no. 75 (June, 1952), pp. 531-48.

Mavrodin, V. V., "Nekotorye momenty iz istorii razlozheniya rodovogo stroya na teritorii Drevney Rusi," *Uchenye zapiski*, vol. 19 (Leningrad, 1939), pp. 145-74.

——, *Ocherki po istorii feodal'noy Rusi* (Leningrad, 1949).

——, *Narodnye vosstaniya v Drevney Rusi* (Moscow, 1961).

——, *Sbornik dokumentov po istorii SSSR* (Moscow, 1970).

——, "Chernigovskoe knyazhestvo," *Ocherki istorii SSSR*, part 1, pp. 393-400.

Mazour, A., *Modern Russian Historiography*, second edition (London, 1958).

"Mazurinskiy letopisets," PSRL 31 (Moscow, 1968).

Molchanovsky, N., *Ocherk izvestiy o Podol'skoy zemle do 1454 g.* (Kiev, 1885). [Not available to me.]

Mongait, A. L., "Staraya Ryazan'," *Materialy i issledovaniya po arkheologii SSSR*, no. 49 (Moscow, 1955).

——, *Ryazanskaya zemlya* (Moscow, 1961).

Monumenta Poloniae Historica, ed. A. Bielowski, vol. 2 (L'vov, 1872).

"Moskovskiy letopisnyy svod kontsa xv veka," PSRL 25 (Moscow-Leningrad, 1949).

Murav'eva, L. L., "Novgorodskie izvestiya Vladimirskogo letopistsa," *Arkheo-graficheskii ezhegodnik za 1966* (Moscow, 1968), pp. 37-40.
——, "Ob obshcherusskom istochnike Vladimirskogo letopistsa," *Letopisi i khroniki, sbornik statey 1973 g.* (Moscow, 1974), pp. 143-9.

Nasonov, A. N., *Mongoly i Rus'* (Moscow-Leningrad, 1940).
——, "Iz istorii Pskovskogo letopisaniya," *Istoricheskie zapiski*, vol. 18 (1946), pp. 255-94.
——, *Istoriya russkogo letopisaniya xi-nachala xviii veka* (Moscow, 1951).
——, *Russkaya zemlya i obrazovanie territorii drevnerusskogo gosudarstva* (Moscow, 1951).
——, "Letopisnyy svod xv veka," *Materialy po istorii sssr*, vol. 2 (Moscow, 1955), pp. 275-321.
——, "Moskovskiy svod 1479 i ego yuzhnorusskiy istochnik," *Problemy istochnikovedeniya*, vol. 9 (Moscow, 1961), pp. 350-85.
——, "Moskovskiy svod 1479 i Ermolinskaya letopis'," *Voprosy, sotsial'no-ekonomicheskoy istorii i istochnikovedeniya perioda feodalizma v Rossii. Sbornik statey k 70-letiyu A. A. Novosel'skogo* (Moscow, 1961), pp. 218-22.
——, "Vladimiro-Suzdal'skoe knyazhestvo," *Ocherki istorii sssr*, part 1, pp. 320-34.
"Nikanorovskaya letopis'," psrl 27 (Moscow-Leningrad, 1962).
Nikitin, P., *Istoriya goroda Smolenska* (Moscow, 1848).
Nikitsky, A. I., *Istoriya ekonomicheskago byta Velikogo Novgoroda* (Moscow, 1893).
Nikol'skaya, T. N., "Voennoe delo v gorodakh zemli Vyatichey (Po materialam drevnerusskogo Serenska)," *Kratkie Soobshcheniya*, no. 139 (*Slavyano-russkaya arkheologiya*) (Moscow, 1974), pp. 34-42.
"Novgorodskaya chetvertaya letopis'," psrl 4 (Petrograd, 1915).
Novgorodskaya pervaya letopis' starshego i mladshego izvodov, ed. A. N. Nasonov (Moscow-Leningrad, 1950).
"Novgorodskaya vtoraya (Arkhivskaya) letopis'," psrl 30 (Moscow, 1965).

Ocherki istorii sssr: period feodalizma ix-xv vv., 2 vols., gen. ed. B. D. Grekov (Moscow, 1953).
"Otryvok iz letopisi o vremenakh tsarya Ivana Vasil'evicha Groznago," rib, vol. 3 (Saint Petersburg, 1876).

Palauzova, S. N., *Rostislav Mikhaylovich', russkiy udel'nyy knyaz' na dunae v xiii veke* (Saint Petersburg, 1851).
Pashuto, V. T., *Ocherki po istorii Galitsko-volynskoy Rusi* (Moscow, 1950).
——, *Geroicheskaya borba russkogo naroda za nezavisimost' (xiii veka)* (Moscow, 1956).
——, *Obrazovanie Litovskogo gosudarstva* (Moscow, 1959).

——, *Vneshnyaya politika Drevney Rusi* (Moscow, 1968).

——, "Mesto Drevney Rusi v istorii Evropy," *Feodal'naya Rossiya vo vsemirno-istoricheskom protsesse* (Moscow, 1972), pp. 188-200.

——, "Vnutripoliticheskoe polozhenie Rusi v nachale xiii v.," *Ocherki istorii sssr*, part 1, pp. 768-776.

"Patriarshaya ili Nikonovskaya letopis'," psrl 10 (Saint Petersburg, 1885).

Perfecky, G. E., trans., *The Hypatian Codex Part Two: The Galician-Volynian Chronicle* (Munich, 1973).

Plano Carpini, John de, *The Journey of Friar John of Pian de Carpini to the Court of Kuyuk Khan 1245-47 as narrated by himself*, ed. and trans. W. W. Rockhill (London, 1900).

——, *Istoriya Mongalov*, ed. and trans. A. I. Malein (Saint Petersburg, 1911).

Pletneva, S. A., "Polovetskaya zemlya," *Drevnerusskie knyazhestva x-xiii vv.*, ed. L. G. Beskrovnyy (Moscow, 1975), pp. 260-300.

Podobedova, O. I., *Moskovskaya shkola zhivopisi pri Ivane iv* (Moscow, 1972).

Pogodin, M., "Mezhdousobnyya voiny 1055-1240," voidr, books 2 and 3 (Moscow, 1849).

——, *Drevnyaya russkaya istoriya do mongol'skago iga*, 2 vols. (Moscow, 1872).

Potin, V. M., *Drevnyaya Rus' i evropeyskie gosudarstva v x-xiii vv.* (Leningrad, 1968).

"Povest' o razorenii Ryazani Batyem," *A Historical Russian Reader: A Selection of Texts from the xith. to the xvth. Centuries*, eds. J. Fennell and D. Obolensky (Oxford, 1969), pp. 76-85.

"Predislovie o velikikh knyazekh Litovskikh, otkudu oni poshli," psrl 17 (Saint Petersburg, 1907).

Presnyakov, A. E., *Knyazhoe pravo v Drevney Rusi* (Saint Petersburg, 1909).

——, *Obrazovanie Velikorusskogo gosudarstva* (Petrograd, 1918).

——, *Lektsii po Russkoy istorii*, vol. 2 (Moscow, 1939).

Priselkov, M. D., *Istoriya russkogo letopisaniya xi-xv vv.* (Leningrad, 1940).

Pronstein, A. P. and Y. Ya. Kiyashko, *Vspomogatel'nye istoricheskie distsiplini* (Moscow, 1973).

Pskovskie letopisi, ed. A. N. Nasonov, 2 vols. (a.n. sssr, 1941, 1955).

Ramm, B. Ya., *Papstvo i Rus' v x-xv vekakh* (Moscow-Leningrad, 1959).

Rapov, O. M., *Knyazheskie vladeniya na Rusi v x-pervoy polovine xiii v.* (Moscow, 1977).

Rappoport, P. A., "Voennoe zodchestvo zapadnorusskikh zemel' x-xiv vv.," *Materialy i Issledovaniya po Arkheologii sssr*, no. 140 (Leningrad, 1967).

——, "Goroda Bolokhovskoy zemli," *Kratkie Soobshcheniya o dokladakh i polevykh issledovaniyakh instituta istorii material'noy kul'tury*, vol. 57 (Moscow, 1955), pp. 52-59.

Rashīd al-Dīn, *The Successors of Genghis Khan*, translated from the Persian by J. A. Boyle (New York and London), 1971.

Révai Nagy Lexikona az Ismeretek Enciklopédiáia, 20 vols. (Budapest, 1911-27).

"Rodoslovie velikikh knyazei Litovskago knyazhestva," PSRL 17 (Saint Petersburg, 1907).

"Rodoslovnaya kniga," VOIDR, book 10 (Moscow, 1851), pp. 1-286.

"Rogozhskiy letopisets," PSRL 15 (Petrograd, 1922).

Rozhkov, N., "Politicheskie partii v Velikom Novgorode XII-XVI vv.," *Istoricheskie i sotsiologicheskie ocherki, sbornik statey*, part 2 (Moscow, 1906).

Rubruquis, William of, *The Journey of William of Rubruck to the Eastern Parts of the World 1253-55 as narrated by himself*, ed. and trans. W. W. Rockhill (London, 1900).

——, *Puteshestvie v vostochnyya strany*, ed. and trans. A. I. Malein (Saint Petersburg, 1911).

Rybakov, B. A., "Chernigovskoe i Severskoe knyazhestva," *Istoriya SSSR*, ed. B. A. Rybakov, vol. 1 (Moscow, 1966), pp. 591-7.

Sakharov, I. P., *Zapiski dlya obozreniya russkikh drevnostey* (Saint Petersburg, 1851).

Sedov, V. V., "Smolenskaya zemlya," *Drevnerusskie knyazhestva X-XIII vv.*, ed. L. G. Beskrovnyy (Moscow, 1975), pp. 240-259.

Semenov, P., *Geografichesko-statisticheskiy slovar' rossiyskoy imperii* (Saint Petersburg, 1862-85).

Serebryansky, N., *Drevne-russkiya knyazheskiya zhitiya (Obzor redaktsiy i tektsy)* (Moscow, 1915).

Shakhmatov, A. A., "K voprosu o kriticheskom izdanii Istorii Rossiyskoy V. N. Tatishcheva," *Dela i Dni*, Kniga pervaya (Peterburg, 1920), pp. 80-95.

Shchapov, Ya. N., *Knyazheskie ustavy i tserkov' v Drevney Rusi XI-XIV vv.* (Moscow, 1972).

——, *Drevnesrusskie knyazheskie ustavy: XI-XV vv.* (Moscow, 1976).

Shchapova, Yu. L., "Steklyannye braslety Izyaslavlya," *Kul'tura srednevekovoy Rusi, posvyashchaetsya 70-letiyu M. K. Kargera* (Leningrad, 1974), pp. 85-7.

"Simeonovskaya letopis'," PSRL 18 (Saint Petersburg, 1913).

Skripil', M., *Russkie povesti XV-XVI vekov* (Moscow-Leningrad, 1958).

"Sochineniya knyazya Kur'skago," vol. 1, RIB, vol. 31 (Saint Petersburg, 1914).

"Sofiyskaya pervaya letopis'," PSRL 5, second edition (Leningrad, 1925).

Sofronenko, K. A., *Obshchestvenno-politicheskiy stroy Galitsko-Volynskoy Rusi XI-XIII vv.* (Moscow, 1955).

Sokolov, P., *Russkiy arkhierey iz Vizantii i pravo ego naznacheniya do nachala XV veka* (Kiev, 1913).

"Sokrashchennaya Novgorodskaya letopis', ot nachala zemli slavyanskoy do vzyatiya Moskvy Takhtamyshem v 1382 godu," *Suprasl'skaya rukopis'*, ed. M. A. Obolensky (Moscow, 1836).

"Sokrashchennyy letopisnyy svod 1493 g.," PSRL 27 (Moscow-Leningrad, 1962).

"Sokrashchennyy letopisnyy svod 1495 g.," PSRL 27 (Moscow-Leningrad, 1962).

Solov'ev, S. M., "Ob otnosheniya Novgoroda k velikim knyazyam," *Chteniya*, no. 1 (Moscow, 1846).

——, *Istoriya Rossii s drevneyshikh vremen*, 29 vols. in 15 books (Moscow, 1962-1966).

Sontsov, D., *Spravochnaya kniga dlya zanimayushchikhsya udel'nym periodom russkoy istorii 1015-1238* (Moscow, 1869).

Sotnikova, M. P., "Serebryanyy slitok s Izyaslavlya-gorodischa," *Kul'tura srednevekovoy Rusi, posvyashchaetsya 70-letiyu M. K. Kargera* (Leningrad, 1974).

Specimen Historiae Polonae Criticae, ed. J. A. Zaluski (Warsaw, 1735).

Speransov, N. N., *Zemel'nye gerby Rossii xii-xix vv.* (Moscow, 1974).

Spuler, B., *Die Goldene Horde. Die Mongolen in Russland, 1223-1502* (Wiesbaden, 1965).

——, *History of the Mongols*, trans. Helga and Stuart Drummond (Berkeley: University of California Press, 1972).

Sreznevsky, I. I., *Materialy dlya slovarya Drevne-Russkago yazyka po pis'menym pamyatnikam*, 3 vols. (Graz, 1955-6).

Stokes, A. D., "Kievan Russia," *An Introduction to Russian History*, eds. R. Auty and D. Obolensky (Cambridge, 1976), pp. 49-77.

Stroganovskiy ikonopisnyy litsevoy podlinnik kontsa xvi i nachala xvii stoletiy (Moscow, 1868).

"Suzdal'skaya letopis' po Akademicheskomu spisku," PSRL 1 (Leningrad, 1928).

Svyatsky, D. O., "Astronomicheskie yavleniya v russkikh letopisyakh s nauchno-kriticheskoy tochki zreniya," *Izvestiya otdeleniya russkogo yazyka i slovestnosti Akademii Nauk*, vol. 20 (Petrograd, 1915-16).

Tatishchev, V. N., *Istoriya Rossiyskaya*, 5 vols. (Moscow-Leningrad, 1962-8).

Tikhomirov, M. N., "Istochnikovedenie istorii SSSR s drevneyshikh vremen do kontsa xviii v.," *Kurs istochnikovedeniya istorii SSSR*, vol. 1 (Moscow, 1940).

——, "Vladimir Nikitich Tatishchev," *Istorik-Marksist*, book 6 (1940), pp. 43-56.

——, *Istoricheskie svyazi rossii so slavyanskimi stranami i vizantiey* (Moscow, 1964).

——, "Letopisnye pamyatniki byvshego Sinodal'nogo (Patriarshego) sobraniya," *Istoricheskie zapiski*, vol. 13 (1942), pp. 257-62.

——, *Krest'yanskie i gorodskie vosstaniya na Rusi xi-xiii vv.* (Moscow, 1955).

——, *The Towns of Ancient Rus'*, trans. Y. Sdobnikov (Moscow, 1959).

——, "Zabytye i neizvestnye proizvedeniya russkoy pis'mennosti," *Arkheografi-cheskii ezhegodnik za 1960* (Moscow, 1962), pp. 234-43.

——, "Russkiy letopisets v 'istorii Pol'shi' Yana Dlugosha," *Istoricheskie svyazi Rossii so slavyanskimi stranami i Vizantiey* (Moscow, 1969).

——, *Drevnyaya Rus'* (Moscow, 1975).

——, and S. S. Dmitriev, *Istoriya SSSR*, vol. 1 (Moscow, 1948).

Tikhonravov, K. N., "Arkheograficheskiya zametki o gorodakh Suzdale i Shue,"
    *Zapiski otdelenia russkoy i slavenskoy arkheologii imperatorskago arkheolo-
    gicheskago obshchestva*, vol. 1 (Saint Petersburg, 1851).
Tizengauzen, V., *Sbornik materialov otnosyashchikhsya k istorii Zolotoy Ordy*,
    vol. 1 (Saint Petersburg, 1884).
Tolochko, P. P., "Kievskaya zemlya," *Drevnerusskie knyazhestva x-xiii vv.*,
    ed. L. G. Beskrovnyy (Moscow, 1975), pp. 5-56.
Tolstoy, M., *Drevniya svyatyni Rostova velikago* (Moscow, 1847).
Tomashiv'skiy, S., "Predtecha Isidora. Petro Akerovich, neznaniy mitropolit
    rus'kiy (1241-1245)," *Zapysky chyna sv. Vasyliia Velykoho*, vol. 2, vypusk
    3-4, god 1926 (Zhovkva, 1927), pp. 221-313.
Troitskaya letopis', rekonstruktsiya teksta, ed. M. D. Priselkov (Moscow-Lenin-
    grad, 1950).
Troubetzkoy A., le Prince, *La Russie Rouge* (Paris, 1860).
Tupikov, N. M., *Slovar' Drevne-Russkikh lichnykh sobstvennykh imen'* (Saint
    Petersburg, 1903).
"Tverskaya letopis'," PSRL 15 (Saint Petersburg, 1863).

"Ukazatel' k Nikonovskoy letopisi," PSRL 14 vtoraya polovina (Petrograd, 1918).
Ukazatel' k pervym os'mi tomam polnago sobraniya russkikh letopisey, 2 vols.
    (Saint Petersburg, 1898, 1907).
Ustyuzhskiy letopisniy svod, ed. K. N. Serbina (Moscow-Leningrad, 1950).

Valk, S. N., *Gramoty Velikogo Novgoroda i Pskova* (Moscow-Leningrad, 1949).
Vernadsky, G., *The Mongols and Russia* (New Haven: Yale University Press,
    1953).
"Vladimirskiy letopisets," PSRL 30 (Moscow, 1965).
Vlas'ev, G. A., *Potomstvo Ryurika: materialy dlya sostavleniya rodosloviy*, vol. 1
    (Saint Petersburg, 1906); vol. 2 (Petrograd, 1918).
"Voskresenskaya letopis'," PSRL 7 (Saint Petersburg, 1856).
"Vykhody Patriarshie (1666-74)," *Dopolneniya k aktam istoricheskim*, vol. 5
    (Saint Petersburg, 1853), pp. 98-154.

Yablonsky, I., *Pakhomy Serb* (Saint Petersburg, 1908).
Yanin, V. L., *Novgorodskie posadniki* (Moscow, 1962).
——, *Aktovye pechati Drevney Rusi x-xv vv.*, 2 vols. (Moscow, 1970).

Zakrevsky, N., "Letopis' in opisanie goroda Kieva," *Chteniya*, book 2 (Moscow,
    1858).
Zaytsev, A. K., "Chernigovskoe knyazhestvo," *Drevnerusskie knyazhestva
    x-xiii vv.*, ed. L. G. Beskrovnyy (Moscow, 1975), pp. 57-117.
Zimin, A. A., *Pamyatniki prava feodal'no-razdroblenoy Rusi xii-xv vv.* (Moscow,
    1953).

——, "Novgorod i Volokolamsk v xi-xv vekakh," *Novgorodskiy istoricheskiy sbornik*, vol. 10 (Novgorod, 1961).

——, "Kogda bylo napisano 'Slovo'?" *Voprosy literatury*, no. 3 (Moscow, 1967), pp. 135-53.

Zotov, R. V., *O Chernigovskikh knyazyakh po Lyubetskomu sinodiku i o Chernigovskom knyazhestve v Tatarskoe vremya* (Saint Petersburg, 1892); also published in *Letopis' zanyatii arkheograficheskoy kommissii 1882-84 gg.*, vypusk devyatyy (Saint Petersburg, 1893).

Zvegintsev, A., trans., "Two National Saints," *The Russian Review*, vol. 2, Aug. no. 3 (Liverpool: University of Liverpool, 1913), pp. 21-44.

Author Index

Source Index

General Index

Acre, town in Palestine, 77

Agafia, sister of Mikhail Vsevolodovich and wife of Yury Vsevolodovich, 9, 10

Aleksandr Ivanovich Yaroslavov, prince, 150

Aleksandr Vsevolodovich, prince of Bel'z, 70, 161

Aleksandr Yaroslavich *Nevskiy*, prince of Novgorod, 23, 25, 28, 36, 37, 43, 49, 160, 164, 166

Alexis I, tsar, 146

Anastasia, mother of Mikhail Vsevolodovich, 9, 10

Andrew II, king of Hungary, 95, 97, 103, 126

Andrew, prince of Hungary, 58, 60-62, 69-71, 96, 97, 99, 103, 127, 165

Andrey, priest, 152, 153

Andrey Yaroslavich, prince of Suzdal', 160

Andrey Yur'evich *Bogolyubskiy*, grand prince of Vladimir, 81, 157

Andrey Vsevolodovich, prince, 10

Antony, archbishop of Novgorod, 24, 30, 31, 120

Antony, metropolitan of Moscow, 142-144

Antony, St., monk, 141, 142, 144

Arbuzovich, family of boyars in Galicia, 99

Arseny, monk (archbishop ?) of Novgorod, 24, 26, 30

Artemy, bishop of Galich, 105, 106, 119-121, 127, 141

Athanasius, St., beard of, 147

Avraamka, monk, XII

Avraamy, martyr, 140

Bakota, town in Galicia, 115-120, 167, 171

Baltic Sea, 26, 32, 48, 76

Bánáts, "client states" of Hungary, 122

Bartholomew, merchant, 77

Baty, Khan, XVI, 6, 83, 86, 87, 89-91, 94, 100, 107, 109-112, 120-122, 124-126, 129-135, 148, 151, 154, 167, illustrations Nos. 3 and 4

Béla IV, king of Hungary, 73, 79, 80, 88, 90, 94, 96, 107, 110, 113, 125-128, 135, 154; daughter of, 108, 109, 122, 123, 166, 167; coronation of, 97, 101, 103; military alliance with Ol'govichi (1236), 103, 121, 124, 165

Beloozero, town in Rostov-Suzdal', 170

Bel'z, town in Volyn', 62, 171

Benedict, friar from Poland, 77, 132, 133

Berestovo, near Kiev, 39

Berestya (Brest), town in Volyn', 111, 171

Black Sea, 76

Blagoslovennoe voinstvo, see "Blessed Host"

"Blessed Host", icon, 146, 148

Bohemia, 77, 125

Bolesław, prince of Mazovia, 112-114, 118; father of, 113

"Bolokhov", princes of, 32, 98-100, 102, 114, 116-119, 125, 165; lands of, 117-119, 171; towns of, 117-118

"Bolokhovtsy", 119

Boris, boyar from Mezhibozh'e, 99, 100

Boris, prince of Polotsk, 54

Boris and Gleb, Saints, 140-142, 144, 154

Boris, Negochevich, *tysyatskiy*, 24, 42, 45, 47, 48

Boris Vasil'kovich, prince of Rostov, 130, 131, 134, 141, 151, 152, 160

Boris Vsevolodovich, prince, 160

Bosnia (Rama), state, 122, 123

boyars, 71; see also Chernigov, Galich, Kamenets, Novgorod, Rostov

Bozh'skyy (Buzh'skyy), town in the "Bolokhov" land, 117-119, 171

Breslau, see Wrocław

Brest, see Berestya

"brothers", 27, 28; in "Bolokhov", 32, 99, 119; in Chernigov, 30, 32, 33, 49, 63, 92, 137; in Novgorod, 16, 25, 27, 43; in Pskov, 26-28; of Vnezd Vodovik, *posadnik*, 28, 42, 45, 164

Bryansk, town and principality, 169

Holy Saviour, Monastery of the (Novgorod), 24
Holy Trinity Monastery (Zagorsk), 151
Il'inskiy Monastery (Chernigov), 143
Michael the Archangel, St., Monastery of (near Kiev), 126
White Lake Monastery (Beloozero), 151
Yur'ev Monastery (Novgorod), 30, 47
Mongolia, xvi, 77, 132
Mongols, see Tatars
Monomashichi, descendants of Vladimir Monomakh, 12, 53, 143
Mordva, tribes east of Murom, 36, 65, 170
Mosal'sk, town in the principality of Chernigov, 45, 52, 169
Moscow, town and principality, 37, 45, 142-146, 148-149, 151, 153, 168, 170; fire (1812), xiii; metropolitan of, 142-144, 153; Napoleonic invasion, 144
Msta, river, 15, 168
Mstislav Daniilovich, prince of Volyn', 161
Mstislav Davidovich, prince (d. 1187), 159
Mstislav Davidovich, prince of Smolensk (d. 1230), 25, 29, 54, 68, 159
Mstislav Glebovich, prince of Chernigov, 10, 66-67, 72, 84-86, 88, 92-94, 107, 110, 114, 115, 121, 129, 134, 137, 158, 163, 166
Mstislav Izyaslavich, grand prince of Kiev (d. 1172), 157, 161
Mstislav Mikhaylovich, prince, 158
Mstislav Mstislavich Udaloy, prince of Novgorod and Galich, 12, 17-19, 54, 58-64, 66-68, 91, 96, 159, 164
Mstislav Romanovich, grand prince of Kiev (d. 1224), 12, 19, 53-54, 59, 66, 68, 74-75, 88-89, 136, 159
Mstislav Rostislavich, prince (d. 1180), 54, 55, 159
Mstislav Svyatoslavich, prince of Kozel'sk and Chernigov (d. 1224), 6, 12, 55, 57, 66, 158
Mstislav Svyatoslavich, prince of Ryl'sk (d. 1241), 158
Mstislav Vladimirovich, prince (d. 1132), 157, 159, 161
Mstislav Vsevolodovich, prince, 10
Mstislav Yaroslavich Nemoy, prince of Lutsk, 161
Mstislav Yur'evich, prince (d. 1238), 160
Murom, town and principality, 170
Muscovy, 2; people of, 145, 154-155; princes of, 143; saints of, 142

Nicolas Pisani, merchant, 77
Nikita, stylite of Pereyaslavl', 10, 150
Nikita Romanovich Odoevsky, prince, 150
Nizhniy Novgorod, town on the Volga, 36, 48, 170
nomads, see tribes and nomads
novaya, unit of currency, 17, 21
Novgorod, town and district, viii, 3, 11-12, 37, 52, 55-56, 61, 65, 67, 69, 79, 80, 82, 84, 86, 91, 93, 120, 121, 137-139, 141, 145, 151, 163, 166, 168, 170 : suburbs (kontsy), 24 ; Plotnitskiy konets, 24 ; Slavenskiy konets, 24 ; Nerevskiy konets, 24; Zagorodskiy konets, 24; Goncharskiy or Lyudin konets, 24; market side (Yaroslav's court), 24 ; Sofiya's side, 24; archbishop's residence, ix, 24, 26; prince's residence, 29, 30; bridges in, 23, 30, 31;
——: inhabitants of, 16-22, 24-35, 39, 41-51, 57, 63, 78, 164; prominent citizens, 30, 33, 42; boyars, 15-16, 20, 24, 26, 30, 42-43, 45-48, 164; peasants and serfs, 20, 23, 29, 31, 42, 44, 49; chernye lyudi, 15, 20; prostaya chad', 24, 26, 43;
——: administration in, 15-16, 30-31; veche, 6, 15-16, 19-22, 24-32, 34, 39, 41-45, 48-50, 64, 92; posadnik, 15-16, 19-21, 26-28, 30-32, 41-43, 45, 47, 164; tysyatskiy, 15-16, 24, 26-27, 42, 45, 47; archbishop, 15, 17, 24, 26, 30-31, 39; prince, 15-16, 18-19, 22, 25, 28-31, 34, 36, 38-41, 43-44, 49-50, 63, 70; commercial weights and measures, 15; commercial court, 16; ecclesiastical court, 15; "vassal" towns of, 15, 26, 30, 47; judges, 25-26, 31-32; taxes, 29, 31-32, 44, 49; zabozhnits'e, 25-26, 31; reforms of Mikhail Vsevolodovich (1229), 29-32, 49;
——: factions in, 16, 20-21, 41, 63-64; unrest in (1228), 24, 26, 28, 31, 43, 49, 164; feuding in (1230), 41-43; faction supporting Mikhail Vsevolodovich, 32, 41-43, 45-50, 81, 164; faction supporting Yaroslav Vsevolodovich, 24-27, 29-32, 43, 46, 49;
——: chronicle writing in, ix; rains in, 23-24, 26, 164; fire in (1217), 25; foreign incursions, 28, 41
Novgorod Severskiy, town and principality, 23, 47, 57, 60, 62, 63, 92, 169
Novyy Torg, see Torzhok

198 GENERAL INDEX

gorod land, 15-17, 22, 25, 30, 32, 36,
42, 57, 164, 168
trade, Baltic Sea, 76; Eastern, 35-36;
German, 76; caravans, 36, 76, 78, 117;
through Novgorod, 15, 16, 21-22, 25-
26, 32-33, 35-36, 48, 79, 81, 93;
through Chernigov, 21-22, 48; through
Kiev, 52, 74, 76-77, 138; through
Rostov-Suzdal', 17, 36, 48
traders, see merchants
tribes and nomads, Finnish, 41; in northwest Rus', 36, 65; in southwest and
southern Rus', 65, 115
Trubchevsk (Trubetsk), town and principality, 47-48, 169
Trubetsk, see Trubchevsk
Turkey, 144, 147
Turov, town and principality, 54, 60, 62,
169, 171; house of, 157
Tver', town and principality, 150, 168, 170
Tverdislav Mikhaylovich, *posadnik*, 42

Udech, town in Galicia, 117
Ugedei, Khan, 120
Ultra-March (*ul'tramartovskiy*) year, see
calendar
Ushitsa, town in Galicia, 115, 171
ustav, see rule

Varangians, chapel of (Novgorod), 25;
Prince Mina Ivanovich, 23
Vasiliev, town in Galicia, 115, 171
Vasil'ko, prince of Kozel'sk, 158
Vasil'ko Konstantinovich, prince of Ros-
tov, 16, 23, 33, 35, 38, 110, 113, 140,
141, 160, 163; wife of, 113
Vasil'ko Mstislavich, prince (d. 1218), 159
Vasil'ko Romanovich, prince of Volyn',
61-62, 73, 84, 98-99, 101, 118-119,
121, 125, 161
Vasil'ko Rostislavich, prince (d. 1125), 157
Vasily III, grand prince, 134
Vasily Yaroslavich, prince of Kostroma,
160
Vasius, merchant, 77
Velikie Luki, town on the Lovat', 15, 168
Venice, 77
Vera, sister of Mikhail Vsevolodovich, 9,
10
Vladimir, St., see Vladimir Svyatoslavich
(d. 1015)
Vladimir, town in Volyn', 61-62, 70, 73,

83, 90, 98-100, 108-109, 111, 113, 171;
bishopric of, 121
Vladimir, town on the Klyaz'ma and
principality, 10, 18-19, 21, 29, 35-36,
45, 51, 56, 59, 82-84, 100, 124, 126,
128, 136, 140, 143, 153, 166, 170
Vladimir, prince of Pinsk, 114
Vladimir Igorevich, prince of Galich
(d. 1212), 158
Vladimir Ingvarevich, prince of Lutsk, 161
Vladimir Konstantinovich, prince of
Uglich, 33, 160
Vladimir Konstaninovich Kurlyatev,
prince, 150
Vladimir *Monomakh*, see Vladimir Vsevo-
lodovich *Monomakh*
Vladimir Mstislavich, prince of Brest
(d. 1173), 161
Vladimir Mstislavich, prince of Smolensk,
159
Vladimir Ryurikovich, grand prince of
Kiev, 29, 35, 39-40, 50-53, 55-56, 58-
80, 83, 85-88, 91-94, 96-104, 107, 110,
114, 121, 127, 134, 138, 159, 163-166;
daughter of, 35, 65; wife of, 74
Vladimir Svyatoslavich, prince of Cherni-
gov, 19, 158
Vladimir Svyatoslavich, Christianizer of
Rus' (d. 1015), 52, 120, 141-142, 144,
157
Vladimir Vasil'kovich, prince of Volyn',
161
Vladimir Volodarevich, prince of Galich
(d. 1153), 120, 157
Vladimir Vsevolodovich, prince (d. 1229),
160
Vladimir Vsevolodovich *Monomakh*,
grand prince of Kiev (d. 1125), 5, 53,
65, 81, 119, 143, 157, 159-161
Vladimir Yaroslavich, prince (d. 1199), 95,
157
Vladimir Yaroslavich, prince (d. 1052), 95,
120, 157
Vladimir Yur'evich, prince (d. 1238), 160
Vnezd Vodovik, *posadnik*, 28, 30-31, 42-
43, 45, 47, 164
Vodovik, see Vnezd Vodovik
Volga Bulgars, see Bulgars
Volga, river and region, 16, 35-36, 65, 67,
79, 92, 126, 140, 168, 170
Volkhov, river, 15, 23-24, 30
Volodar Rostislavich, prince (d. 1124), 157